Jonathan Franzen at the End of Postmodernism

Continuum Literary Studies Series

Also available in the series:

Active Reading by Ben Knights and Chris Thurgar-Dawson
Beckett's Books by Matthew Feldman
British Fiction in the Sixties by Sebastian Groes
Canonising Hypertext by Astrid Ensslin
Character and Satire in Postwar Fiction by Ian Gregson
Coleridge and German Philosophy by Paul Hamilton
Contemporary Fiction and Christianity by Andrew Tate
Ecstasy and Understanding edited by Adrian Grafe
English Fiction in the 1930s by Chris Hopkins
Fictions of Globalization by James Annesley
Joyce and Company by David Pierce
London Narratives by Lawrence Phillips
Masculinity in Fiction and Film by Brian Baker
The Measureless Past of Joyce, Deleuze and Derrida by Ruben Borg
Milton, Evil and Literary History by Claire Colebrook
Modernism and the Postcolonial by Peter Childs
Novels of the Contemporary Extreme edited by Alain-Phillipe Durand and Naomi Mandel
The Palimpsest by Sarah Dillon
Recalling London by Alex Murray
Romanticism, Literature and Philosophy by Simon Swift
Seeking Meaning for Goethe's Faust by J. M. van der Laan
Sexuality and the Erotic in the Fiction of Joseph Conrad by Jeremy Hawthorn
Such Deliberate Disguises: The Art of Phillip Larkin by Richard Palmer
Women's Fiction 1945–2000 by Deborah Philips

Jonathan Franzen at the End of Postmodernism

Stephen J. Burn

continuum

Continuum International Publishing Group
The Tower Building   80 Maiden Lane
11 York Road   Suite 704, New York
London SE1 7NX   NY 10038

www.continuumbooks.com

© Stephen J. Burn 2008

All rights reserved. No part of this publication may be reproduced or transmitted in any form or by any means, electronic or mechanical, including photocopying, recording, or any information storage or retrieval system, without prior permission in writing from the publishers.

Stephen J. Burn has asserted his right under the Copyright, Designs and Patents Act, 1988, to be identified as Author of this work.

British Library Cataloguing-in-Publication Data
A catalogue record for this book is available from the British Library.

ISBN: PB: 978-1-4411-9100-7

Library of Congress Cataloging-in-Publication Data
A catalog record for this book is available from the Library of Congress.

Typeset by Newgen Imaging Systems Pvt Ltd, Chennai, India
Printed and bound in Great Britain by Biddles Ltd, King's Lynn, Norfolk

For Julie

Contents

Acknowledgements	viii
Preface	ix
Abbreviations and Note on Editions	xv
Chapter 1 A Map of the Territory: American Fiction at the Millennium	1
Chapter 2 Genealogy: Franzen's Early Writing	28
Chapter 3 In the Concrete Waste Land: *The Twenty-Seventh City*	52
Chapter 4 Midnight in the System Rooms: *Strong Motion*	68
Chapter 5 Millennial Fictions: *The Corrections*	88
Notes	129
Bibliography of Works by Franzen	141
Works Cited	146
Index	157

Acknowledgements

Farrar, Straus and Giroux, LLC and HarperCollins Publishers Ltd have kindly granted permission to reprint: Excerpts from *The Corrections* by Jonathan Franzen Copyright © 2001 by Jonathan Franzen; Excerpts from *The Twenty-Seventh City* by Jonathan Franzen. Copyright © 1988 by Jonathan Franzen; Excerpts from *Strong Motion* by Jonathan Franzen. Copyright © 1992 by Jonathan Franzen; Excerpts from *How to be alone* by Jonathan Franzen. Copyright © 2002, 2003 by Jonathan Franzen; Excerpts from *The Discomfort Zone* by Jonathan Franzen. Copyright © 2006 by Jonathan Franzen.

Preface

Jonathan Franzen occupies a revealing position amongst America's millennial novelists. While critics at century's end began to anatomize the end of postmodernism, mapping "postmodernism's wake" (Harris), or announcing the emergence of "post-postmodernism" (McLaughlin), the conflict between postmodern innovation and more conventional narrative forms was internalized and played out in Franzen's novels and essays.[1] His work has tried to absorb the story-based narrative energies of writers such as Isaac Bashevis Singer and Alice Munro, while it has been simultaneously shaped and distorted by the achievements of American postmodernism.

Given the recent interest in new directions after postmodernism signaled by critics such as Charles B. Harris and Robert L. McLaughlin, Franzen's attempt to fuse disparate traditions would seem to make a study of his work particularly timely, but for a variety of reasons his reputation has developed somewhat unevenly. His novels have often received distractingly overblown praise from reviewers eager to find and praise a major talent,[2] but at the same time, his work has attracted less serious academic attention than might be expected. While Franzen is frequently compared to Richard Powers and the late David Foster Wallace—more prolific and more explicitly innovative writers—there is a notable discrepancy in their critical profiles. Entire books and special issues of journals have been devoted to explicating Powers and Wallace's fiction,[3] but while references to Franzen can often be found in unusual places—in the *British Medical Journal* or the *Journal of the American Academy of Psychoanalysis and Dynamic Psychiatry*, for example[4]—two decades after the publication of his first novel only a handful of essays solely devoted to Franzen's work have appeared.[5]

Some of the reasons why scholars have overlooked Franzen's novels aren't difficult to locate. On a basic level, Franzen's hostility toward the academy may have discouraged critics from exploring his relationship to academic constructions of postmodernism. This is particularly unfortunate, however, because even Franzen's hostility toward the academy seems to be entwined with postmodern fiction and the arguments that surrounded its emergence. Although Franzen confessed that he began writing novels with the belief that "the highest compliment . . . Art could be paid was to be taught in a university" (*A* 245), by the mid-1990s he had reconceived of academia as a "nursing home for terminally ill arts," and claimed it would be "better the novel die with honor in the gutter than enter those gates" ("I'll Be Doing More of Same" 34). Yet, in framing his rejection of the academy in these terms, Franzen is basically paraphrasing Gore Vidal who 20 years earlier complained that after reading works by John Barth, Donald Barthelme, and Thomas Pynchon, he "would prefer for [novels] to die rather than to become teaching-tools, artifacts stinking of formaldehyde in a classroom" (39).

More materially, however, the distracting details of Franzen's dispute with Oprah Winfrey seem to have exerted an almost magnetic attraction for writers interested in Franzen, and what little critical attention he has received has tended to circle morbidly around the implications of this dispute: is Franzen racist? Elitist? Sexist?[6] Instead of recycling these questions, my critical method concentrates on the novels, rather than the novelist, so this study has little to add to the host of increasingly fine-grained dissections of what is, after all, an argument over whether or not someone wanted to appear on a late afternoon TV show—a subject that ought to be less intriguing than the novels themselves. Nevertheless, because Franzen draws on his own life in his novels, and so frequently appeals to his own experience in his nonfiction, I have included a biographical overview in this study. At the very least, this sketch might serve to fill out the two-dimensional cartoon figure of Franzen who sometimes functions in accounts of the Oprah affair.

In the rest of this study, however, my interest is in larger formal and rhetorical questions: what tensions emerge from the intersection of form and content in a given work? What opaque language games are hidden in Franzen's ostensibly transparent prose? How does Franzen employ intertextual allusion to enrich the texture of his fiction? Unifying each of these investigations—and compromising the heart of the book—is an attempt to map the shifting coordinates of Franzen's engagement with postmodern aesthetics across the arc of his early career. This is a subject that divides Franzen's readers. In the wake of his first two novels, critics saw few problems in placing him directly in a line extending from the experimental heart of postmodernism. In 1996, for example, Melvin Jules Bukiet classified Franzen with Powers and Pynchon as exponents of what he called "Crackpot

Realism," a form of fiction that registers the deep technological changes of our times while also elevating the role of coincidence and interconnection beyond the level we ordinarily find in conventional novels. But by the time *The Corrections* was published, Franzen's apparent midcareer shift toward the mainstream market made such a designation doubtful. By 2002, Tom LeClair argued that in spite of the comparisons with Pynchon that Franzen's early novels elicited, the less-nuanced fictions of Tom Wolfe now provided a more valid reference point ("Shortfall"). In this study, I maintain that such divergence over how to categorize Franzen's novels is an inevitable consequence of his approach to the novel. As I argue in the second chapter, Franzen's imagination characteristically works by fusing opposites on every level—formal, thematic, geographic—so his novels become a kind of synthesis of divergent forces. A given novel might squeeze together experimental and traditional narrative templates, religious and scientific worldviews, and evoke a running comparison between the Midwest and the Eastern seaboard. This conflation of opposites inevitably leads to conflicting interpretations, but elucidating how this blend alters on a novel-by-novel basis and, crucially, how it illuminates Franzen's relationship to postmodernism is the burden of the last three chapters of this study.

In making a case for the intricate qualities of each novel, I am not arguing that Franzen is a neglected novelist—in fact, he has mocked the critical industries that emerge around underappreciated writers ("Your contribution of just 15 minutes a week can help assure Joseph Roth of his rightful place in the modern canon" ["Alice's Wonderland" 1]). But I do think that his works are more complexly layered hybrids than they may at first appear, and that his relationship to postmodern fiction is more tangled than it initially seems. Because Franzen is not the kind of novelist who explicitly foregrounds his learning, or draws attention to his efforts to undermine generic conventions, he is sometimes praised or blamed too simplistically for withdrawing from the complexity of postmodern narrative strategies in favor of evoking the traditional rewards of storytelling.[7] To try to establish a more nuanced understanding of Franzen's extensive relationship to postmodernism, I have sought to provide an outline of the state of American literary postmodernism in the 1990s as part of this study's first chapter. Until its last third, this chapter is less concerned with Franzen than it is with constructing a snapshot of the reaction against the forms and techniques of postmodernism in the 1990s that might help contextualize the ambivalent position of writers, such as Franzen, who grew up in the age of postmodernism. At the end of this chapter, I tentatively outline some of the ways that the work of Franzen and his contemporaries—who I suggest might be thought of as post-postmodern—can be distinguished from their postmodern predecessors.

In Chapter 2, I move from Franzen's literary context to his personal context and outline the temporal coordinates of the life behind the books. While I address a number of issues as part of this discussion—the role of lists in Franzen's fiction, the distinctions that might be drawn between his fiction and nonfiction—the biographical sketch in this chapter principally serves to introduce the large body of writing that precedes his first novel. Because most of this early writing is little known—and probably awkward to locate for most readers—my method in Chapter 2 is mostly descriptive, rather than analytical, attempting to provide a fuller understanding of Franzen's literary background.

Chapter 3 marks the beginning of a more sustained analysis of Franzen's novels. Concentrating on *The Twenty-Seventh City*, this chapter compares Franzen's novel to first books by Wallace, Powers, and William T. Vollmann in an attempt to identify some common characteristics of early post-postmodern fiction. Each of these works, I argue, share formal similarities and display a fascination with figures from the early twentieth century, which in Franzen's novel bleeds into a larger ecocritical investigation.

My focus shifts to *Strong Motion* in Chapter 4, though I also try to stress connections between Franzen's first and second books. Amongst these many connections, I note that his first two novels share a fascination with the literary history associated with the cities he writes about, while ecological catastrophes haunt both works. But while the contemporary atmosphere of his first novel was preoccupied with literary modernism, the ecological argument of *Strong Motion* is filtered through the techniques of what Tom LeClair calls the "Systems Novel," a scientifically informed branch of postmodern fiction. Chapter 4 elucidates Franzen's use of the Systems Novel with particular reference to his interest in chaos theory, while it also introduces one of Franzen's characteristic approaches to structuring his fiction: what I call his use of "Temporal Form."

Because *The Corrections* is currently Franzen's most famous, and I think least understood, novel, I devote the longest chapter in this book to its explication. Most reviewers and critics argue that this novel represents a move toward the techniques of realism, a regression that might be seen as a narrowing of the novel's intellectual bandwidth. This shift was apparent even in early reviews, which argued that the novel owed "more to Salinger" than to "something along the DeLillo, Powers, Wallace axis" (Birkerts, "Novel" 71). Later reviews and essays have extended this argument, insisting that the novel prioritizes "character" rather than form, and critics have likened the novel's formal arrangement to a loosely strung-together series of novellas. Though these critics often have Franzen's implicit support, I try to demonstrate in Chapter 5—with these arguments specifically in mind—that *The Corrections* is deeply preoccupied with the significance of form and structure—especially in extending the idea of Temporal Form introduced in my previous chapter—and fundamentally suspicious of traditional notions of "character." In its form and content, the book is, I argue, engaged in a four-way conversation with William Gaddis, Don DeLillo, Powers, and Wallace. Precisely because such intertextual dialogues have been relatively unexamined by earlier critics, I think this aspect of Franzen's work is worth exploring.

I am aware that Roland Barthes's conception of literary texts as a "tissue of quotations drawn from the innumerable centers of culture" could be used to excavate Franzen's intertextual references (146). Equally, my discussion of metafiction and the Systems Novel could have been framed by Niklas Luhmann's systems theory and his study of the way "art splits the world into a real world and an imaginary world" (142). But rather than limit Franzen's three books to one recurrent theoretical angle, my approach in the last three chapters of this study—when I move away from close examination of Franzen's work—has been to set other texts alongside each novel, to attempt to illuminate his fiction from as many angles as possible. I have drawn these texts from a variety of disciplines—literary criticism, turn-of-the-century anthropology, neuroscience, chaos theory—but this is a book of literary, rather than cultural, criticism, so in each chapter I have supplemented these interdisciplinary perspectives by outlining comparisons with parallel works by Franzen's contemporaries, Wallace and Powers. Taken together, these arguments are intended to articulate a larger argument about how Franzen's work can be conceptualized within a wider literary ecology and to test the possibility of a post-postmodern fiction.

Begun in England and completed in America, this book was written in a kind of exile that was made easier by my parents, Sam Burn, Audrey and Denis Ferguson, Marek Haltof, Austin and Alisa Hummell, Dana Schulz, John Smolens, Ray Ventre, and Jonathan Wilson. I would like to thank Jonathan Franzen for taking the time to confirm or disdain my conjectures as I worked on this book and for drawing my attention to some of the influences upon his fiction that I would otherwise have missed. Göran Ekström helped me locate a seismology article I had been unable to track down. William Harmon, president of the T. S. Eliot society, helped direct my queries to affiliates of the society whose help I greatly appreciated.

At Continuum, the support and wisdom of Anna Fleming and David Barker were invaluable.

Between 2004 and 2006, I taught Franzen's work to six classes at Northern Michigan University and I am grateful to the many students—especially Todd Dodson and Jason Shrontz—who surprised me or forced me to rethink the conclusions that I had come to about his books. Also at NMU, I'm grateful for the advice and support of Jim Schiffer, the assistance of Michelle Kimball, while I appreciate the help of the Faculty Grant committee, who awarded me a research grant in 2006. A portion of Chapter 1 is based upon my essay "The End of Postmodernism," which was originally published in Jay Prosser's *American Fiction of the 1990s* (Routledge, 2008). A paragraph from Chapter 5 first appeared in a review I wrote of David Foster Wallace's *Infinite Jest* for the *Times Literary Supplement*. I'm grateful for permission to draw upon both.

Abbreviations and Note on Editions

A complete list of works cited is included at the end of this volume, which I've split into two sections so that works authored by Franzen can be conveniently located. The first lists works authored by Franzen; the second lists works by other authors, as well as interviews with Franzen. Quotations identified as "personal correspondence" come from my own discussions with Franzen. All references to Franzen's books are from the following editions and are signaled by the abbreviations below:

TS   *The Twenty-Seventh City.* 1988. New York: Noonday-Farrar, 1997.
SM   *Strong Motion.* New York: Picador-Farrar, 1992.
C   *The Corrections.* 2001. New York: Picador-Farrar, 2002.
A   *How to Be Alone.* Rev. ed. New York: Farrar, 2003.
DZ   *The Discomfort Zone.* 2006. New York: Picador-Farrar, 2007.

On only one occasion do I refer to an earlier published extract from one of these novels—"Chez Lambert"—and that work is referenced in the second list of works cited. I have always used paperback reprints because Franzen has consistently made corrections to each of his texts after the first printing. In some instances the changes involve relatively minor corrections. For the paperback of *The Twenty-Seventh City,* for instance, Franzen made such changes as correcting the first edition's "Dharari" to "Dharavi" (18), and removing the exclamation point from the middle of "Luisa should turn eighteen the same year! Probst turned fifty" (220). In others books, however, the revisions address more substantive matters. In the case of *The Corrections,* Franzen made quite extensive changes, such as the revisions made to the pages detailing Denise's visit to Vienna. In the first edition, for example, Franzen writes:

> she finally called Cindy von Kippel (née Meisner) and accepted an invitation to dinner at her seventeen-room apartment on the Ringstraße . . .

The von Kippel living room was half a block long and furnished with gilt chairs in sociability-killing formations. Ancestral Watteauery hung on the walls. (392–3)

While in the paperback this becomes:

she finally called Cindy Müller-Karltreu (née Meisner) and accepted an invitation to dinner at her cavernous "nouveau penthouse" overlooking the Michaelertor . . . The Müller-Karltreu living room was furnished with baroque loveseats and Biedermeier chairs in sociability-killing formations. Soft-core Bouguereaus or Bouguereau knockoffs hung on the walls. (390)

Along with the shift in local detail, here, come a cluster of other minor changes. The name of Cindy's maid, for example, changes from Annerl in the first edition to Mirjana in the paperback, their chalet moves from St. Moritz to Kitzbühel, and their sideboard is no longer "Louis XIV-ish" (393) but rather "vaguely *Jugendstil*" (390).

Chapter 1

A Map of the Territory
American Fiction at the Millennium

Why are terminal events so pleasing?

Don DeLillo, Great Jones Street *(223)*

This book is a study of the novels of Jonathan Franzen, but it is also about the context in which these novels were written as it attempts to outline a tentative map of American fiction at the millennium, a time when numerous writers struggled through what they seemed to believe were the last days of postmodernism. But to begin a survey of American writing by referring to the American writer's self-conscious awareness of a critical framework requires some explanation, since American literature is, after all, famously resistant to traditional modes of classification. As far back as 1841, for example, Thomas Carlyle questioned the applicability of critical categories to American writing and warned readers encountering Ralph Waldo Emerson to not worry about classifying the American, for "ists and isms are rather a growing weariness" (x). Emerson, himself, extended this sentiment by imagining in "The American Scholar" a mind "tyrannized over by its own unifying instinct" and remorselessly categorizing everything it encountered (86).

From Emerson through to Wallace Stevens's reflections on the "rage for order" (130), American literature is fascinated and revolted by the classifying impulse, and much postmodern fiction may seem to replicate that relationship. In Thomas Pynchon's *Gravity's Rainbow* (1973), for example, the fear is distilled into almost pure form when Pynchon imagines a text that is "to be picked to pieces, annotated, explicated . . . squeezed limp of its last drop" by the "scholar-magicians of the Zone" (520). Nevertheless, the generation of American writers who came to be associated with the rise of postmodernism in the 1960s were unusual not just in their self-conscious efforts to classify their relationship to literary history, but also in their tendency to dramatize that self-consciousness within their fiction. This anxious awareness of literary history shadows the work of many major postmodernists. Robert Coover, for example, began his career by invoking the shade of Cervantes in an attempt to neatly define the beginning of a new literary era that his work would help usher in. In *Pricksongs and Descants* (1969)—a volume that gathers many of his earliest fictions—Coover tells the ghost of the Spanish novelist that he finds himself "standing at the end of one age and on the threshold of another," addressing the need for "new . . . fictional forms" (78, 79). To an even greater extent, John Barth internalizes and recasts the tensions of his generation in his late fiction. In *Once Upon a Time* (1994), for instance, Barth presents a writer working on what he "can't resist thinking of as [his] Last Book" (382), an elegiac sentiment that is reinforced by the acronym yielded by Barth's title: this writer is on his way *OUT*. Barth's writer acknowledges that he is driven by "the record-keeper in me" (11), and the skeleton of the novel is provided by a survey of, and a progression through, Barth's fictional productions that is, in turn, prefaced by a sketch of literary history's production of a "division between high art and commercial 'prolefeed,' polarizing novelists into James Joyces on the one hand and James Micheners on the other" (24–25). Trying to establish "who in the fluxing world he is" (323), these maps of both literary history and his own works locate him in time and space, affirming for Barth his position at the confluence of modernism and popular fiction, as "a confessed Postmodernist" (25).

Once Upon a Time and *Pricksongs and Descants* stand at opposite ends of postmodernism, but both texts illustrate an impulse within the movement to imagine the writer's work as a kind of historical marker, illuminating the self's relationship to the literary past. Although earlier literary periods were constructed by critics, these texts embody the efforts of postmodernism—as Brian McHale has argued in "What Was Postmodernism?"—to "periodize . . . itself." McHale writes: "From the very outset, postmodernism was self-conscious about its identity *as* a period, conscious of its own historicity, because it conceived of itself *as* historical."

As much as any writer of his generation, Jonathan Franzen has been preoccupied by the question of how a writer who grew up in the heyday of postmodernism might relate to a movement that so forcibly established and policed its own borderlands. In 2001, Franzen told Donald Antrim that he had begun writing novels as a way of creating a "conversation with the . . . great sixties and seventies Postmoderns" (73), and his reviews of other novels, as well as the essays where he meditates on the state of fiction, indicate how deeply he is concerned with the place of his fiction within a larger literary ecology that has been predominantly shaped by the energies of American postmodernism. But to excavate Franzen's relationship to his literary ancestors—and so, implicitly, to theorize about the end of postmodernism—requires a reader to revisit and reconsider both the mode of postmodernism's initial construction in the early 1960s and the messy cluster of meanings that have congealed around the term over a much longer period.

A genealogy of the end of postmodernism: Order and chaos

Summaries of postmodernism are commonly framed in terms of the movement's supposedly derivative relationship to modernism, a relationship that is just as commonly introduced with reference to the first book to use the designation *modernist* in its title: Laura Riding and Robert Graves's *A Survey of Modernist Poetry* (1927). The problem that immediately besets such constructions, however, is that by the time Riding and Graves's study was published, the term *postmodernism* had already appeared in the title of a book: Bernard Iddings Bell's *Postmodernism and Other Essays* (1926). The break in linearity implied by these titles may seem appropriately postmodern, but the discontinuity can be explained by the fact that Bell is positioning himself *post-* a different kind of *modernism* to that addressed by Riding and Graves. *A Survey of Modernist Poetry* largely circles aesthetic issues asking how punctuation might be deployed in a poem, or what relation might exist between a poem's length and its structure, and arguing that the self-conscious criticality of the modernist period meant that "poetry becomes the tradition of poetry" (261). Bell's interests, by contrast, are theological. He is preoccupied with the disintegrating certainties of Christianity—the infallibility of the scriptures, the power of the individual mind—that have made of Protestantism "a collapsing system" (4). Trying to square the scriptures with modern science, Bell imagines a "Postmodernist" today as "a man without a Church" (65), but he has little to say about difficult poetry.

The divergent focus of these two books introduces the first problem faced when addressing the history of postmodernism. The term not only has different meanings in different disciplines and contexts, but those varied usages are also attached to different chronologies for the term. So while, in theology, the first use of *postmodernism* predates the canonization of literary modernism, in artistic circles the term is not proposed for another 10 years, eventually appearing in a 1936 issue of the *Journal of Higher Education* to describe the emergence of surrealism (Rusk 379).[1] With such tangled histories and often conflicting usages, it makes little sense, then, to explore what the end of *postmodernism* might mean in an interdisciplinary sense.

While I'm going to suggest that many novelists and critics have already posited the end of literary postmodernism, to a social theorist concerned with the logic of late capitalism, postmodernism might show few signs of weakening. The difficulty here, as Terry Eagleton argues at the start of *The Illusions of Postmodernism* (1996), is that with its many distributed meanings "postmodernism is such a portmanteau phenomenon that anything you assert of one piece of it is almost bound to be untrue of another" (viii). But if it is impossible to anatomize the widescale end of postmodernism, it is possible to isolate different moments in the evolution of literary postmodernism, to ask which strands survived and which died as postmodernism approached the millennium. To detach postmodern techniques from the complexities of the literary field in which they're deployed goes against the stated beliefs of postmodern novelist John Barth, who argues that "what makes a text postmodern" is not "literary strategies in isolation, but rather 'their connection through complex feedback loops with postmodernism as a cultural dominant'" (*Further Fridays* 308). But I think there is some taxonomic value in separating two aspects of literary postmodernism, in particular, that I would like to examine from opposite ends of the movement's construction.

In *Constructing Postmodernism* (1992), Brian McHale argues that as literary histories are constructed, "each successive cultural phase recuperates what has been excluded and 'left over' from the preceding phase" (56). This is certainly true of the emergence of critical debate about literary postmodernism in the late 1960s and 1970s, as scholars constructed a movement characterized in terms of its opposition to modernism.[2] I'm particularly interested, here, in the tendency of early critics of postmodernism to identify the movement as a deliberate attempt to subvert the emphasis that the modernists placed on artistic form. For disillusioned critics, this subversion of form would be the triumph of the Pound Error that Ezra Pound describes in the fragmentary last phase of *The Cantos*, an "Error of chaos" (802)[3]:

> my errors and wrecks lie about me.
> And I am not a demigod,
> I cannot make it cohere. (810)

The classic works of modernism insisted upon an order that was both formal and intellectual, controlled by both their careful textual arrangement and the nonliterary grids—drawn from Frazer's *The Golden Bough*, Greek myths, and so on—their narratives followed. "Order, order, order," as Joyce insists—twice—in *Finnegans Wake* (1939) might properly be taken as the movement's governing principle (337, 338). Early postmodernism, by contrast, seemed to deliberately stress disorder. In artistic manifestos, such as Raymond Federman's *Surfiction: Fiction Now . . . and Tomorrow* (1981), a new fiction was presented whose "most striking aspects" would "be its semblance of disorder and its deliberate incoherency" (13). Federman explained: "it will be deliberately . . . non sequitur, and incoherent. . . . The new fiction will not create a semblance of order, it will offer itself for order and ordering" (13–14). Critics were presenting similar diagnoses. De Villo Sloan, for example, (who was already detecting "The decline of American Postmodernism" in 1987) constructed an irrational, chaotic postmodernism by arguing that while "modernism considered itself high art, postmodernism tends toward nonart . . . [it] seeks to cultivate the irrational" (32–33). In its purest form, this subversion of artistic order was indicated by chance methods of composition. Leonard B. Meyer was one of the earliest critics to identify the role of "random operations" in the production of what he called *antiteleological* art (173), but the idea was elaborated by later writers. Christopher Butler, for example, wrote in *After the Wake* (1980) about William S. Burroughs's use of chance juxtapositions to develop an "art which repudiates rational control" (102). Equally, Richard Kostelanetz described less well-known works, such as Marc Saporta's *Composition No. 1* (1962) and Peter H. Beaman's *Deck of Cards* (1989), as examples of chance literary composition in *An ABC of Contemporary Reading* (1995).

There are certainly examples of recent postmodern fiction that incorporate the role of chance. Lee Siegel's *Love and Other Games of Chance* (2003), a carefully constructed novel that nevertheless encourages the reader to select chapters according to their progress on "the great aleatory game" of snakes and ladders (224), springs to mind. But as American fiction has evolved, the importance of disorder has significantly diminished. Partly this is the function of a generation of critics attuned to emerging sciences of chaos and complexity—as well as work in other disciplines—who have revealed that the illusion of disorder in many postmodern works has rather indicated, as William Gaddis notes in *The Recognitions* (1955), the presence of a "perfectly ordered chaos" (18).[4] But at the same time, the diminished importance of disorder is partly a function of the simple passage of time: as postmodernism has progressed, it has become easier to trace fuller arcs for the careers of the early postmodern writers, which makes it easier to distinguish their major works and to reconceive their artistic ambitions. From this long perspective, it becomes clear that many American postmodernists—like the authors of encyclopedic narratives Northrop Frye describes, who "build their creative lives around one supreme effort" (322)—conceived of their careers as culminating in a capstone masterpiece, often encyclopedic in scope, that they constructed over a number of decades. While DeLillo and Pynchon each spent at least 6 years working on a single long book, each designed to encapsulate what *Mason & Dixon* (1997) calls "some Zero-Point of history" (152), their investment of time is dwarfed by the efforts of Gaddis, Coover, and William H. Gass.

Gaddis spent around 50 years researching (and wrestling with) a history of the player piano. A character in his first novel, *The Recognitions*, boasts that this piece of nonfiction would have "everything in it" (579), and Gaddis's notes for the book suggest a landmark work of awesome scale, tracing endless connections through art, science, and music. But as he sensed the scope of the project would defeat him, Gaddis was forced on his deathbed to recast the book as *Agapē Agape* (2002), a more modest 96-page monologue. In a similar vein—though his final work, presumably, is closer to its initial conception than Gaddis's—William Gass spent 30 years working on the dense, allusive journal that makes up his 653-page novel, *The Tunnel* (1995), a text that Gass's narrator describes as "a kind of encyclopedia" (157). Despite the acclaim that greeted his earlier essays and short fiction, Gass often insisted that his reputation should ultimately rest upon this long book. In the early 1970s—more than 20 years before the book was published—he told an interviewer that *The Tunnel* must be considered his "crucial work," while his other projects should be relegated to the status of mere "exercises and preparations" ("William H. Gass" 39). More than any other novel, *The Tunnel* encapsulates this postmodern ambition, taking as its subject a writer who announces that "it was time for 'the Big Book,' the long monument to my mind I repeatedly dreamed I had to have" (4).

To some extent, this drive is surely a product of the same anxious pressures that encouraged the postmodern writer to periodize postmodernism. But the example of Robert Coover, in particular, stresses that when a fuller sense of a postmodernist's career trajectory is considered, a similar level of formal control can be found in their encyclopedic capstone work to that found in the work of the high modernists. Less than 5 years after the publication of his first book, *The Origin of the Brunists* (1965), Coover had evidently begun to plan a long work entitled *Lucky Pierre*, that he would work on for more than 30 years.[5] Despite the fact that he published 11 other (sometimes short) novels and built an impressive reputation with *Pricksongs and Descants*, *The Universal Baseball Association* (1968), and *The Public Burning* (1977), dazzling examples of metafiction that are inescapable in any primer of postmodern fiction, this big project preoccupied him and eluded completion until the year of Coovers' 70th birthday. In its final form *The*

Adventures of Lucky Pierre: Directors' Cut (2002), like much of Coover's earlier work, is composed of a dense verbal tapestry of puns and repetitions, with a central character's narrative caught up in a complex blurring of ontological layers that makes it difficult to locate what's real and what isn't, and—as in all good postmodern tales—this is, of course, partly the point and partly the subject of a critique that's carried within the novel itself. One character's self-conscious outburst "Storyline! It's an associative free-for-all" (116), recasts the complaints of those critics for whom randomness and incoherence overlap with postmodernism, but a more precise examination of the novel reveals a rigid and careful order that underpins the novel's anarchic action. The book's two-part title provides one key to revealing *Lucky Pierre*'s latent order.

The first half of the title alludes to an old joke (also referenced in *Gravity's Rainbow* [497]) about the so-called lucky member in the middle of a homosexual threesome and introduces the reader to at least one of the novel's subjects: pornography. In the porn- and film-dominated setting of the novel, named Cinecity by Coover, Lucky Pierre has long been the most famous porn actor. His career has gradually shifted through six phases that encapsulate the passage from his early days as a child actor, when he was known as "Wee Willy," to his last aged incarnation as "Pete the Beast." The subtitle "directors' cut" may be an ironic allusion to the massive editorial process Coover must have gone through to organize more than 30 year's worth of notes and drafts into a 405-page narrative, but the position of the apostrophe is also significant. Unlike Gass's novel, which describes itself as a "domestic epic . . . that took place entirely in the mind" of one narrator (32), there is not a single controlling director who has produced this text, but instead there are nine female directors whose attempts to direct and entice Lucky are dramatized in different chapters. The combination of Pierre's six incarnations and his nine directors produces what Coover calls a "structural pun" ("An Interview" 72): 6 plus 9 in this pornography-suffused world equals one 69 for the reader.

The artistic sympathies of each of these directors adds further shading to the underlying order of the novel, as Brian Evenson has demonstrated that "each director is associated . . . with one of the nine daughters of Zeus and Mnemosyne . . . who served in ancient Greece as the goddesses of music, art, literature, and intellectual pursuits" (257). But even given this fundamentally modernist patterning, a reader might still fairly ask why a 400-page book required a gestation period of more than 30 years? The first answer is apparent all over the novel's surface in the brilliant verbal exuberance of Coover's prose. The world of pornography is surely one of the most limited and clichéd arenas a novel can enter, but Coover escapes these confines with characteristic verbal dexterity. In an example that could be taken as an algorithm for Coover's technique, the reader can mark the steps as he sheds the constriction of his subject matter in the following passage: "Stand up to be counted these days, you get counted out, swept away in the conflux, the profusion pollution, the sea of faces. The sea of farces. Faeces. Phases. Phrases" (106). In the last 11 words Coover sets out with the raw material of cliché and then seamlessly associates his way to higher ground, passing through comedy and scatology to reach the true subject of his generation: language.

But it is not simply these linguistic pyrotechnics that must have been time consuming for Coover. It is also the exacting precision of that language within the larger frame of the book. The first word of the novel, for example, is *Cantus*, a musical term from the fifteenth and sixteenth centuries that denoted a choral piece in polyphonic style. The suggestion of polyphony neatly introduces the role of the nine directors whose many voices script Pierre's life, but in Coover's careful structure the opening word has more work to do. Appropriately for a novel that promises "secret acrostics" on its second page, if the first letter of each chapter's first word is selected, a clear order emerges that runs c-d-e-f-g-a-b and so on. As the subject of music has been introduced by "Cantus," this is presumably designed to imitate a musical scale, and the pattern holds almost to the end of the book. But the ordering impulse doesn't stop here. There's a parallel movement whereby the last word of each chapter begins with the letter that opens the following chapter. This pattern, again, lasts up to the final chapter and gives some indication of the precision with which Coover has constructed his book.

This sort of careful deployment of language and rigid underlying order reveals lines of continuity between modernism and postmodernism, and, on one level, it encourages a reassessment of the initial emphasis placed upon disorder in the early construction of postmodernism. At the end of postmodernism, the movement seems rather to be obsessed by formal order; thus when Franzen announced in 1996 that "an era of (critically privileged) formal innovation [was] coming to an end" and that the time had come "for form's dialectical counterparts, content and context, to return as the vectors of the new" ("I'll Be Doing More of Same" 38), it makes sense to think of him specifically reacting against the example of such writers as Coover, Gaddis, and Gass. On another level, however, *Lucky Pierre*'s long gestation and its intricate structure encourage recognition of a characteristic impulse within American postmodernism toward producing an encyclopedic capstone work. This recognition runs counter to a critical tradition that has its roots in the work of such eminent modernist critics as Hugh Kenner and Harry Levin, and that continues through to today.[6] In a similar vein, while Jay Clayton (appropriately) cautions in *The Pleasures of Babel* (1993) that evaluative discussions of greatness "may circumscribe the range of valid cultural experiences and privilege a canon tailored to the interests of a small but dominant group of taste makers," his praise for a society that is "constructing a literature without masterpieces" (148) has helped obscure the way that writers such as Coover, Gaddis, and Gass self-consciously strove to create career-affirming masterpieces.

The existence of encyclopedic postmodern masterpieces, predicated on an obsession with formal schemes, is the first element I would like to highlight in the changing shape of postmodernism. But if postmodernism's perceived use of disorder has been almost entirely transformed as the movement evolved, there are other aspects of literary postmodernism whose duration has been more extended. Postmodernism's use of self-referring forms—techniques that bend away from the act of representation to remind the reader, as Coover writes in *The Public Burning* (1977), to "BEWARE THE MAD ARTIST" (288)—has, in particular, gradually emerged to the point where it rests at, or near, the center of the movement. Paul Maltby has noted that although the earliest accounts of postmodernism "understated, if not overlooked, its preoccupation with problems of representation," this oversight was corrected in the late 1970s and early 1980s through the "ascendancy of what we may call the metafictionist paradigm," a paradigm that was underwritten by critical work from Larry McCaffery, Robert Scholes, Christine Brooke-Rose, Patricia Waugh, and others (99). But while Wendy Steiner has asserted that "outside the United States . . . metafictionists . . . are still enthusiastically received; in America, however, critical taste has moved on" (529),[7] the metafictionist paradigm in American literature remains a crucial component of postmodernism, but to explain its centrality, it's necessary to focus upon accounts of the end, rather than the beginning, of postmodernism.

Closing time in the funhouse: Constructing the end of postmodernism[8]

Looking back from the perspective of the millennium, the 1990s appears to have been a transitional decade for American fiction, torn between the emergence of a generation of writers seeking to move beyond postmodernism and the prolonged vitality of many writers—Barth, Gaddis,

Pynchon, Coover—associated with the original rise of the movement. But, while for many critics the end of the century seemed to overlap with the end of postmodernism, the pivotal moment, when the twilight of postmodernism shaded into the dawn of whatever lies beyond, is understandably difficult to locate. One of the problems, here, is that there are several competing accounts of the last days of postmodernism, each of which outlines an alternative chronology for the movement's demise.

From the very start of the 1990s both critics and writers seemed eager to draw a line under the postmodern era in the hope of defining a new imaginative space for fiction. In 1990, for example, William T. Vollmann published a prescient short essay, "American Writing Today: A Diagnosis of the Disease," in which he argued that the "games of stifling breathlessness" associated with postmodernism and structuralism had robbed fiction of its essential weight (358). Just a year later, a more systematic attempt to pinpoint the moment of transition came when a seminar series entitled "The End of Postmodernism" was held in Stuttgart in August 1991. Attended by prominent postmodern novelists, such as John Barth, William Gass, and Raymond Federman, the philosophy of the conference was ostensibly to divine what new directions might be possible after postmodernism. Though many of the participants seemed to doubt whether postmodernism had really come to an end, seminar organizer, Heide Zeigler, evidently believed that it had, and she argued that its demise could be more or less directly traced to the postmodern fascination with self-reference. Metafiction, she argued, had trivialized the postmodern aesthetic, degenerating into mere "playfulness and narcissism" (7).

Just 2 years later, David Foster Wallace published an important essay on the end of postmodernism, "E Unibus Pluram: Television and U.S. Fiction," in the *Review of Contemporary Fiction*, and he, too, traced the movement's collapse to what he described as the corrosive power of postmodern metafiction. Wallace believed that postmodern irony and metafictional strategies had become unworkable because television (the initial target, in Wallace's eyes, of much postmodern fiction) had co-opted these tactics. In place of postmodernism, Wallace saw a group of writers—whose work, he suggested, might be classified as "post-postmodernism" or "image-fiction" (171)—that he hoped would ultimately be able to reestablish the idea of writing as a symbiotic exchange between reader and writer.

Wallace, Vollmann, and Ziegler are noteworthy indicators of the growing dissatisfaction critics and writers felt with postmodernism in the early 1990s. But if there is a moment when postmodernism comes to an end, it seems to be located later in the decade, in or around a 27-month period bracketed by the publication of Larry McCaffery's *After Yesterday's Crash* in August

1995,[9] and November 1997, when Richard Rorty claimed in the *New York Times* that we had reached a point where "nobody has the foggiest idea" what postmodernism meant (13). At this point I would like to briefly break my own rule about respecting the borders of literary postmodernism in order to stress some of the wider resonances of this cultural moment. Within this time frame we find a dense cluster of attempts to smooth down the soil atop the grave of postmodernism: McCaffery's *After Yesterday's Crash* presented Avant-Pop as a movement that was more attuned than postmodernism to the America that had been shaped by the massive media expansion of the late twentieth century. In the same year, Mark Amerika and Lance Olsen introduced a volume, provocatively titled *In Memoriam to Postmodernism: Essays on Avant-Pop* that (in terms that closely mirror those of Wallace's essay) described Avant-Pop as an outgrowth of postmodernism, which had become necessary because the "metafictional strategies of postmodernism got totally absorbed by . . . mainstream media marketers" (2). In 1996, events accelerated. Art critic Hal Foster concluded his study, *The Return of the Real*, with a chapter entitled "Whatever Happened to Postmodernism?" in which he argued that the idea of a postmodernism that suggested the possibility of alternative forms beyond modernism had failed because it had been gradually "emptied by the media" (206). Franzen published his famous *Harper's* essay, "Perchance to Dream" in April in which he outlined his reasons for abandoning his desire to critique and "Address the Culture" in a way that he believed postmodernists had (54). At the same time, urban designer Tom Turner introduced the term *post-postmodernism* in a study of city planning to designate a period that challenged "the 'anything goes' eclecticism of its predecessor"(v). Finally, in 1997, Wallace's essay was republished and brought to a wider audience in his nonfiction collection *A Supposedly Fun Thing I'll Never Do Again*, and philosopher Richard Rorty denounced postmodernism as merely a "word that pretends to stand for an idea" in a *New York Times* symposium on the "Most Overrated Idea" (13).

Clearly something has taken place, here. There are too many different attempts to map a route beyond postmodernism in too many different disciplines in the mid-1990s to dismiss such efforts as either untimely or entirely misguided. Yet, one of the problems for all these accounts is not just that, as Charles B. Harris observed, the corpse of literary postmodernism "remains suspiciously lively" ("PoMo's Wake" 1), but that postmodernism has co-opted reports of its demise and bent them toward the end of *more* postmodernism.

The clearest example of postmodernism's absorption of its own decline is surely to be found in the work of John Barth. A participant at the 1991 Stuttgart seminar, Barth noted in *Once Upon a Time* that "that blank space after *1991*—look[ed] disagreeably gravelike" (10), but he, nevertheless, rapidly transformed the conference into an example of postmodern fiction with the appropriately paradoxical title, "The End: An Introduction," in *On with the Story* (1996). Barth's story diagnoses the impetus behind the conference (which he sees as a millennial fascination with "the end of this, the end of that" [15]) as a "terminary malady" (14) and announces incredulously: "And not long ago, believe it or not, there was an international symposium on 'The End of *Post*modernism'—just when we thought we might be beginning to understand what that term describes!" (14). But this story about endings resists the ending scripted by the Stuttgart conference not just by mocking how premature the idea of the conference was, but also by encoding a resistance to, or refusal of, endings in the story's form. The story begins and ends in midsentence as if to reinforce the narrator-author's belief that he "expect[s] this series to extend ad infinitum" (13). Note, too, that on the microlevel of the sentence, this idea is reinforced by the fact that the sentence describing the symposium does not have a proper beginning, but rather begins with a conjunction. Both the form and the content of this story react against the notion of clear starts and ends and reach instead toward perpetuity.

Although "The End: An Introduction" lasts for only 11 pages, the importance of its response to the end of postmodernism for Barth is indicated by the fact that he recognizably reworked the same imaginative material in *Coming Soon!!!* (2001), the novel that preoccupied him for most of the 1990s. Barth structures this millennial novel around a fiction writing contest between an aging novelist-surrogate for Barth[10] and a young novelist aspirant, but the difference between these two combatants is not simply one of age. The aging writer is a devotee of both print fiction and "literary postmodernism" (329), whereas the younger writer is a proponent of the "post-postmodern" (74), an aesthetic that is much more technologically up-to-date—the young writer is preparing a "cunningly hypertexted magnum opus" (362).[11] In tracing what he considers this new direction to entail, Barth obliquely reveals that the germ of his novel lies in David Foster Wallace's critique of postmodern fiction.

On the brink of the 1990s, Wallace published *Girl with Curious Hair* (1989), a short story collection that concluded with a novella-length metafictional story about metafiction titled "Westward the Course of Empire Takes Its Way." Despite preceding Wallace's essay on television and American fiction by 4 years, "Westward" is intimately linked to his later essay on the failure of postmodernism,[12] and this is absolutely apparent in the skeletal story of the novella, which follows the students of a creative writing instructor named Ambrose on their way to the opening of a Funhouse chain of restaurants that's being developed in association with McDonalds. Ambrose is, of course, the name of a character from Barth's famous metafictional story, "Lost in the Funhouse," and Wallace's character is a very thinly veiled persona for Barth. Ambrose, however, mainly lurks in the background because he is, it seems, soon to be superseded by the younger characters who will "divine a nation's post-postmodern . . . future" (354). Wallace, then, connects Barth's metafiction with the progress of both empire and consumer capitalism, but on a technical level he attempts to counter the elder writer's influence by employing metafictional strategies to (as he later told Larry McCaffery) "expose the illusions of metafiction" (142). All of this seems to add up to a potentially devastating critique of Barth's work, but Wallace's attack funnels into *Coming Soon!!!* because the post-postmodernism of the younger writer in the novel is, Barth tells us, characterized by a tendency to deploy (as Wallace did) "the tradition of the Postmodernist novel . . . with a kind of impatience, like a bored virtuoso illusionist warming up for the main event" (13), as well a tendency to appropriate not simply "certain field-identification marks of Postmodernist taletelling but, on occasion, the tellers themselves" (14). Wallace's attempt to expose the limitations of postmodernism, then, ironically becomes the engine for Barth's postmodern novel, but the end this conflict drives toward is not the end of postmodernism. In Barth's account it is the younger writer who gives up on his electronic fiction, to leave the aging postmodernist to complete his work. In the absence of a valid new movement, we are driven back to enjoy what the novel calls "postmodern nostalgia" (22): Barth quotes Donald Barthelme (283), alludes to Robert Coover (14), and recycles or alludes to several of his earlier works (*The Floating Opera, LETTERS, Further Fridays, On with the Story*), perhaps as a way of "closing the circle on his own life's work" (194–5).

Similar strategies can be located in the works of other postmodernists. *The Adventures of Lucky Pierre*, for example, can be less directly mapped onto one specific critique of postmodernism, but it is, nonetheless, suffused with and inspired by an elegiac tone that records the passing of the movement. While Coover brilliantly rehearses the staples of his brand of postmodernism, "a deep melancholia has stolen in" to his work (402), as Coover's central character reflects "It's over, isn't it" and falls to "Retrospectives, memorials, relics" (367). Like Barth's movement toward postmodern nostalgia, however, Coover's fascination with relics leads him to embed a subtle catalogue of postmodernism's greatest hits in Cinecity's film titles. William Gaddis's *The Recognitions* and *Agapē Agape* are alluded to in the movie *Randy*

Recognitions (32) and the film script that includes "our little love feast. Our agape" (386). There are also more direct echoes of works like Italo Calvino's *Invisible Cities* (1974), which is recast as "*Invisible Titties*" (390); Barth's *Giles Goat-Boy* (1966) and short story collection, *Lost in the Funhouse* (1968), which are melded together in an early Pierre movie, "a goatish knockabout comedy called *Lust in the Funhouse*" (297), while "*Horsebuns and Whines & Feeling Blue: The Travelling Salesman and the Lonesome Wife*," a film featuring "who else but the master himself, Willie," contains a double pun on William Gass's *Willie Masters' Lonesome Wife* (1968) and *On Being Blue* (1975) (366–7).

Coover and Barth's works, then, are gravestones to postmodern metafiction, which paradoxically remind us of the obituaries to the movement, while simultaneously testifying to its continued vitality. But postmodern fiction's peculiar resistance to accounts of its last days should not be considered entirely surprising. Indeed, in 1991—the year of the Stuttgart seminars—Fredric Jameson began his landmark study, *Postmodernism, or, The Cultural Logic of Late Capitalism* by identifying one of the movement's distinguishing features to be "an inverted millenarianism in which premonitions of the future, catastrophic or redemptive, have been replaced by senses of the end of this or that" (1).[13] Or earlier still, consider Barth's contention that a postmodernist should deal "with ultimacy, both technically and thematically," in his important essay "The Literature of Exhaustion" (*Friday Book* 67). A fascination with the new beginnings to be found in endings seems to have been deeply etched into the core of postmodernism.

But what counternarratives existed in the 1990s for the writer who had mastered postmodernism's theoretical toolkit, but who sought to move beyond its premises? Where do Barth and Coover leave the younger writers they influenced? The first thing to note, here, is that examples of younger writers finding their material in the same accounts of the end of postmodernism that inspired writers such as Barth are quite scarce. One rare exception would be Mark Leyner, who published a short ironic and funny fiction entitled "Geraldo, Eat Your Avant-Pop Heart Out" in 1997. Taking Richard Rorty's rejection of postmodernism as its starting point, Leyner imagines a recovering postmodernist called Alex who appears on Jenny Jones's talk show to discuss why he "believes that his literary career and his personal life have been irreparably damaged by [postmodernism], and who feels defrauded by the academics who promulgated it" in the wake of Rorty's "shocking admission" (11). But Leyner is not satisfied to just draw on Rorty as a source text; he also incorporates a parody of David Foster Wallace (who concluded "E Unibus Pluram" with a fairly devastating demolition of

Leyner's *My Cousin, My Gastroenterologist* [1990]), and his insistence that postmodernism could not be followed by writing that simply redeployed postmodern irony. Leyner writes:

Dissolve back to studio. In the audience, JENNY JONES extends the microphone to a man in his mid-20's with a scruffy beard and a bandana around his head.[14]

MAN WITH BANDANNA: I'd like to say that this "Alex" is the single worst example of pointless irony in American literature, and this whole heartfelt renunciation of postmodernism is a ploy—it's just more irony. (11)

Leyner's parody, however, is a fairly isolated example and, in general, younger writers have inevitably been less likely to find their imaginative materials in metafictional games drawing on the literature of last things that so fascinated their predecessors. The development of what might be called *post-postmodernism* has a more ambivalent relationship to the recursive narrative strategies of the earlier generation.

Post-postmodern topographies: A short history and tentative definition

"The Map," Gregory Bateson notes in *Steps to an Ecology of Mind* (1972), "is not the territory" (455), a caveat that is restated in many of the novels that provide the immediate context for my discussion of Franzen's work.[15] But if my map of postmodernism has so far been deliberately based upon only a partial survey of the territory—drawing on just two dimensions of American literary postmodernism—then the movement beyond postmodernism introduces a territory that is so complex that, if not fundamentally unmappable, at least introduces increased danger of distortion. The multiple branching developments of recent American fiction mean that even provisional map making seems an almost hopeless task. Even if discussion is limited to the use of metafiction by writers who seem to have been molded by the influence of postmodern fiction, there are a host of vastly divergent developments. At one pole, there are writers who have diluted the metafictional impulse to the status of a plot device, such as Jhumpa Lahiri, whose stolidly realist *The Namesake* (2003) uses the relationship between books and naming as a plot mechanism that never disrupts her novel's ontological status. At the other extreme, there are writers who are closer to postmodern metafictional practice, such as Marisha Pessl, whose *Special Topics in Calamity Physics* (2006) unfolds according to the principle that each character "is responsible for the page-turning tempo of his or her Life Story" (71) and in which chapters are named after books that control or illuminate their action. Faced with such an eclectic literary field, a reader might feel like the characters in Jorge Luis Borges's treatment of the map paradox, who after futile efforts to establish a map "which coincided point for point with" their territory, abandoned cartography, leaving a land in which "there is no other Relic of the Disciplines of Geography" (325).

To try to make some useful distinctions without generating reductive principles that flatten the diversity of a broad swath of contemporary writing, I'm going to limit my discussion of writing after postmodernism to the three writers—Franzen, Richard Powers, and David Foster Wallace—whose work I discuss throughout the rest of this book. In the chapters that follow I set each Franzen novel alongside parallel works of fiction by his contemporaries Wallace and Powers, to attempt to put Franzen's conception of the future of fiction into context. I select Wallace and Powers as points of reference not just because I believe these two writers have produced some of the most significant work from the last two decades, but also because Franzen himself situated his fiction in relation to their work in the mid-1990s when he was working out the latest phase of his approach to the novel. In 1996, he identified Powers as one of his "classmates in the Neo-Furrowed-Browist school of American fiction" ("FC2" 116).[16] He has also frequently referred to Wallace's work, and in the same year that Franzen noted affinities with Powers, Wallace revealed that he and Franzen had been arguing about the future of fiction ("Quo Vadis" 8). Wallace and Franzen evidently met in the late 1980s, after Wallace sent a letter to Franzen expressing his admiration for *The Twenty-Seventh City*, and his massive novel, *Infinite Jest* (1996), was a particularly important influence upon *The Corrections*, even though both authors ultimately pursue different aesthetic solutions.

Each work by Franzen, Powers, and Wallace bears the thumbprint of their author's idiosyncratic approach—Franzen, as I note in the next chapter, works with a kind of double vision; Powers is fascinated by isomorphism; Wallace was obsessed with self-referring forms—and, by setting their works alongside each other, I do not wish to suggest that these writers are interchangeable, or even that they seek the same intellectual ends. Instead I argue that their novels can be viewed as what biologists call homologous forms. Their essays and interviews, as well as their novels, make it clear that these three writers all emerge from the same origin, having been immersed in the fiction of American postmodernism. Wallace dated his birth as a writer from the day he read Donald Barthelme's "The Balloon" ("Salon

Interview") and he identified the formative influence of Gaddis and DeLillo in "E Unibus Pluram." Powers alludes to Pynchon in both his novels and in nonfiction such as his "Pynchon Appreciation." He has also described DeLillo as "an enormous influence" ("A Conversation"), while he acknowledged in a conversation with me that there was a "direct line" of descent between Gaddis's work and his own. But from this common origin, each writer's fiction has evolved in a different direction.

Despite that divergence, and because of their common roots in postmodernism as well as their parallel attempts to move beyond the work of their literary ancestors, I'm going to classify the work of these three writers as *post-postmodern*. Nobody sensible can feel happy about promoting a new term in a discipline that so often involves itself in hermetic discussion, especially when the term is as ungainly as *post-postmodern*. Yet, out of the available terminological options, *post-postmodern* has the benefit of indicating a simultaneous degree of overlap and separation from the practice of the earlier postmodernists while it has already been used by numerous critics and by several important writers. Not least significant, here, is Wallace, who used the term in his essay "E Unibus Pluram" (171), in his short story collection *Girl with Curious Hair* (354), and in his long novel, *Infinite Jest* (142). But while the term may recently have gained increased currency, its early history is inescapably less auspicious.

In its early literary-critical usage, post-postmodernism was used to indicate the failure of postmodernism to adequately define itself as a distinct phenomenon from modernism. By 1984, Joe David Bellamy had apparently lamented that he had to use the term *postmodern* because although it stressed the fact that the new movement had to be calibrated in relationship to modernism, it led "to absurd consequences like the need to define a Post-Postmodernism" (qtd. in Newman 22).[17] Earlier usages still mock the fashion-driven need for new terminology. In 1975, for example, the *New Yorker* included a satirical "letter to a literary critic" that announced that "Post-Modernism [was] dead."[18] Mocking the rapid succession of literary fashions ("If we're going to slap a saddle on this rough beast, we've got to get moving"), the letter toys with "Post-Post-Modernism" as a descriptive term for the movement after postmodernism, before dismissing it as "lumpy" sounding ("Talk of the Town" 19). Yet, just a year after the *New Yorker*'s parody appeared, the term *post-postmodern* was being used with increasing seriousness in literary-critical circles. In 1976, Alan Wilde tentatively proposed that Barthelme's later work signaled the emergence of a "possibly, post-postmodern?" morality that would be centered around "a humanism of sorts" (68). Two years later, Kimberly Benston shifted the issue from morality to aesthetics when she suggested, in an interview with poet

Amiri Baraka, that a "post-postmodern" poetics might be detected in the work of poetry that emerged after Robert Creeley, Charles Olson, and Allen Ginsberg (307). By 1980—and still on the subject of American poetry—Charles Altieri felt that he had to explain (in a discussion of a division between poetry that sought to represent the immediacy of experience through referential language and poetry that stressed language's role as a cultural system) that he was not offering "statements of a post-postmodern faith" (217).

As if to confirm Bellamy's intuition that simply naming a movement *postmodern* would imply the emergence of a later *post-postmodernism*, in 1986, Larry McCaffery—while ostensibly canonizing postmodernism in the introduction to *Postmodern Fiction: A Bio-bibliographical Guide*—concluded his initial sketch of postmodernism by describing a "Post-postmodernism," which would illustrate "the evolution of contemporary consciousness" (xxv). The new movement, McCaffery presciently suggested, would represent a synthesis between formal innovation and traditional literary modes, though he noted that "this is not to say that experimentalism has dried up completely, but certainly it is obvious that authors today are less interested in innovation per se than they were ten or fifteen years ago" (xxvi). Within a little over 10 years, the term's meaning splinters further. Even though Alan Thiher dismissed the term as a "bizarre expression" (239) in 1990, during the same year David Porush proposed what he called a "post-postmodern model" for the study of science and literature. This model would move "beyond the tail-biting ahistorical 'paradoxy' of postmodernism" (59) by connecting the insights of deconstruction to "recent scientific theory and speculations that have entailed problems with both the limits of logic and classical assumptions about the simplicity of nature" (40). One year later, Malcolm Bradbury described Saul Bellow's novels as taking place in "a post-postmodern time" (38), while by 1995 W. M. Verhoeven was classifying Raymond Carver's contribution to American literature as "post-postmodern moral realism" (58). Other uses abound in the late 1990s.

Obviously the haphazard and conflicting deployment of the term already suggests that it will be no more precise than its predecessor, postmodernism. It's hard to feel good about the explanatory value of a term whose usage collapses the differences between such different writers and contexts. Its bandwidth is just too broad. Nevertheless, for want of a better alternative, I have adopted it in this study, and through the course of the later chapters I will try, on a novel-by-novel basis, to elucidate what developing post-postmodernism means in reference to Franzen's fiction. In preparation for those later discussions, however, it is useful to sketch out an initial skeleton definition of the field identification marks of post-postmodern fiction as I conceive of them.

1. Post-postmodernism explicitly looks back to, or dramatizes its roots within, postmodernism. As such it is a development from, rather than an explicit rejection of, the preceding movement, and so—just as modernist works have affinities with postmodernist works—post-postmodernist novels betray (as Harris noted in "PoMo's Wake") a family resemblance to the previous generation's work.[19] It is the burden of much of the rest of this study to demonstrate how Franzen's intertextual dialogues make plain his postmodern origins, but it is worth briefly noting here that his work consistently includes knowing winks to the reader about his postmodern ancestors—Duane Thompson's attempt to make a joke about Pynchon and paranoia in *The Twenty-Seventh City* (*TS* 55); the copy of Barth's *The Sot-Weed Factor* (1960) that Renée Seitchek discards in *Strong Motion* (*SM* 239); or Chip's email address in *The Corrections*, "exprof@gaddisfly.com" (*C* 428). In a similar fashion, Wallace interspersed references to DeLillo, Gaddis, and Pynchon throughout *Infinite Jest*, in particular. The "M.I.T. language riots" (987n24) mentioned toward the end of the novel refer to a fictional event from DeLillo's 1976 novel, *Ratner's Star* (31)[20]; Steven Moore has identified the fictional location "Erythema AZ" (227) as an allusion to the skin disease plaguing Wyatt Gwyon in *The Recognitions* ("First Draft"), while one character, Orin Incandenza, steals the last name of Pynchon's Pig Bodine as a pseudonym, a ruse that he defends as "a private chuckle" (1014n110). Equally, Powers has said that he has "always tried to write [his] personal landmarks directly into my books in some way . . . by some quotation or homage or identifiable theft that brands the book's indebtedness" ("An Interview" 21), and his books clearly mark his postmodern heritage. Powers's *The Time of Our Singing* (2004), for example, subtly echoes Pynchon's work. When Powers describes Marian Anderson singing on the brink of the Second World War and reflects that "a state takes shape, ad hoc, improvised, revolutionary, free—a notion, a nation that, for a few measures, in song at least, is everything it claims to be" (48), the reader is meant to hear the dark echo of *Gravity's Rainbow*: "a State begins to takes form in the stateless German night, a State that spans oceans" (566).[21]

Beyond these allusions to literary ancestors, a more serious dimension of post-postmodernism's filial relationship to postmodernism is the continuity of the kind of ambition to produce an encyclopedic masterwork that I identified earlier in this chapter as a characteristic impulse within postmodernism. The encyclopedic ambition of such writers as Gaddis, Pynchon, Coover, and Gass provides a model that controls and sets the standard for the younger generation of writers. In constructing *Infinite Jest* and *The Gold Bug Variations,* both Wallace and Powers clearly attempted to reproduce the intellectual range and formal care that characterized the encyclopedic masterpieces of the older writers.[22] In the case of Franzen, however, I argue in Chapter 5 that it is the legacy of this impulse that deformed his early attempts to write *The Corrections* as a work that would shift between first and third person (like Wallace and Powers's books), and would orientate itself in relationship to a character who was "full of data" ("How He Came" 123). The model of the postmodern masterwork, then, is important both as it is imitated, and departed from, in the work of the next generation.

In identifying this line of continuity between postmodernism and post-postmodernism, it is clear that the role of form is the dimension that fluctuates the most both between and within generations. Although Franzen, Powers, and Wallace have each produced works that stress homologies between form and content, in each of these works the balance between the importance of form and something closer to a conventional plot grounded in a recognizable world, is weighted toward plot to a much greater degree than in the work of the postmodernists. Even between the three post-postmodern writers, however, there is fluctuation. In their work, the importance of form might be conceived of on a sliding scale, with Powers at the most formal extreme at one end and Franzen at the most story-based extreme at the other. This is not to suggest that Franzen's works are not carefully arranged—in fact, it is their formal dimensions that have perhaps been most overlooked by critics—but, as I'll argue in Chapters 4 and 5, in particular, the precise nature of the formal arrangement, what I call his use of "temporal form," is deliberately and carefully set to reinforce the importance of story.

2. Post-postmodern novels are informed by the postmodernist critique of the naïve realist belief that language can be a true mirror of reality, and yet they are suspicious of the logical climax to this critique: Derrida's famous statement that "there is nothing outside the text" (158). The consequences of this are both aesthetic and political. From an aesthetic standpoint, this means that metafictional techniques are employed with less regularity and toward different ends by post-postmodernists, and so their fiction tends to

produce hybrid novelistic forms.[23] From a political point of view, this means that the younger novelists *more obviously* address the idea of a real world beyond the problems raised by nonreferential systems of discourse.

After their apprentice fictions, Franzen, Powers, and Wallace produced their first major works in the 1990s in the midst of the debates over the end of postmodernism that I traced earlier in this chapter. What was surely notable in these debates was that so many critical efforts to mark the end of the movement identified metafiction as the malignant tissue within the flesh of the postmodern novel. However the concept of metafiction was treated by different critics, the reaction against self-referring postmodernism is absolutely the atmosphere within which the post-postmodern writer works. The influence of this atmosphere, for Wallace, often meant attempting a kind of meta-metafiction, as he did in short stories such as "Westward" or "Octet," and he described the earlier story as an attempt "to get the Armageddon-explosion, the goal metafiction's always been about, I wanted to get it over with, and then out of the rubble reaffirm the idea of art being a living transaction between humans" ("An Interview" 142).[24] Employing rather different techniques, Powers—as I discuss in some detail at the end of Chapter 5—sees in the selective deployment of metafictional techniques another way to reengage with the world beyond the book. Utilizing self-reference to create what he calls a "jump shift in epistemic levels" ("A Dialogue" 187), Powers hopes his novels will reawaken the reader "to the irreducible heft, weight, and texture of the entrapping world" ("Literary Devices" 15).

I consider parallels between narrative strategies employed by Powers and Franzen at the end of Chapter 5, but out of these three writers, it is clear that Franzen's work reacts most strongly against self-referential strategies, and he rarely engages in moments that are purely metafictional. While I note in the next chapter that Franzen's early writing—indeed his very first publication, *The Fig Connection* (1977)— flirts with self-conscious frame breaking, the proportions of his later fiction are weighted much more heavily toward emphasizing language's referential qualities. Nevertheless, even *The Corrections* reminds the reader of a word's dual existence as print sign and referential signifier when, on the novel's first page, Franzen invokes a word you can "stare at until it resolves itself into a string of dead letters" (*C* 3). The synthesis between realist and self-reflexive modes is perhaps most pronounced in Powers's work,[25] though the tendency of the post-postmodern writer, in general, to effect some compromise between the two has typically made their works variegated forms, stitching together a hybrid of different literary styles. This tendency to mix modes may be one reason why Robert McLaughlin detects in *The Corrections* "an inconsistent attitude toward language" (63).

McLaughlin also notes in his valuable essay on reactions against postmodernism that "a good way to think about the agenda of post-postmodernism" is that "literature has been and continues to be valuable as a way of critiquing our social world . . . but only if we understand that all . . . things are mediated through language" (67).[26] The question of an engagement with the social world (which, McLaughlin correctly insists, is not altogether absent from postmodern fiction) is an element that is more strongly emphasized by post-postmodernist novelists and perhaps promotes a more direct political engagement. There is consequently less of the element of silliness that sometimes creeps into the postmodern novel's defamiliarizing strategies—the talking dogs, the satirical songs—and a more earnest (not necessarily more sophisticated) attempt to address global issues. In "American Writing Today," Vollmann urges contemporary novelists to address "important human problems" (358), and the post-postmodern novel frequently considers ecological questions, in particular.

In *The Comedy of Survival* (1997), Joseph W. Meeker asks "from the unforgiving perspective of evolution and natural selection, does literature contribute more to our survival than it does to our extinction?" (4), and Powers, Wallace, and Franzen have frequently answered this question by examining the different ways in which literature can contribute to survival by encoding warnings about the environmental future. *Infinite Jest* probes the intersection of commerce, state, and environment to imagine the effects of "a kind of ecological gerrymandering" (403). *The Gold Bug Variations* maps the "increasingly complex web of interdependent nature" (411–12), while *The Echo Maker* (2006), moves toward its conclusion with an image of a posthuman ecosystem, "when the surface of the earth is parched and spoiled, when life is pressed down to near-nothing . . . Nature and its maps will use the worst that man can throw at it. The outcome of owls will orchestrate the night, millions of years after people work their own end" (443). In an essay about Powers, Scott Hermanson suggests the term *econovelist* to describe such writers, whose understanding of the environment is shaped by both a knowledge of science and an awareness of the complexities of literary representation ("Just Behind the Billboard" 62), and Wallace and Franzen seem to fit this category. More specifically, Franzen's first two novels move toward an examination of what Lawrence Buell calls a "mythography of betrayed Edens," threatened by "occult toxic networks" (37, 38), that climaxes in *Strong Motion*.

3. Post-postmodernism is more obviously preoccupied with notions of character than postmodernism, and yet this development is not as straightforward as it may seem. First, each successive major literary movement in the past 100 years has routinely announced that it had a more tenacious grasp on character than its predecessor. Virginia Woolf, for example, tried to clear a space for modernist fiction in "Mr Bennett and Mrs Brown" (1924), by announcing that while the earlier Edwardian novelists "were never interested in character in itself" (77), her generation's work would get closer to the "surprising apparition" that approximated real human identity (86). In a parallel gesture, when John Barth promoted his brand of postmodernism in "The Literature of Exhaustion," he presented it as an opportunity to "rediscover validly . . . such far-out notions as . . . characterization" after the era of modernist experimentation had neglected to do so (*Friday Book* 68). By the time Franzen issued his 2002 complaint that in postmodern fiction "Characters, properly speaking, weren't even supposed to exist. Characters were feeble, suspect constructs," but that he "seemed to need them" as a reader and writer (*A* 247), it becomes clear that we are not dealing with some straightforward notion that is either included in fiction or is not; rather we are dealing with a continuum of at least a 100 years in which writers working within different cultural matrixes each give a different inflection to the concept of character.

Some of these inflections seem to be more important to specific writers than others. During David Foster Wallace's attempts to probe "the soul's core systems" (692) in *Infinite Jest*, for example, he has one character identify a "hip cynical transcendence," which he associates with "the U.S. arts" (694), which he implicitly suggests is the attitude that prevents us from encountering people "being really human" (695) in postmodern fiction. For Franzen, however, I offer a more developed account of how *The Corrections* might map onto specific postmodern debates about character in Chapter 5, an account that suggests that Franzen's attitude is more ambivalent than earlier critics have detected. But, in spite of individual distinctions, some foundational work describing larger generational overlaps and divergences can be outlined here. Although some critics—normally those who are orchestrating some agenda against postmodern fiction—identify character as a concept that is systematically refined out of the postmodern novel, there are presumably few postmodern writers who would support such a claim. Besides Barth, Thomas Pynchon, for example, has distinguished his mature fiction from his early work in terms of his apprentice effort's failure to establish "some grounding in human reality" because "plot and characters" were subservient to "something abstract—a thermodynamic coinage or the data in a guidebook" (*Slow Learner* 17–18). Where the emphasis on character seems to differ between postmodern and post-postmodern fiction, however, is in the degree of personal history dramatized by the author, and this is linked to alternative treatments of time. As Ursula Heise has argued, "postmodernist novels focus on the moment or the narrative present at the expense of larger temporal developments" (64). In, say, William Gaddis's *JR* (1975), Coover's *Lucky Pierre*, DeLillo's *Great Jones Street* (1973), or *White Noise* (1985), the central characters—JR Vansant, Pierre, Bucky Wunderlick, Jack Gladney—may largely seem to be psychologically credible, but they do, however, seem to have emerged more or less out of nowhere. Because in each of these novels—even in *Lucky Pierre* with its shifting ontological layers—the author largely respects the integrity of time's arrow, we pick up only fragments of a character's history as the dramatic necessity of the novel's present dredges them up. We learn, then, in Gaddis's novel that JR comes from a family named Vansant only after reading nearly 500 pages when his teacher, Amy Joubert, finds occasion to mention his last name to Jack Gibbs (497). Equally we only learn JR's mother's occupation when a conversation with composer Edward Bast prompts him to blurt out that "she's like this here nurse" (134). Similarly, in *White Noise*, we only discover that Jack has been married five times as the necessities of the immediate moment present the reader with children whose parentage Jack needs to explain: the possible return of his daughter Bee reveals that Jack had a "marriage to Tweedy Browner" (16); a discussion with his daughter Steffie prompts Jack to explain that his "first and fourth marriages were to Dana Breedlove" (213). We piece these artfully displaced fragments together, and construct whatever backstory we can.

In post-postmodern novels, however, we get a fuller sense of a character's personal history because these younger authors more freely interrupt time's passage through strategically deployed analepses.[27] In *The Corrections*, for example, the story of Chip Lambert's struggles, as they progress from his parent's visit in September (when he is 39 years old) through to his return from Lithuania, are enriched not just by the lengthy flashbacks relayed in "The Failure" (which cover the preceding 6 years), but also by the protracted ventures into time past in "At Sea," when Franzen gives us snapshots of Chip's childhood from 32 years earlier. *Infinite Jest* works on a similar axis. While Wallace's novel opens in 2010,[28] by presenting the reader with a 15-page scene introducing Hal Incandenza, the novel drops into the past for the rest of the book, excavating a mosaic of scenes from a 50-year period (going back beyond Hal's birth to introduce his father and grandfather) that help to explain how Hal became the character we briefly encounter in 2010. In a more muted fashion, Powers's *Gain* (1998) interrupts its story of Laura Bodey with brief memories of the earliest funerals she attended as a young girl (14), or of her previous hairstyles (109). This shift, I suggest, represents a younger generation's more fundamental belief in the shaping influence of temporal process—that the things that happen to you in the past make a difference to who you are in the present—and it entails a number of consequences for the post-postmodern novel. Most importantly, the idea of the shaping influence of genetic inheritance figures more prominently in post-postmodern fiction. In this respect, it is remarkable how many recent books by postmodern-influenced American authors have focused on generational succession or lost ancestors. As well as *The Corrections* and *Infinite Jest*, a short list of such works would include Powers's *Gold Bug*, Dave Eggers's *A Heartbreaking Work of Staggering Genius* (2000), Mark Costello's *Big If* (2002), Lahiri's *The Namesake*, Jonathan Safran Foer's *Everything Is Illuminated* (2005), Nicole Krauss's *The History of Love* (2005), and Pessl's *Special Topics in Calamity Physics*.

But if the relationship between time and character varies between postmodernism and post-postmodernism, then there are other divergences in terms of character where the borders between the two movements seem to shade into each other. Perhaps the most important of these areas concerns the influence of ideas drawn from neuroscientific research, which suggest that the neurophysiology of the brain underpins character motivation. Though most postmodern writers have not engaged with research into the brain, Tom Robbins alluded to "recent neurological research" in *Even Cowgirls Get the Blues* (1976); Joseph McElroy based his 1976 novel, *Plus*, around a disembodied brain floating in space; and, since 1973, Don DeLillo's novels have consistently addressed neuroscientific ideas, provocatively asking whether behavior was "all a question of brain chemistry, signals going back and forth, electrical energy in the cortex?" (*White Noise* 45). Perhaps partly because commentators such as Howard Gardner and Clifford Geertz have suggested that "mind-science be viewed as a quasi-literary rather than strictly scientific enterprise" (Horgan 264), and surely in large part because the 1990s was designated "The Decade of the Brain," neuroscientific explanations of behavior form a much more prominent part of the worldview of the post-postmodern novelist. This is not to suggest that these writers have simplistically absorbed reductionist conceptions of selfhood from science—just as frequently the neuronal conception of character is a model writers have reacted against—but their attention to the nonliterary realities of their world have increasingly presented them with scientific explanations of what DeLillo calls "the violent chemistries of men" (*Ratner's Star* 256).

Amongst post-postmodern writers, Richard Powers has most successfully mined the interface between neuroscience and fiction. Drawing on Paul D. MacLean, Joseph LeDoux, Daniel Dennett, Antonio Damasio, and many others, Powers has explored how the evolution of the neuronal circuitry of the brain has left it "hardwired to fear" (*Gold Bug* 546), while *The Echo Maker* provides a comprehensive analysis of the neuroscientific self. Neuroscience sits further from the center of Wallace's work, but in *Infinite Jest* he named a character after the Russian neurologist A. R. Luria and explores the actions of characters who draw on "some deep reptile-brain level" of cognition (548).[29] For Franzen, the conceptual underpinnings of neuroscience are linked to the philosophical substratum of postmodernism. He explains that the neural map of the mind "with its image of neural networks effortlessly self-coordinating, in a massively parallel way, to create my ghostly consciousness and my remarkably sturdy sense of self . . . [seems] lovely and postmodern" (*A* 10). Perhaps because he associates neuroscience with postmodernism—in spite of its appeal—Franzen largely reacts against this materialist explanation of selfhood in the plot of *The Corrections*, though the novel's structure nevertheless invokes specific neuroscientific research. Despite the broad spectrum of positions toward neuroscience, the importance of the neuronal explanation of character seems to be a crucial component of the way character is conceived in the contemporary world, and by extension in the post-postmodern novel. As I've tried to stress, however, such explorations of scientific ideas are not without their postmodern precedents—especially in DeLillo's fiction—so the difference here is perhaps one of degree rather than kind.

In outlining these tentative categories, I've limited my sample of post-postmodern writers to Franzen, Wallace, and Powers, though it seems to me that a comparable case could be made (though not always with the same uniformity or with the same confidence) for such writers as Evan Dara, Marisha Pessl, George Saunders, Lynne Tillman, and William T. Vollmann. But it should be stressed that the post-postmodernism outlined here is not an achieved position that exists rigidly across Franzen's three novels. If postmodernism, as Patricia Waugh argues, represents a mood of intense "dissatisfaction or loss of faith in the forms of representation . . . associated with modernism and modernity" (3), then Franzen's work consistently strains to move beyond such disaffection. Viewed in isolation, however, his novels seem to reflect shifting aesthetic dialogues that—as I argue in later chapters—might be classified as modernist (*The Twenty-Seventh City*), postmodernist (*Strong Motion*), and post-postmodernist (*The Corrections*). Without neglecting the developmental arc of his work, what I'd like to suggest, and explore throughout the rest of this book, is first, that in spite of the fact that Franzen's intertextual dialogues sometimes reach back to modernism, what we see in his early novels is an emergent post-postmodernism that only gradually becomes an achieved position as the millennium approached. Second, I'd like to suggest that although Franzen's work relies much more heavily on the norms of conventional—even generic—fiction than Powers and Wallace's novels do, his fiction rewards the kind of careful elucidation that Powers and Wallace have enjoyed. But before I turn to these novels, it is helpful to set the overview of the end of postmodernism I have mapped, here, against Franzen's personal development, by introducing his earlier—more obviously self-referential—writing and considering the relevance of the construction of his relationship to postmodernism that he offers in his nonfiction.

Chapter 2

Genealogy
Franzen's Early Writing

When we are confronted with a list, we have to ask what the purpose of the list is, for a list is a purposeful collection.

William H. Gass, Tests of Time *(89)*

Near the middle of Franzen's second novel, *Strong Motion*, the seismologist Renée Seitchek filters her old books, deciding which works to keep and which to throw away:

> she flipped books into the carton, *A Separate Peace, Franny and Zooey, Zen and the Art of Motorcycle Maintenance, The Women's Room. The Glass Bead Game, The Sot-Weed Factor*, a stack of Vonnegut, some Frank Herbert and Robert Heinlein, *Watership Down, Fear of Flying, The Sunlight Dialogues*, a boxed set of Tolkien, more Salinger, some P. D. James, *The Bell Jar, 1984* . . . D. T. Suzuki, *The World According to Garp* and *Ragtime* followed. (*SM* 239–40)

Renée's attempt to catalogue these books takes place on the margins of the real drama of *Strong Motion*—its seismic upheavals and street protests—but, for a number of reasons, it's possible to read the list she produces as an introduction to both Franzen's life and work, a way of starting to think about how he relates to a reaction against postmodernism, because the list provides a kind of grammar of his novelistic method, distilling some of his obsessions and characteristic strategies. First of all, the list draws our attention to one of Franzen's habitual characterization techniques. John Frow has argued that the list is "postmodernism's preferred genre" (vii), and Franzen affirms that we live in an "age in love with lists" (*A* 187). In each of his novels, when a character is beset by some sort of trauma their list-making instinct is stimulated, and they respond by trying to bring their world to order by preparing a list. Here, for example, is how Alfred Lambert responds in *The Corrections* when he is tormented by the sexual energy and indiscretion of his fellow humans:

> He lay awake . . . and catalogued the faults of humanity . . . Alfred blamed the girl . . . He blamed the man . . . He blamed God . . . He blamed democracy . . . He blamed the motel's architect . . . He blamed the motel management . . . He blamed the frivolous, easygoing townspeople . . . He blamed his fellow guests. (*C* 244)

For Alfred, this kind of list making is a temporary solace for his ills. His list rotates the offending couple through a series of larger systems—moving from church and state down to the microcosm of his immediate companions—to search for an explanation why people do not behave as he believes they should. Alfred faces a situation that he finds painful, so he makes it explicable by cataloguing the personal failures that allowed the situation to arise.

Though less hierarchical, Renée's catalogue is an example of the same urge. In the instance above she is regrouping in the wake of a torturous experience with her family, and her list of books to discard is an attempt to regain control of her sense of self. Along with these books, she throws out shoes, posters, jackets, records, cartoons, and a pair of polyester bell-bottoms with giant green-and-white checks. As she unfolds the bell-bottoms, she reveals the directing principle behind her list: "I'm supposed to go through life feeling good about myself, knowing there was a time I was seen in public in these?" (*SM* 240). Her list of books, then, is restorative. It is an attempt to cleanse herself of the contamination of her previous personal failures.

Yet, while Renée's list introduces a compulsion that Franzen explores in each of his novels, the motivation behind her catalogue also highlights an anxiety that haunts many of Franzen's meditations on literature: which books will survive, and which will be discarded in a world where "the novel is dying?" (*A* 171). This obsession is not without its postmodern inflection. In the year of *Strong Motion*'s publication, Robert Coover published an essay on hypertext with the threatening title "The End of Books," and in both his fiction and nonfiction, Franzen circles gloomily around the questionable survival prospects of the contemporary novel and sets them against his fear that in millennial America "every hour of the year" is "a good hour for staring at a screen" (*C* 522). The relationship between electronic media and literature explored by Coover is polarized into an opposition in Franzen's essays, in particular, but Renée's rejection of her books does more than simply introduce the threat of literature's obsolescence. The specific books she decides to discard are revealing, too.

There are several preliminary observations that can be made about these rejected books. First of all, with the exception of D. T. Suzuki's text, all are works of fiction. Second, it's notable that amongst these fictions, Franzen does not include any novels that have already stood the test of time. The oldest book he names is Herman Hesse's *The Glass Bead Game* (1943), published just 46 years before Renée compiles her list in *Strong Motion*.[1] Equally, the most recent book is John Irving's *The World According to Garp* (1978), so Renée's list evaluates a precisely delineated slice of 35 years of literature. Finally, of the 18 fiction writers listed, nearly three quarters are American. In its broad outlines, then, the list offers a snapshot of 35 years of mainly American literature. Already we have a sign that Franzen's fiction is preoccupied with the American fiction produced by the generation that precedes his own.

But regardless of these narrowed parameters, what is the reader to deduce from a list of books as eclectic as this? The list permits no easy reductions, although it can be parsed in several ways. There are "popular" and "literary" works (perhaps Herbert, P. D. James, and Tolkien, lining up against Orwell, Plath, Hesse, and Salinger); postmodernist and realist works (Barth and Vonnegut rather than Gardner, Irving, and Knowles); works with direct political messages alongside works whose dialogue tends to be self-referring (Orwell, French, and Jong versus Barth, Doctorow, and perhaps Salinger)[2]; and there is even an uneasy mix of subgenres, with science fiction (Herbert, Heinlein) nestled next to fantasy (Tolkien) and crime fiction (P. D. James). The problem, however, is that there are just too many options here. It would be convenient if the list could be easily reduced to one particular genre or aesthetic strategy that Franzen wants the reader—like Renée—to reject, but the list does not offer such a simple solution.

Instead, Renée's list introduces two artistic strategies that help to illuminate Franzen's fiction. First, one of the contentions of each of the following chapters in this study is that a Franzen novel, like those by Powers and Wallace, insistently establishes an implicit dialogue with earlier books. In elucidating this dialogue, I don't mean to suggest that Franzen's work has a purely literary component. Amongst the dense spectrum of nonliterary influences that have shaped his novels, contemporary cinematic works, for example, have also been quite influential. While his first two books certainly owe part of their conception of conspiracy as a structuring device for narrative to Pynchon and DeLillo, they also draw their dark, paranoid atmosphere from movies such as Ivan Passer's *Cutter's Way* (1981) and Wim Wender's *The American Friend* (1977). Similarly, Chip's adventures in Lithuania, as they are dramatized in *The Corrections*, reflect the influence of the postsocialist Albania sketched in Gianni Amelio's *Lamerica* (1994), a movie Franzen watched while working on the novel.

Equally, even though the "problem of originality" is a theme in Franzen's first two novels (*TS* 343, cf. *SM* 170), I don't mean to suggest that Franzen is unable to write a sentence without desperately reaching back to some earlier work for support. In his *Anatomy of Criticism*, Northrop Frye insists that "poetry can only be made out of other poems; novels out of other novels" (97), but I am not necessarily arguing in support of this vast interlinked framework of literary history. Instead, the intertextual dialogue I outline in Franzen's work emerges because he deliberately conceives of books not in isolation, but as nodes in a larger network, and his allusions are partly a way of acknowledging his debts to that network and partly a way of articulating distinctions between his own fiction and earlier novels. However the intertextual conversation functions, books for Franzen are a means of connection, which is one of the reasons why in both his first two novels he has major characters employed by libraries.

Second, I argue that the synthesis of apparently opposed literary qualities embedded in Renée's list—popular versus literary, postmodernist versus realist, and so on—are indicative of the fundamental curve of Franzen's imagination. For reasons that appear both personal and aesthetic, division and its flipside, synthesis, seem to be the underlying principles of Franzen's life and fiction. Near the end of the first book on Renée's list, *A Separate Peace* (1959), the narrator complains that he "was trying to cope with something that might be called double vision" (185). Mixing opposites, and resisting simple unities, a kind of double vision shapes each of Franzen's novels. While I analyze how this strategy informs or deforms each of Franzen's novels in Chapters 3 and 5, in particular, in this chapter I explore the personal ramifications of this double vision for Franzen.

Origins

One way to approach Franzen's double vision, and to attempt to read Renée's list, is to refract the list through the lens of his biography. According to "On Being Unable to Read," an essay by Valerie Cornell—Franzen's ex-wife and the dedicatee of *Strong Motion*—Franzen himself had to decide which books he wanted to keep and which he could discard when he and Cornell faced "the bisection of a shared library" after their marriage disintegrated (405). Like Renée, Franzen was evidently willing to give up *Franny and Zooey*, but Cornell reports that he wanted to keep DeLillo's novels and volume II (but not volumes I and III) of Proust.

But while it might be possible to map connections between life and art, Franzen's beloved Proust cautions that "one ought never to know an author except through his books" (2: 53). Although there seem to be large overlaps between what we know of Franzen's biography and the lives of some of his characters, Franzen has echoed Proust's warning in terms of both his novels and his essays. In *The Twenty-Seventh City* he mocks people's interest in biography when Susan Jammu ironically summarizes a conversation about her background as a list of "everything you wanted to know about my private life but were too bored to ask" (*TS* 379). Circling the same issue in 2002, Franzen told Kevin Canfield that the "I" addressing the reader in his essays should be considered as just "a rhetorical construction. It's a version of me. The novels are versions of me," but "the real private self is a much blurrier and messier and multivalent thing." This is a book primarily about Franzen's novels, rather than about Franzen himself, but—bearing Proust and Franzen's warnings in mind—it is still worth outlining a chronology of Franzen's life, even if only to provide a framework in which the large body of his mainly unknown early writing can be contextualized.

Jonathan Earl Franzen was born on August 17, 1959, in Western Springs, Illinois, and even the year of his birth signals division, as he has noted that 1959 marks "the cusp of a great generational divide" (*A* 164). His father, Earl T. Franzen, had been raised in northern Minnesota and was employed by several engineering and railroad companies in Minnesota, Wisconsin, Illinois, and Missouri, before he worked as a chief engineer for the Missouri Pacific Railroad (MoPac, then, seems to provide the model for MidPac in *The Corrections*) between 1967 and his retirement in the summer of 1981. Franzen's mother, Irene Super, shared Earl's roots in Minnesota. She was a bartender's daughter, but before her marriage she worked as a receptionist in a doctor's office (*DZ* 13). The couple evidently met in a philosophy night class at the University of Minnesota, when Earl worked for the Great Northern Railroad, but their marriage, according to Franzen, turned out to be "less than happy" (*A* 11). By the time of Franzen's birth Earl and Irene already had two sons, but because of the difference in their ages—Tom (a contractor in Seattle) is 9 years older than Jonathan, while Bob (a doctor in Portland, Oregon) is 11 years older—he spent much of his childhood feeling like an only child. He recalls, "my parents had me late in life, and my most typical experience as a child was to be left to my own devices while adults went to work and had parties" (*A* 299).

In 1964 the Franzens moved to St. Louis, settling a year later in suburban Webster Groves where they lived in an attractive home at 83 Webster Woods. In *The Discomfort Zone,* Franzen offers this description of his childhood home as it stood in 1999:

> Two story solid brick three bedroom center hall colonial home on shaded lot on cul de sac on private street. There are three bedrooms, living room, dining room with bay, main floor den, eat-in kitchen with new G.E. dishwasher, etc. There are two screened porches, two wood-burning fireplaces, two car attached garage, security burglary and fire system, hardwood floors throughout and divided basement. (*DZ* 7–8)

Webster Groves is, of course, also home to the Probst family in *The Twenty-Seventh City,* but Franzen situated them in "a three-story stucco house" about a mile away on Sherwood Drive (*TS* 27). Franzen chose this house for the Probsts because he toured the home's gardens when he was at school, and recalled that "it seemed the essence of earthly comfort . . . not quite characteristic of the rest of the town" ("Don't Judge" 3). The Franzens, themselves, were more clearly a part of the town, attending the First Congregational Church of Webster Groves, while Jonathan was enrolled at Webster Groves High School. Although Franzen recalls that he considered himself "on the outside" at High School, mixing with friends "who were not headed in traditional directions," he did take part in some traditional activities (at age 15 he played the baritone for the Marching Statesmen of Webster Groves [*A* 290]) and he evidently remembers his time at the school fondly ("Don't Judge" 3). The teachers, Franzen notes, "thought it was their job or privilege to encourage creativity of all kinds," and they provided the inspiration behind his first publication, as Franzen's former physics teacher, Bill Blecha, who describes Franzen as an "outspoken but not sassy" student, persuaded the pupils to produce a play ("In the Mind's Eye" G11). Following these instructions, Franzen set to work with Kathy Siebert and the outcome was *The Fig Connection,* a play that was deemed so successful at Webster Groves that Franzen and Siebert were encouraged to publish it. When Franzen was just 17, they managed to sell the play for $100, a windfall that encouraged him to pursue a career as a writer.

The Fig Connection is a one-act play, split into four scenes and a finale, and like Franzen's later novels it relies on unlikely juxtapositions in terms of both plot and technique for much of its impact. Mixing east and west, modernity and anachronism, the play takes as its dramatic situation the efforts of some apparently modern Russian spies to capture Isaac Newton before he discovers gravity in London in 1666.³ The title, then, is a pun on Nabisco's *Fig Newtons,* and the odd unions that create the plot are replayed in the dramatic texture of the play which mixes slapstick routines, which are meant to recall the Keystone Cops, alongside scenes that parade a metadramatic awareness of the play's artificiality, such as this excerpt from near the end of the play:

> WINSTON: By the way, what happened to your lovely lab assistant?
> NEWTON: Oh, she's just offstage somewhere.
> WINSTON: (a bit baffled) Where?
> NEWTON: Oh, you know, offstage. (38)

Elsewhere in the play Franzen and Siebert indulge in similar postmodern frame breaking—characters leave the stage and chase each other up the theater's aisles; a character who has been hiding in the audience throws off a disguise shortly after the play opens and joins the actors onstage—and there seems to be a faint echo of Samuel Beckett's *Endgame* (1957) in a scene where two actors hide in trashcans.

Franzen discusses his personal relationship with Siebert in *The Discomfort Zone,* but his creative partnership with her is significant for several reasons. First, his collaboration with Siebert introduces Franzen's tendency to work alongside female writers—in her wake, Franzen produced books while involved with Valerie Cornell and Kathy Chetkovich. Both had books dedicated to them, but each seems to have experienced a degree of ambivalence about Franzen's success.⁴ But Siebert is also important to Franzen's later work because after finishing *The Fig Connection* the two also collaborated on an untitled play⁵ about British colonial India that featured a character who would serve as a prototype for Susan Jammu, the Indian American police officer who dominates Franzen's first novel. He recalled Jammu's first incarnation in this play in an interview in 1988:

> It was just an absurd, long, anachronistic comedy-mystery . . . but there was a police inspector named Jammu, who was male at the time, and a while later I had the idea of putting this character, whom we all had liked, into a story set in St. Louis. The idea basically started with the collision of this character, this strange Indian police officer, with what in my mind is a pretty ordinary Midwestern city. ("Don't Judge" 3)

After graduating from Webster High in 1977, Franzen left this ordinary city to study at Swarthmore College, Pennsylvania, a school that appears several times in his fiction.[6] Franzen's remembers it as an intellectually challenging environment, noting that his first paper for an English class was written for Professor Chuck James who deemed his work to only merit a C+. This experience, Franzen recalls, taught him that good writing was hard work (Mills).

At Swarthmore

Swarthmore, in the late 1970s and early 1980s, seems to have offered a vibrant, stimulating atmosphere for a young writer. During Franzen's 4 years of study, the college hosted an Auden symposium and a presentation on Faulkner's South. There were also readings from such writers as John Knowles (lecturing in 1977 on "Why I Write"), Alice Walker (reading in 1981 from *You Can't Keep A Good Woman Down* [1981]), and E. L. Doctorow (who gave a poetry reading in 1981). Each of these writers is named, or alluded to, in Franzen's novels,[7] and Franzen would later call Doctorow "our most exciting historical novelist" ("Where Our Troubles Began" 1), but as well as visits from celebrity novelists, there were also the more routine cultural events of student life. Franzen's earlier work on drama may have drawn him to student productions of Anton Chekhov's *The Cherry Orchard* (staged in November 1977) and Beckett's *Waiting for Godot* (staged in April 1981). Similarly, his interest in cinema may have attracted him to local screenings of Stanley Kubrick's *Dr. Strangelove*, *A Clockwork Orange*, and *Lolita*.

Less speculatively, Swarthmore clearly offered Franzen the opportunity to explore different kinds of writing. In his first semester, he volunteered to be an investigative reporter for the *Phoenix*, Swarthmore's student newspaper, but he evidently experienced such tortures conducting interviews that he vowed to be a fiction writer, because "the great thing about fiction—I remember actually thinking this—was that you got to invent all the quotes" ("Swarthmore Commencement"). In spite of these misgivings, Franzen worked variously as a copy editor, feature editor, and opinion editor for the *Phoenix*, and his contributions are surprisingly numerous and surprisingly diverse. Across more than 30 articles, Franzen considers a variety of academic topics—grade inflation, debates surrounding the redefinition of the core curriculum, and controversy over Swarthmore's past admission policies for African American students—while he also seems as comfortable discussing the life of pizza delivery boys as he is examining the work of Swarthmore's Sproul Observatory in refining its galactic star maps. His work often demonstrates a politically alert edge, as when (in the wake of Steven

Biko's death) he wrote an article outlining Swarthmore's investments in multinational companies with dealings in South Africa. Equally, however, he is not above engaging in some student silliness, such as a cowritten letter submitted to the paper to defend the Acorn Squash as "one of the most intelligent and culturally advanced members of the fruit family" ("SAGA Slaughter" 2).

Amid this diversity, it is possible to detect hints of subjects that will turn up in his later novels. The fascination with food that runs through *The Corrections* is prefaced by articles that register the "traces of pastry aroma" and "smells of starch and spice" around an Italian market ("Italian Market" 4), while an article that mentions Teamsters in Philadelphia ("Union Maids" 6) foreshadows the fascination with "unreconstructed Teamsters" in the same novel (*C* 339). But what is striking, in terms of both the literary activity at Swarthmore and Franzen's later career trajectory, is how rarely his journalism explicitly addresses literary matters. Though he published a poem in the *Phoenix* in 1977, Franzen—perhaps driven by the responsibility to "Address the Culture" that he would later describe (*A* 95)—often devotes his articles to attempts to grapple with broader social commentary, rather than directly reporting on literary matters. One surprising way this fascination with broader trends manifests itself is in a series of humorous fashion overviews.

Franzen's fashion articles direct the "aspiring fashion baron" ("What's in Vogue" 3) toward the styles that are, and are not, deemed acceptable on campus and beyond. An almost unreasonable emphasis seems to be placed upon footwear. The year 1978, he promises, "is Year of the Clog" ("Fashion" 5), but "hightops," he cautions elsewhere, "are not in vogue, and anyone who ignores this must be willing to accept being termed avantgardist or Midwestern" ("What's in Vogue" 3). Beyond the footwear, there's often subtle self-directed humor—an article entitled "Campus in Style" is accompanied by an unacknowledged photograph of Franzen himself and his style is dismissed as that of a "preppie impostor" (4)—but what stands out in these essays is Franzen's emerging confidence with language, his willingness to showcase his verbal skills. "Fashion," Franzen notes, "runs like a language, only quicker" ("Fashion" 5), and he develops this analogy at length in an article ostensibly about whether or not it's acceptable to wear a sweat suit:

> As the semester ends, the tide of campus clothing trends begins to ebb, leaving new fashion debris strewn on the beach, and taking outdated styles back out to sea. When this ebb and flow works on language, philogists *[sic]* call it amelioration and pejoration, referring to the promotion

of a once base word to high station, and vice versa. Nearly illiterate, fashion observers have no such fancy words, but they do see similar patterns in people's everyday choice of clothing. ("Fashion" 5)

Elsewhere, literature and language similarly creep in at the edges of other articles—an overview of Swarthmore's board of managers, for example, leads Franzen to reflect that one manager "was Ezra Pound's lawyer during his struggle for release from a Washington D.C. mental hospital" ("Board of Managers" 3)—but there are other essays that engage more directly with language. In an amusing coauthored article entitled "Attention Staffers: The *Phoenix* Style," Franzen and Nick Burbank offer guidelines to aspiring student journalists, with the caveat that "these are not rules to be followed to the letter, but rather are suggestions to be taken dogmatically" (6). In this short article, Franzen and Burbank explain that "Brevity . . . should be avoided at all costs" and parodically summarize Kant's *Critique of Pure Reason* as "a sensitively drawn portrait of a boy and his dog on the 19th Century Mississippi River"(6). In a gesture that looks forward to the intertextual dialogue of the later novels, the article concludes by affirming that "Literary Allusion is Bliss" (6).

But writing about language in these essays often circles Franzen back to reflections on larger social issues. Prefiguring the fascination with names in his later novels, Franzen's second article for the *Phoenix*, "Dick Falls, Kathy Triumphs," found him trawling through the college telephone directory as a "diligent directory scholar" trying to quench his "demographic thirst" by establishing quantitatively, the most common first and full names on campus. After determining that there were 53 Davids and 32 Katherines at Swarthmore, Franzen cautions: "in most cases a personality makes a name, rather than vice-versa" (4). This may seem like an isolated journalistic assignment, but Franzen's early journalism betrays a taste for tracking down statistical data that permits him to map broad social trends. In the same year as his article on names—1977—Franzen also dug up data on enrollment in the Honors program and different disciplines in an article entitled "Pol. Sci. Leads Sex Imbalance in Honors." This data, along with an earlier study he located, led into speculations on the role of cultural biases in producing a gender imbalance in different majors. This was evidently more fraught territory than the campus directory, and the *Phoenix*'s next issue featured letters accusing him of using "rather dubious statistics" (Shinkle 2) and criticizing his decision to interview only one student to represent the career choices of Swarthmore's female population. Unperturbed, the following April found Franzen working through data stretching back to 1873, recording the number of Swarthmore students who married a fellow graduate of the college. "The Alumni Office," Franzen wryly notes, "has no divorce records for more morbid investigators," though within the next 20 years he would go on to marry and divorce a Swarthmore alumna ("Marriage" 5).

In Franzen's last academic year at Swarthmore, his contributions to *The Phoenix* were largely confined to his own column, entitled "Issues and Issues." In anticipation of the divisions that characterize his later novels, he used this forum to agonize over questions that he found irresolvable. In 1991 he recalled: "All I was really interested in was saying 'I can't decide about anything because where there is strong controversy, both sides have really good arguments'" ("PW Interviews" 54). An article from February 1981, however, outlines this philosophy as he saw it at the time and places a greater emphasis on objectivity: "the *inquiring intellectual* mind reels at . . . simplicity . . . the inquiring mind admits issues and issues; it takes no propaganda at face value; it strives at all costs to remain objective" ("A New Vietnam" 5). The focus of this column is impressively diverse, often drifting beyond the continental United States to evaluate "healthy local chauvinism" in a global context ("Dateline" 4). Franzen variously wrestles with political violence in El Salvador, with comparisons between European and American attitudes to war and apocalypse, with changing American attitudes toward health, and with the relationship between national breakfasts and intellectual breadth. Franzen's range of external reference is impressive, too, quoting from Nietzsche as well as the *New England Journal of Medicine*, but frequently the intellectual inquiries of his late journalism are interesting because they become vehicles for rehearsing the techniques of fiction, and imagined dialogues abound. In an essay on the role of coffee in the rise of modern society, for example, Franzen ends by creating a surreal conversation between two lab rats, who reflect on the merits of being offered alcohol following a caffeine injection:

> Silenus: I *am* beat. Got on that exercise wheel after lunch, and my legs just ran away from me. Couldn't get off the thing until now. I need a shot of that new water they've got in Compartment 2 . . . the new water's got some kind of painkiller in it. Tastes like hell, but you get used to it after a while. Excuse me a sec—
>
> Rhadamanthus: Wait! Look, Sil, you've got to take better care of yourself. This life's no good for you. Lay off that stuff, OK?
>
> Silenus: And sit around gnawing my claws all afternoon like you? You crazy? I tell you, Rhad, Compartment 2 is where the action is . . . ("Vice" 9)

This may not be, in itself, the most impressive example of Franzen's student writing, but the extravagant names show a young author experimenting with broadening the implications of his work by using names to filter contemporary questions through a long historical lens. *Rhadamanthus*, for example, was a judge in the underworld, who Virgil describes holding "sway with his unbending laws, chastising men, hearing all the frauds they have practiced" (150), while *Silenus* was, appropriately, a follower of Bacchus, who Ovid describes "staggering from . . . inebriation" (372). In Franzen's last column for the *Phoenix*, however, he made his most explicit statement of his literary affiliation and focused directly upon the present. As he prepared to leave Swarthmore he explained that "our generation lives in the unprecedented *[sic]* fear. Any moment all of humanity might be exploded to extinction," and he identified this experience of nuclear terror with postmodern fiction by naming his graduating class the "Kurt Vonnegut generation" ("What's Growing" 3).

Although the bulk of Franzen's student writing appeared in *The Phoenix*, he was also involved with student literary magazines. Befitting a member of the Vonnegut generation—and following the metadramatic elements of *The Fig Connection*—this work sometimes draws attention to its construction out of language, as in the case of his poem "Rainy Season," which momentarily diverts from description into the matter of language:

But you can tell Pim-Wee this too (tucked in among
The Subjunctive and the Predicate Nominative): (10)

"Rainy Season" is part of a linked series of poems attributed to a "Sir Winston Cook," who reports "helplessly" from different locations, but while in other poems Franzen alludes to the weight of literary history—one poem's speaker describes "humming old poets' poems" ("Mixed Review")—as well as writing, Franzen also briefly adopted editorial duties. When Franzen arrived at Swarthmore, a student literary magazine entitled the *Nulset Review* had just been launched, and after placing three poems in the magazine (including one in his first semester), he was eventually appointed editor in fall 1980. His first action in this position—as he recounts in "The Foreign Language"—was to "organize a contest to rename" the magazine (*DZ* 143), and he settled upon the title *Small Craft Warnings*. That the magazine should share its name with a play by fellow-St. Louis native Tennessee Williams is not coincidental—as I argue in Chapter 3, Franzen has a particular fascination with literary ancestors whose geography overlaps with his own—but the new title of the magazine lasted longer than its new editor. By the second issue of *Small Craft Warnings*, Franzen had relinquished his editorial duties, though he remained on the magazine's staff and contributed a photograph to one more issue.

A more substantial piece of early writing appeared in another Swarthmore magazine. Taking its title from a word that Susan Kelz Sperling's *Poplollies and Bellibones* (1977) defined as meaning *daybreak*, *Sparrowfart* presented itself as "a modest magazine of Quaker humor from Swarthmore College" and it concluded with a short dramatic work by Franzen. The title of this work, "This Is Not a Play," echoes the distinction between representation and reality in René Magritte's *The Treachery of Images* (which famously offers an image of a pipe accompanied by the explanation: "*Ceci n'est pas une pipe*"), and the play itself is like a surreal Beckett short, updated into the age of American bureaucracy. Centered around a character called Jerry, sat at a microfilm viewer in "a quiet filing room in a large corporate office" (27), the play documents him being tormented by taunting, sometimes rhyming voices that intrude into his slim engagement with other workers:

BOB: (approaching JERRY) Jerry, have you filed that Trenton series yet?
JERRY: Um. (He sorts through some computer cards.)
VOICE ONE: Trenton.
VOICE TWO: Benton.
VOICE THREE: Scranton.
ONE: Troy.
TWO: Illinois.
THREE: Iroquois. (28–9)

Yet, apart from all the writing opportunities Swarthmore afforded during this period, his academic responsibilities also provided a seminal exposure to German literature and culture. In his junior year Franzen spent 4 months in Munich as part of an exchange program, and he recalls that "Goethe's poetry particularly infected" him during this period (*DZ* 132). Upon returning to college, Franzen took a seminar with George C. Avery that focused on German modernism. Avery had published *Inquiry and Testament* (1968), a study of the Swiss writer, Robert Walser, as well as articles on German literature by the time Franzen appeared in his class and he seems to have been an important influence upon the young novelist.[8] In Avery's class Franzen read: "Nietzsche's *Birth of Tragedy*, stories by Schnitzller and Hofmannsthal, and a novel by Robert Walser . . . an essay by Karl Kraus, "The Chinese Wall"" as well as Rainer Maria Rilke's *The Notebooks of Malte Laurids Brigge* (1910), Franz Kafka's *The Trial* (1925), Alfred Döblin's *Berlin Alexanderplatz* (1929), and Thomas Mann's *The Magic Mountain* (1924)

(*DZ* 135–6). The impact this reading had upon Franzen's fiction is evident in many small allusions spread across his work. In both *The Twenty-Seventh City* and *The Corrections*, characters visit Germany, and (as I briefly note in Chapter 4) Kraus's satirical attacks on the news media lie behind Franzen's critique of the media in his first two books. *The Trial* seems to have been particularly important, as Franzen evidently saw Joseph K. as a model for *The Twenty-Seventh City*'s Martin Probst. The *St. Louis Post-Dispatch* reported that Franzen said "that originally he was influenced by Kafka and the idea that the things that happen to a person externally are in some intimate relationship with his internal processes." Franzen expanded:

> I do basically see [Probst] as incredibly lucky and leading a wonderful life, but he hasn't had to take any responsibility for it—and he knows it, knows that he's not really a better person than others less fortunate. He even has some desire to be corrupted. He resents the ease with which people who are less upright and moral get what they want. ("Don't Judge" 5)

There is also a subtle nod to Kafka's character embedded in the lawyer Joseph K. Prager's name in *The Corrections* (*C* 72),[9] and Franzen has gone so far as to claim that "all along, I've considered myself a kind of German writer" ("Intimately Connected").

Franzen's experience at Swarthmore with all things German also provided the foundation for his first major post-Swarthmore publication, a short story called "Facts" that appeared in *Fiction International* in 1986. In the April of his last semester at Swarthmore, Franzen apparently wrote the story in one afternoon (he recalls, with chagrin, that none of the 25 or 30 other stories he wrote in the 1980s were as successful), and submitted it to the college's annual fiction contest, which was judged that year by novelist Richard Price. The story placed third in the competition, but "Facts" marks an interesting junction in Franzen's career as a writer. Submitted to a Swarthmore competition, and partially set in Munich, the story looks back to Franzen's years as a student in America and abroad. Yet, the story's juxtaposition of international events with murder and conspiracy in the Midwest, filtered through a series of snapshots in different locations, looks forward to the themes and techniques of his first novel, *The Twenty-Seventh City*.

Writing the novels in Europe and America

Franzen was keen to return to Europe in the wake of his time in Munich, and after graduating in 1981 with a BA in German, he traveled to Berlin's

Freie Universität (through the aegis of the Fulbright Student Program) with the intention of continuing his study of German literature. At Freie Universität, Franzen extended his immersion in the work of the Austrian satirist Karl Kraus, taking a seminar devoted to Kraus's apocalyptic drama, *The Last Days of Mankind* (1918), and writing a long paper on the relationship between the Grumbler's monologues from that play and two of Kraus's essays "Heine and the Consequences" and "Nestroy and Posterity." But in Berlin, Franzen's own writing also began to absorb his attention. He began to work on his first novel, while he also recalls "I feel I grew up intellectually there, largely through writing letters to the person I married when I came back" ("Don't Judge" 5). The recipient of those letters was Valerie Cornell, the editor of *The Nulset Review* who Franzen had met in 1980, and the couple married on October 2, 1982. During the same period, Franzen was reunited with Göran Ekström, a Swedish physics student with whom Franzen shared a dorm room while at Swarthmore. Ekström had returned from a year in Moscow to work on a PhD in seismology at Harvard, and he told Franzen about a job that was available in the Earth and Planetary Sciences department at the university.

Franzen accepted the position of research assistant in 1983, and he remained at Harvard until 1987. During this period he worked as a "research drudge" (personal correspondence) eventually appearing as coauthor on 20 surveys of seismic activity, which appeared in *Physics of the Earth and Planetary Interiors* between 1983 and 1988. This appointment allowed both Franzen and Cornell to spend the majority of their time working on novels. Franzen recalls:

> it became an absolutely ideal job for a writer because I worked weekends, and the two of us, by living frugally, could live on what I made at a two-day-a-week job, plus having all the privileges of the school associated with the job—the libraries and other resources. In my work I looked at seismograms, basically, and at a computer screen where seismographs were plotted, rejecting bad data and accepting good data. It was routine work for the money. ("Don't Judge" 5)

Between September 1982 and September 1987 Franzen and Cornell lived in what he called the "student slum" of Somerville, north of Cambridge ("A Writer Basking" D7), a location that Franzen drew upon in *Strong Motion*, where Louis Holland is also a resident of "Cambridge's budget-class neighbor" (*SM* 5), sharing a rented apartment in Somerville's Clarendon Hill. Paying $300 in rent, Franzen and Cornell undertook a writing regime that was famously spartan. Emily Eakin reports that "separated by only 20 feet, they wrote eight hours each day and then, after a dinner break read for five more . . . The novelist David Foster Wallace who met the couple around this time, remarked that they were living with 'faces pressed against the inside of the bell jar'" ("Jonathan Franzen's Big Book" 20–1).[10]

Although Franzen continued to be fascinated by German literature—he worked on a translation of the two Kraus essays he had studied in Berlin, between 1983 and 1984—he also relied on "the excellent public library in Somerville" (*A* 246) to locate the major works of American post-modernism. The immediate product of this working arrangement for Franzen was the first draft of *The Twenty-Seventh City*, a manuscript of 1,100 pages. The idea for this novel had been gestating since his early dramatic work, but he labored over the first few chapters, writing and rewriting them to his satisfaction, before completing the bulk of the book in a burst of writing in 1985. Franzen took the novel—which filled three manuscript boxes—to a young agent, Susan Golomb. In September 1987, Franzen and Cornell moved to Jackson Heights, Queens, and within 3 weeks of their move Golomb sold the book to Farrar, Straus, and Giroux.

Backed by a promotions budget of $50,000, the first printing of *The Twenty-Seventh City* (some 40,000 copies) was published in September 1988. An aggressive media campaign preceded the novel's appearance—including a two-page advert in the *New York Times Book Review* announcing "It's 1984 in St. Louis and Big Brother is a Woman" (28–9)—and the book was well received in most of the major reviewing outlets. Many reviewers were struck by how young the author of this ambitious, polished, novel was, and his emerging fame even merited a photo shoot in *Vogue*. The unexpected success of *The Twenty-Seventh City* allowed Franzen and Cornell to travel more widely at the end of 1988. In late October they took a holiday in Rome, and though they returned to New York when Franzen was awarded a $25,000 Whiting Award, by mid-November they had moved to Spain. Borrowing a house owned by the parents of friends in the small inland village of Llíber in Alicante, they spent the winter writing. Cornell was working on a novel "about a psychopathic county politician," while Franzen drafted *Strong Motion* ("A Writer Basking" D7). Between May and June in 1989, Franzen and Cornell were on the move again, staying in Italy, Germany, and France.

In retrospect, Franzen describes this period as an attempt to save his marriage, by "trying to solve non-geographical problems geographically" ("Jonathan Franzen's Big Book" 21). Cracks had evidently been appearing in their marriage, and in 1990, Franzen and Cornell separated.

In 1991, he withdrew to Yaddo, an artist's colony in upstate New York, to complete the final chapters of *Strong Motion*, but the couple reunited in "a too-expensive house" in Philadelphia (*A* 63), and Franzen's second novel was published in January, 1992.

Strong Motion clearly draws upon and recasts Franzen's years in Massachusetts, working with earthquakes and living in Somerville, but the novel was greeted with less extravagant praise than *The Twenty-Seventh City*. Franzen cites a number of reasons for this disappointing reception—an ill-coordinated marketing campaign, an unappealing dust jacket—but the next few years were to be marked by more difficulties and confusion.

In early 1992 Franzen was back at Swarthmore. Living (like Chip in *The Corrections*) in a college faculty sublet, Franzen served as a visiting associate professor. This was one of two occasions when Franzen taught at Swarthmore (he returned in 1994), but on both occasions he taught basically the same works. The reading list only ever included one entire book—Paula Fox's *Desperate Characters* (1970)—but each week Franzen assigned stories by writers such as Anton Chekhov, Denis Johnson, Charles Johnson, David Foster Wallace, Joy Williams, Jane Smiley, and Lydia Davis. Franzen also brought in Wallace and Fox to judge the college fiction contest, in 1992 and 1994 respectively, and Wallace gave one of the first readings from *Infinite Jest* at Swarthmore.

Whether Franzen's portrait of academia in *The Corrections* derives from his time at Swarthmore or from the spring of 1997 when he taught a fiction workshop to 11 graduate students at the Columbia University School of the Arts, it clearly was a form of employment that didn't sit well with the rhythm of his life as a novelist. He explains: "I thought a teaching job was the ultimate reward for writing a good book . . . But when I did finally do some teaching, it completely ate me up. I was spending three days a week on one class, and it just didn't seem compatible with writing novels in the long run" (qtd. in Amsden). Several of Franzen's students have evidently gone on to make a living through their writing,[11] though Franzen's diagnosis of his students in his second spell at Swarthmore was mixed: "although I spent way too much time on it, I loved the work. I was heartened by the skill of my students . . . I was depressed, though, to learn that several of my best writers had vowed never to take a literature class again" (*A* 78).

Off campus, the mid-1990s were evidently a difficult period for Franzen. Although he was a Guggenheim fellow in 1996, the profits from his first two books were gone, his marriage to Cornell finally dissolved in 1996, and his father died from Alzheimer's on Tuesday, May 16, 1995, at Bethesda-Dilworth Memorial Home in Kirkwood, Missouri. Earl Franzen was cremated with a memorial service on June 3, the last time Franzen was seen in public with Cornell. This cluster of landmark events signaled the end of an era for Franzen, who told Donald Antrim: "Not long after that, something loosened up. There was a space in which I could actually start to write again, a little bit, something that was mine and not ours" ("Jonathan Franzen" 75). During this period Franzen had entertained serious doubts about his vocation. He reflected: "I reached such a low point. I was so discouraged with fiction . . . I was even thinking of temping or maybe becoming a paralegal or something. And it occurred to me that I had written these two good novels, and it was not really appropriate for me to go and word-process at a law firm. And that maybe I should think about doing some journalism" ("Making the Corrections" 29). On the strength of his novels, Henry Finder and Chip McGrath at *The New Yorker* agreed to commission a 15,000 word essay on the Chicago post office in June 1994.

The return to journalism seemed to satisfy Franzen's desire to engage more directly with the culture, and during the years in which he struggled with his conception of what kind of novel *The Corrections* should be,[12] he undertook a number of projects, many of which are collected in *How to Be Alone*. The most famous of these appeared in *Harper's* as "Perchance to Dream"—a title that Franzen never seems to have been happy with and which was given to the essay by Colin Harrison, an editor at *Harper's* in the mid-1990s—and as "Why Bother?" in *How to Be Alone*. This essay began as an assignment for the *New York Times Magazine*, which allowed Franzen to make contact with a number of other writers, such as Don DeLillo and Donald Antrim, both of whom Franzen took to dinner on the *New York Times* expense account ("Making the Corrections" 29).

Franzen views this period, and his contact with writers such as DeLillo and Antrim, as part of a crucial reintegration into the world after years of isolation, and his work evidently began moving again. In 1997 he began working in a studio on 125th Street in East Harlem, which he rented from a sculptor friend, and it was here that he wrote most of *The Corrections*. Although his mother (who is listed in the novel's acknowledgments, along with one of Franzen's brothers), died before the book was completed, his third novel was finally published on September 5, 2001. *The Corrections* won the National Book Award and was a finalist for both the Pulitzer Prize and the PEN/Faulkner award, but this success was somewhat mitigated by Franzen's messy entanglement in arguments about the novel's selection for Oprah Winfrey's Book Club.

Winfrey had evidently called Franzen on the afternoon of August 31, 2001, to reveal that *The Corrections* would be selected by her powerful book club, but she did not make her selection public until September 24 (Schindehette 83). Farrar, Straus, and Giroux apparently printed 500,000 more copies on the strength of her choice, but by October 22, 2001, Oprah Winfrey had decided to withdraw Franzen's invitation to appear on the show because he was "seemingly uncomfortable and conflicted about being chosen as a book club selection" (Winfrey qtd. in Schindehette 84). The fallout from this dispute has already been dissected in several books and countless newspaper columns, but too many of these writers—unfamiliar with Franzen's first two novels and the arc of his career—have failed to see how the roots of this dispute emerge not necessarily from a particular antipathy to Oprah Winfrey, but from a fundamental division that stretches across all his work. In August 1988, for example, before his first novel had even been published, Franzen described his novel for the *St. Louis Post-Dispatch* in terms that clearly prefigure his discomfort over the divide between popular and literary books. Franzen explained that his book "was conceived and written for the most part as a literary book, which I saw as a printing of 7,500 copies and maybe getting good reviews and getting a comfortable little place in the literary scene, but I by no means wrote it for snob appeal" ("Don't Judge" 5). Franzen's sense of division here, between literary elitism and popular appeal, is just one example of the fundamental oppositions that are deeply imprinted upon his DNA as a novelist. But while Franzen has offered further personal reflections on his tendency to maintain "two separate versions of myself" (*DZ* 96) in *The Discomfort Zone*, a memoir that was published on September 5, 2006, and showed some inclination to embrace popular forms by appearing in the eighteenth season of *The Simpsons* on November 19, 2006, to elucidate some of the aesthetic dimensions of his double vision—and to shift focus from life back to work—it's necessary to go back to Renée's list.

Fiction and nonfiction: Franzen and the postmodern novel

Amongst the books that Renée decides to discard are a number of novels that we can be fairly sure Franzen has read. George Orwell's *1984* (1949), for example, presumably belongs in that category since Franzen begins his own novel of political repression, *The Twenty-Seventh City*, in 1984 and includes several references to Orwell's Thought Police (*TS* 111, 266). One reason why *1984* is included on Renée's list also seems relatively clear. Orwell's book famously presents a nightmarish vision of the future, so it fits alongside the other dystopic novels of the future that Renée adds to her list: Herman Hesse's *The Glass Bead Game,* which is set in the twenty-third century; Frank Herbert's *Dune* (1965), with its futuristic vision of an intergalactic empire; and perhaps also Kurt Vonnegut's *Player Piano* (1952) and *The Sirens of Titan* (1959). Franzen, himself, imagines dark times for humanity in his first two novels, but this list is a way of indicating that, unlike Orwell, Hesse, Herbert, and Vonnegut, he situates his crises in a recognizably contemporary setting. For Franzen the apocalypse is much closer than the writers on Renée's list imagine.

But one book on the list that Franzen confessed he had not read is John Barth's 1960 novel, *The Sot-Weed Factor.* Barth belongs on this list not because his baroque novel encapsulates something in itself that Franzen wants the reader to reject. Instead, it stands for a range of artistically complex postmodern American novels that represent the core of Franzen's ambivalent relationship to his literary ancestors. In reconstructions of his literary apprenticeship, Franzen has long stressed his early engagement with postmodernism, describing how he "cut [his] teeth on . . . *The Recognitions* and *Gravity's Rainbow*" as well as books by DeLillo and Coover ("I'll Be Doing More of Same" 36).[13] But while Franzen initially admired postmodernism's critical take on postwar American society—this is the Franzen who as a student describes himself as a member of Vonnegut's generation—he increasingly had to labor to muster the enthusiasm and dedication to make it through many representative postmodernist novels. In fact, in "Mr. Difficult," Franzen recounts how he feared that people would probe his credentials as a smart advocate of postmodern fiction by asking whether he had "read *The Sotweed Factor*" (*A* 247 [*sic.*]). Barth's novel, then, stands in Renée's list as a representative of a list of Franzen's own: "a canon of intellectual, socially edgy, white-male American fiction writers . . .—Pynchon, DeLillo, Coover, Gaddis, Gass, Burroughs, Barth, Barthelme, Hannah, Hawkes, McElroy, and Elkin" (*A* 246). These were writers that Franzen began his career seeking to emulate but—evidently as a result of his struggle to finish their novels—he came to the conclusion that they were writers who were disengaged from their audience, writers who were largely praised by an academic establishment that privileged difficulty over the traditional rewards of narrative (*A* 246).

This, of course, is not a summation that Barth (or for that matter, many of the other writers on this list) would be likely to agree with. In fact, in a metafictional moment in *The Sot-Weed Factor,* Barth has his author-surrogate Ebenezer Cooke exclaim that "it repels me to own the muse sings clearest to professors! 'Twas not of them I thought when I wrote the piece" (137). Nevertheless, Franzen sets these writers against a kind of writing that might take Isaac Bashevis Singer as its representative. While Barth's novel is thrown away in *Strong Motion*, a Singer novel provides the epigraph for Franzen's book, and Franzen has often noted his admiration for Singer's work.[14] Singer placed his belief in the primacy of the conventional components of fiction and often declared his opposition to avant-garde writers who, he claimed, had disdained the reader. He insisted that "the psychologizers and sociologizers of modern fiction have actually declared war on the story," mistaking the fact that the mission of literature was to tell an entertaining story ("I.B. Singer" 118). Singer summarized his beliefs in his 1978 Nobel lecture—which Franzen quotes in *The Discomfort Zone*—when he argued that "the storyteller . . . of our time, as in any other time, must be an entertainer of the spirit in the full sense of the word, not just a preacher of social or political ideals," and this seems to be the model of the writer that Franzen wants to privilege over the fault-finding postmodern author (163). The counters here, then, are not *popular* versus *literary*, as the tired Oprah debate suggests, but might be more accurately classified with the awkward titles: academically-privileged formalist postmodernism versus story-based literature that aims to entertain the reader.

A further distinction, however, is required here. In "Mr. Difficult," Franzen succinctly frames the terms of this division as an opposition between *Status* and *Contract* fiction. A writer who subscribes to the status model creates his novels with indifference for the reader's pleasure, striving instead to fashion a work of historically important art. A writer following the contract model, by contrast, considers a novel to represent "a compact between the writer and the reader" where the writer primarily strives to create "a pleasurable experience" for his reader (*A* 240). But the meanings of these terms are not as straightforward as they first appear. While Franzen argues that Gaddis "frankly endorsed Status and disdained Contract" (*A* 242), at the same time he suggests that *Finnegans Wake* could be considered a contract work (*A* 240), a caveat that presumably empties the explanatory value of Franzen's opposition.[15] But regardless of how muddy these categories may appear, the crucial fact is that *within the confines of this essay Franzen resolves the opposition*. Although he begins the essay by suggesting that he subscribes "to two wildly different models of how fiction relates to its audience" (*A* 239), by the end of the essay it is clear that he allies himself with "many other Contract-minded Americans" (*A* 268). At this point we face one of the crucial distinctions between Franzen's novels and his nonfiction. In his essays, Franzen frequently expresses his divided feelings about a subject, or presents an opposition, but he nearly always reaches some kind of resolution by the end of the essay. Whether he is wringing his hands over smoking or not smoking, writing big socially engaged novels or writing character-based fiction, or wondering whether he is a status or contract reader, by the last paragraph any lingering division is smoothed over and cemented with a pithy final sentence. This, for example, is how any doubt over the place of difficulty in fiction is dispensed with: "A story like this, where the difficulty is the difficulty of life itself, is what a novel is for" (*A* 269).

But within his novels such oppositions are never resolved with this kind of ease. Instead Franzen seems to create each book by maintaining the kind of double vision that I suggested characterized Renée's list. In each of his fictions he maps out the foundations of a novel that will provide the kind of story-based entertainment that Singer praises—he concentrates on characters, and strives (in Singer's words) "to tell a story, where there is tension and where the reader does not know at the beginning what the end will be" ("I.B. Singer" 118)—but despite these underpinnings, his fiction never works on this level alone. At the same time, he indulges in the kind of formal games that are the hallmark of postmodernism. The opposition between these two aesthetic strategies creates an unsettling tension at the heart of his works that is absent from his essays. Are his characters, for example, meant to be taken as imitations of their fleshy counterparts, or are they just linguistic counters in a larger formal scheme? Are Franzen's chronologies meant to impart a tincture of realism, or are they a component of an underlying impersonal grid of meaning? The answer, as I suggest in subsequent chapters, is that both descriptions are accurate, because Franzen's books are built on an opposition between postmodernism and more traditional fiction that is stubbornly unresolved in each novel.

Because Franzen's borrowings from the toolbox of the conventional novel are fairly apparent—his emphasis on strong characterization, his incorporation of traditional plots (family crises, coming-of-age stories, and so on), his preference for resolution rather than indeterminacy—in the following three chapters I offer detailed accounts of how he has spliced these elements with (perhaps less obvious) aspects of the postmodern novel. The proportions between conventional-story-telling-entertainment and postmodern-game playing shift in each work, and it takes me much of the rest of this study to disentangle and elucidate Franzen's dialogue with the postmodern novel. It is, however, worth noting here the major consequence that the distinction outlined above between Franzen's fiction and nonfiction has for critical readings of his work. The prevailing critical view of Franzen's development at present is that Franzen has moved away from postmodernism toward what Robert McLaughlin calls an "essentially conservative" aesthetic (61). On one level, this seems reasonably accurate, and it is an interpretation that certainly meshes with the construction of his career that Franzen offers in his essays. But I'd like to demonstrate that the difference between Franzen's nonfiction and his fiction introduces complications into readings that assume that the former can explain the latter. As "Why Bother?" (or, as it is more frequently identified in its 1996 incarnation, "Perchance to Dream")[16] is by some distance Franzen's most quoted essay, I'll take it as an example.

In virtually every critical interpretation of *The Corrections*, the argument in "Perchance to Dream" is treated as a kind of preface to the novel itself. In "Turncoat," for instance, Rebein takes the essay absolutely at face value, concluding that the essay, "simply put," demonstrated Franzen's initial error in imitating postmodernist fiction, "a theory of fiction writing that did not suit his temperament or talent" (209).[17] With more nuanced caveats, McLaughlin notes that "the ideas" in "Why Bother?" and "I'll Be Doing More of Same" "influenced the writing of . . . *The Corrections*" (62); Catherine Toal argues in "Corrections" (2003) that the essay is "a useful precursor text" to the novel (312); Jeremy Green similarly contends in an otherwise useful discussion in *Late Postmodernism* (2005) that Franzen "mounted his own effort to comprehend the relationship between literary production and media culture in a 1996 *Harper's Magazine* essay" and that "his success" in doing so "may be judged by reading *The Corrections*" (80). The underlying belief that animates each of these interpretations—regardless of the conclusions that the individual critic extracts—is that "Perchance to Dream" represents a successful resolution to the creative problems Franzen suffered in the early 1990s. Because Franzen's nonfiction nearly always resolves dichotomies, there is certainly evidence in the essay itself to support this belief. The essay moves toward its conclusion with a simulated epiphany, a note of breakthrough: "As soon as I jettisoned my perceived obligation to the chimerical mainstream, my third book began to move again. I'm amazed now that I'd trusted myself so little for so long" (*A* 95). The atmosphere of triumph is palpable, but it's important to note that the facts of the composition of *The Corrections* make it clear that "Perchance to Dream" charts the resolution of an aesthetic problem that Franzen had not really resolved and did not resolve for several more years. If "Perchance to Dream" marked the breakthrough in 1996, then why did Franzen not compose the majority of the novel ("80 percent," he told Antrim [78]) until 2000? Why, as late as 1998, was Franzen telling interviewers that the novel was narrated in the first person by "a very depressed staff attorney at the Securities and Exchange Commission" ("A Nonsmoker's Novel" 1865)? The only logical answer to these questions is that the reductive sketch of a solution to the contemporary novel's ills in "Perchance to Dream" actually bears only a marginal relation to the novel Franzen actually wrote, and that the aesthetic foundations of *The Corrections* are more complex than the essay intimates.

Because I believe that Franzen's fiction works on much more complex ground than the rhetorical flourishes of his nonfiction suggests, one of the broader contentions of this study is that Franzen's own comments about his work are often misleading. In terms of *The Corrections*, too, I'll argue that the simplified resolution to "Perchance to Dream" is likely to distort a reader's understanding of Franzen's third novel. The foreground, as it were, of *The Corrections* is increasingly stuffed full of apparently straightforward characterization and obvious plot devices. But at the same time, the background of the novel seems to be proportionately animated with postmodern trickery as a compensation. Despite the local pleasures of his nonfiction, I have little to say, then, in the rest of this book about his essays, and I have rarely adopted the terms Franzen produces in his nonfiction, such as "tragic realism" (*A* 91). Instead, in the remaining chapters I attempt to explore how the shifting proportions of Franzen's fiction, its unresolved divisions between realism and postmodern formalism negotiates his relation to his literary ancestors and charts the possibility of an emergent post-postmodernism.

Chapter 3

In the Concrete Waste Land
The Twenty-Seventh City

These fragments you have shelved.

Ezra Pound, The Cantos *(28)*

Shifting between three continents and balancing several intertwined narrative lines, *The Twenty-Seventh City* is an unusually sophisticated debut novel. Like the first books by Franzen's contemporaries—Richard Powers's *Three Farmers on Their Way to a Dance* (1985) and David Foster Wallace's *The Broom of the System* (1987)—*The Twenty-Seventh City* earned comparisons to earlier postmodern novels for its labyrinthine plot, its manipulation of multiple viewpoints, and its use of systems theory. But unlike Powers and Wallace, Franzen's work also elicited questions about its relationship to more generic works. Although the *Chicago Tribune* detected a heavy debt to Thomas Pynchon as well as "sub currents of Don DeLillo" (Blades 5), the *New York Times Book Review* examined Franzen's novel under the heading "crime/mystery" and concluded that it was a "thriller" that could be judged in terms of its relationship to "more conventional potboilers" (Andrews 22). *Vogue* expressed similar doubts, fearing that the novel came close to "the brute dualities of Robert Ludlum" (Jefferson 454). Given this mixed response, it's perhaps unsurprising to discover that division seems to be built into the novel's foundations. Thematically and chronologically, as I'll demonstrate in this chapter, *The Twenty-Seventh City* is founded upon separation and opposition, and even the geography of Franzen's first novel suggests division, taking St. Louis as its setting, a city that Richard Ford describes as "neither West nor Middlewest, neither South nor North; the city lost in the middle" (68).

Compared to many other novels, *The Twenty-Seventh City* is broad in its geographical focus—not just moving between countries, but taking the whole of a city and its citizens as its subject—but thin in its temporal range, devoting just 8 months to the majority of its action. In Franzen's oeuvre, however, this time span gives *The Twenty-Seventh City* a longer chronology than any of his other novels.[1] Within these geographical and temporal boundaries, the novel is composed of a mosaic of short tableaux that shuttle between different viewpoints. These narrative particles are arranged to move Franzen's characters through a series of concentric circles, which frame the individual in progressively larger and colder environments, and as we move between these loops, Franzen's narrative technique varies subtly.

At the center of the narrative circles, characters are situated in the matrix of the family and their private moments are relayed through the novel's roving third-person camera eye and objective transcripts of conversations (*TS* 31–2, 249, 334–5). In this zone, characters talk about the routine mechanics of suburban family life, reflecting on close friends, speculating about girlfriends. The intimate closed circle of the family, however, is contrasted with the larger arena of urban St. Louis where characters move between their workplaces and the gray weave of "cratered streets" that interlaces the city (*TS* 389). An "atmosphere of fear" (*TS* 393) increasingly dominates this circle, as carefully staged terrorist strikes punctuate the rhythms of urban life, but the city itself is, in turn, set against a larger national context, where metropolitan St. Louis sits in the cosmopolitan "shadow of New York" (*TS* 410). In these two rings, the third-person narrative lens is interspersed with extracts from local and national news media (*TS* 8–13, 137–9, 267, 377, 400, 431), that recast private lives for the public. Finally the individual gets "lost in the larger visuals" (*TS* 241), as Franzen evaluates all these lives in his largest scale, meditating on America's place in the context of global terrorism. The outer edges of this encompassing circle are also the outer edges of the book, as the novel's first and last paragraphs concern characters in Bombay, some 8,000 miles from St. Louis. The guiding principle behind this system of concentric circles seems to be that "parallax correct[s]" and clarifies the reader's views, as Franzen shows how his characters apparently change as he shifts scales (*TS* 157). We see, for example, a leading business man, Martin Probst, appear as a dominant patriarch, towering over his family (*TS* 86). Then Franzen supplements this scene by shifting to the public arena, where an interview in the local *Post-Dispatch* continues to "magnify his person" (*TS* 377). But to make sure that we don't mistake Probst for a figure of real consequence, Franzen then shows him visibly shrinking when confronted by a reporter from outside the city, who interviews him cursorily for *Time* magazine (*TS* 409–12). Local importance, in this book, is partly a myth of scale.

The shifting scales of *The Twenty-Seventh City* represent a characteristic post-postmodern narrative strategy, an effort to reframe the life of the individual within a series of larger systems. Powers has a character in *Galatea 2.2* (1995) summarize this approach as an attempt to transcend local confusion, when she criticizes novelists by asking: "why read in the first place, if the people who are supposed to give us the aerial view can't tell us anything except what an inescapable mess we're in?" (210).² Transcending the mess, Franzen's novel often telescopes his shifts in scale down to a single scene when he makes use of rapid zoom outs within a few sentences, as when he takes a young couple wandering around a construction site and suddenly widens his focus to take in the aerial view, setting them in a narrowing perspective that moves from the light of distant stars, through the neon glare of national media systems, down to their local darkness:

> Through the iron parallelograms above her she could make out the W of Cassiopeia. To the south, two vertical strings of TV-tower lights competed in the night like the stations they belonged to. Trucks rumbled by on Manchester Road, and Luisa swayed in the darkness, and drank her wine, her eyes on Duane. (*TS* 59)

Franzen's use of "a god's eye perspective" (*TS* 354) in such scenes carefully establishes distance between the characters and the reader, strategically prohibiting the kind of empathetic connection with a character and her developed back story that he will emphasize more strongly in his next two books. But this technique also hints at Franzen's larger view of society. The young girl in this scene—Luisa Probst—has just described herself as "basically . . . a net person" (*TS* 56), and while her literal reference is to her interest in entomology, in a sense all of Franzen's characters are "net" people—individual nodes comprising a much vaster interconnected network. The scene on the construction site highlights the individual's connection to larger systems not just because it sets the couple in wider perspectives, but also because the details Franzen picks out in those perspectives—the towers that send and receive signals, the arterial roads that link cities—stress modes of connection. This interlinked vision of society turns viciously incestuous in *The Corrections*, and it shows its darker side at the end of *The Twenty-Seventh City*, when two apparently separate plots come together to cause the death of Luisa's mother. But the novel's macroscopic vision is paralleled by its attention to microscopic process. Below the level of the individual are "parallel worlds—worlds of the invisible" (*TS* 215): Luisa's insects, a bacterial world of "active germs . . . waiting, hopping eagerly into the air" (*TS* 209), and even a "museum of soil types" (*TS* 212). Taken together, these scalar shifts remind the reader of Franzen's novel that life takes place on multiple levels and look forward, in particular, to *Strong Motion*'s emphasis on underlying processes. The post-postmodern novel, as Powers notes, urges the recognition that "the world isn't simply taking place at eye-level view, there's lots going on above us and below us" ("Salon Interview").

The pivotal figures in the "tight circles" of *The Twenty-Seventh City*'s tiered narrative system (*TS* 70) reveal the divide that is central to the novel, its opposition between East and West. The novel's antagonist, Susan Jammu, internalizes these contraries. Born in Los Angeles in 1949—on the cusp of the century's center—Jammu is the daughter of Peter B. Clancy, an American journalist, and Shanti Jammu, a Kashmiri Brahman with a blood link to Indira Gandhi. Through Gandhi's fiat, Susan Jammu was appointed to the Indian Police Service in 1969, rising within the next 10 years to the position of commissioner of the Bombay police. But when the novel opens in 1984, a 35-year-old Jammu has switched hemispheres to take up the role of chief of the St. Louis Police Department. Prefiguring DeLillo's explorations of how acts of terror "alter the inner life of the culture" (*Mao II* 41), Jammu's shadowy methods are centered around using terror to force characters into what she calls the "'State' in which a subject's everyday consciousness becomes severely limited" and they are susceptible to her psychological manipulation (*TS* 30).

In the novel's initial schema, Franzen's protagonist, Martin Probst (who was born in 1934) is poised against Jammu and her associates who see him as a representative "citizen of the West" (*TS* 33). Probst's ancestors came out of Oklahoma, broken by the dustbowl years and poor business decisions, and they came to St. Louis in 1940, where Probst set to work as a contractor, eventually heading the company that built Eero Saarinen's famous St. Louis Arch. By 1984, Probst has established a reputation for real integrity, which has helped him gain the position of chairman of Municipal Growth—a conglomerate of businesses based on a real St. Louis coalition known as Civic Progress. His private life appears to be equally successful, but the lists that his wife, Barbara, and his daughter, Luisa, keep reveal the family to be ripe for corruption.

Unlike Renée's list of books in *Strong Motion*, which is an attempt to control a spiral of new emotions, Barbara and Luisa keep lists that register their openness to new experiences. Luisa is an amateur ornithologist, who ventures out of the family circle to add to her "lifetime list" of bird sightings (*TS* 62), but her catalogue ultimately serves as an opportunity to develop her blossoming romance with Duane Thompson. Barbara, by contrast, makes lists that are a photographic negative of Luisa and Renée's. Rather than expanding, Barbara's lists pare her life down to its bare essentials: "In an average week she made six breakfasts, packed five lunches, and cooked dinners. She put a hundred miles on the car. She stared out of windows for forty-five minutes" (*TS* 89). While the larger resonance of Barbara's name—she shares her name with the patron saint of architects and builders—would seem to make her an ideal wife for Probst, her list reveals her initially subterranean frustrations with the repetitiveness of her married life, hinting at her desire to move beyond this closed circle of routine. This desire ultimately finds expression in her affair with Balwan Singh, one of Jammu's associates, a romance that leads her well beyond the confines of the family.

How to start a post-postmodern novel

As this skeletal plot summary probably suggests, Franzen's first novel—with its dark strangers, extramarital affairs, and psychological pressure—*does* share affinities with the generic crime fiction that several of his first reviewers proposed as a point of comparison. But at the same time, the architecture of the novel—and particularly of the novel's opening—clearly parallels the fiction of more experimental writers who published their first novels within a few years of Franzen's debut. A short survey of Franzen's contemporaries is required, here, to bring *The Twenty-Seventh City*'s relation to post-postmodernism into sharper focus.

Richard Powers, David Foster Wallace, and William T. Vollmann each published their first novel within a 3-year period in the mid-1980s. But while the efforts of each writer to emerge from under the influence of their postmodern predecessors could be categorized as post-postmodern, critics have not yet explored the similarities between their first novels—Powers's *Three Farmers on Their Way to a Dance* (1985), Wallace's *The Broom of the System* (1987), and Vollmann's *You Bright and Risen Angels* (1987). Some of the parallels between these books seem interesting, but somewhat slight. Embedded in each of these novels, for example, is a fascination with a pivotal figure from the first half of the twentieth century (Henry Ford for Powers; Ludwig Wittgenstein for Wallace; Adolf Hitler for Vollmann). More significant, however, is the way that Powers and Vollmann, in particular, present their narratives nested in surprisingly complex paratextual apparatus.

Three Farmer's on Their Way to a Dance is a novel that worries that "Art can only hope to be an anaesthetic" (13) and its opening chapter, which is prefaced by a nursery rhyme and begins with the calming voice of a first-person narrator voice, seems to be calculated to induce a sedative effect. But despite its tranquilizing opening, the action of the first chapter is carefully designed to bristle against the novel's paratextual material. Before the reader reaches the first chapter's nursery rhyme, she encounters two epigraphs, the second of which is from Anne Jardin's *The First Henry Ford* (1970): "'Everybody,' said Knudsen, explaining the demand for the automobile, 'wants to go from A to B sitting down.'" On first inspection, this seems an appropriate epigraph for a book that begins in Detroit and spends some time excavating Ford's ill-fated attempt to end the First World War. Yet, the actions of the first chapter's narrator in "Motor City" (11) carefully undermine the supremacy of the automobile that Jardin recounts. To get to Detroit the narrator has taken a train journey, after which he "walked . . . for a few blocks" noting car-inspired insanity ("two lawyers fist-fought over a parking space") before he plans to take another train (12). In fact, through the novel's 352 pages there are only two car journeys, both of which are terrifying ordeals. Ultimately this narrator—a persona for the author—explains that "a car is for getting from start to finish as quickly as possible. But I earn a living by pointing out what happens between" (341). The epigraph, then, has been a kind of trick, luring the reader into assuming that "everybody" acts upon the same desires, and that technology is the readymade answer to those desires. As the second epigraph fools the reader, it confirms the message of the first epigraph from Proust's *Remembrance of Things Past*: "we guess as we read . . . everything starts from an initial mistake."[3]

A similar trick is evident at the start of Vollmann's *You Bright and Risen Angels*. Like Powers's nursery rhyme in *Three Farmers*, the first section of Vollmann's baroque novel lures the reader into a false sense of security by affectionately addressing the reader directly as "my best beloved" (3). The story is also framed by some helpful-looking paratextual material. Vollmann outlines "a social gazette of the personalities interviewed for this book" and a list of "transcendental contents" as if they'll help navigate through this complex text. But when examined closely, these materials are just as deceptive as Powers's epigraphs: the table of contents lists a second volume that doesn't exist, and the index of characters begins with the essential protagonists only to descend into parody, eventually listing polar bears as the "terrestrial managers of the reinsurance syndicate" (xii).

While Wallace's novel doesn't feature the same elaborate paratextual framework that Powers and Vollmann include, the first chapter of *The Broom of the System* is similarly deceptive, inasmuch as it presents action that takes place 9 years before most of the rest of the novel. But what is clear from this brief survey is that the opening of these post-postmodern novels are somewhat more subtle than they first appear. Unlike the openings of classic works by the postmodern novelists surveyed in Chapter 1—say, William Gaddis's *JR*, William Gass's *The Tunnel*, or John Barth's *Coming Soon!!!*, each of which has a dramatic opening that immediately alerts the reader to the complex formal games the author is playing—these books feature deceptive beginnings that seek to lure the reader in to a traditionally plotted story, before alerting her to the ironies and complexities of the novel itself.

Like Vollmann and Powers, in particular, *The Twenty-Seventh City*, as I'll demonstrate, is wrapped in a deceptively traditional opening, while it also shares a fascination with a key early twentieth-century figure with Powers, Wallace, and Vollmann.

Narrative frames

The Twenty-Seventh City is—like Franzen's later novels—arranged to stress homologies between the novel's plot and its architecture. The conspiracy at the heart of the story Franzen tells in *The Twenty-Seventh City* is centered around a characteristically postmodern fascination with the control and movement of information. Like Joseph McElroy's *Lookout Cartridge* (1974), exploring "great multiple fields of impinging informations" (465), or Pynchon's *Gravity's Rainbow*, where data is the "first real magic" (38), Franzen's novel is full of characters who are obsessed with data. His conspirators identify "informationalists" (*TS* 505) and an "informational elite" in the city (*TS* 393), while even those characters hidden in quiet, domestic settings listen to "Information Radio" (*TS* 88). But this information can be either good or bad, either signal or noise, and the plot of Franzen's novel explores this opposition as Jammu's conspirators begin to either lie or hide information from each other. What is most interesting, however, is the way that this delicate balance between information and misinformation in his plot is replicated in the structure of the novel through the deceptively straightforward frames that surround Franzen's narrative.

The novel's title provides the first of these apparently simple frames. *The Twenty-Seventh City* offers itself as a putative key to the work, providing a straightforward index of St. Louis's urban decline. Franzen encourages this perception at the start of the novel's second chapter by reporting that "in 1870 St. Louis was America's Fourth City . . . Only New York, Philadelphia and Brooklyn had larger populations," but by 1980 St. Louis had "dwindled to America's Twenty-Seventh City. Its population was 450,000, hardly half the 1930 figure" (*TS* 24, 26). The information encoded in this simple equation of decline is, however, misleading at both ends. As Franzen acknowledges in the novel, St. Louis's status as the Republic's Fourth City was founded on falsehood because, as Eric Sandweiss has explained, "the 1870 results had been cooked to make St. Louis's population seem bigger than it actually was" (xxx). But the figure marking St. Louis's 1980s low is equally dubious. Clarence E. Olson confirmed this when he observed in an interview with Franzen shortly before the novel's publication: "St. Louisans know, this is a distortion of the facts, a fluke caused by the separation of the city and St. Louis County in the last century. The St. Louis metropolitan area has always ranked much higher" ("Don't Judge" 3).

The falsehood encoded in this title comprises the first lesson on the danger of received information that Franzen presents the reader. Other lessons soon follow. After the title, Franzen inserts an apparently helpful note informing the reader that "this story is set in a year somewhat like 1984." Although most contemporary reviews of the novel accepted the veracity of this date,[4] the information Franzen offers the reader, here, is exactly a half-truth. In actual fact, the novel is evenly split between 1984 and 1985 (12 of the novel's 24 chapters are devoted to each year), and with only a few exceptions the novel's action can be directly traced onto the calendars for those years.[5]

Franzen follows his prefatory note with more paratextual data to apparently aid the reader, this time presenting a map of St. Louis and vicinity. In constructing his case against postmodernism, Rebein responds enthusiastically to this gesture, explaining that the map is an instance of "Franzen's abiding interest in place," symbolizing an attempt "to do for St. Louis what Joyce's books do for Dublin and Faulkner's for rural Mississippi" (213). Yet, while the map's clear lines seem to offer a neat grid on which the novel's action can be plotted, this is—again—misleading. In fact, the limitations of the map's quaint regionalism are sharply exposed by the very first sentence of Chapter 1, which announces Jammu's arrival from "Bombay, India" (*TS* 5). As the novel progresses it becomes clear that Jammu's transfer is not the only important character movement that takes place beyond the boundaries of the map's neatly fenced-off territory. Luisa Probst has recently returned from Paris, Duane Thompson has come back from Munich, Asha Hammaker and Balwan Singh have traveled from India to St. Louis, and near the end of the book Devi Madan travels to Edinburgh and back. By contrast, several of the local charms that the map does pick out—the planetarium just south of Forest Park, Weiss airport—barely register on the novel's radar.

These frames are an example of Franzen's fascination with imitative form, part of his attempt to match structure to story, but—like the prefatory matter in Vollmann and Powers's novels—they also serve as a kind of narrative anesthetic. Functioning together the paratextual material dulls the reader's sensitivity to the dislocations of Franzen's plot, instilling the belief that this book is more conventional than it actually is. But what should also be clear—even from the first few pages of *The Twenty-Seventh City*—is that Franzen plays a kind of game with the reader, and one of the rules of this game is that comments that Franzen makes about his work may be less straightforward than they seem. With this in mind, it is worth reading several of his other comments about fiction skeptically.

Rites of passage in the modern city

In a review of William Kennedy's *Very Old Bones* (1992), written just 4 years after *The Twenty-Seventh City*, Franzen cautioned that "Kennedy has yielded to the most dangerous of modern temptations and written a novel about writing novels" ("Skeleton Key" 2). His suspicious attitude toward the metafictional turn parallels the reaction against self-reference that would become so prevalent in the 1990s, and each of the first novels by Franzen, Powers, and Wallace explores and critiques the impulse toward a self-consciousness they associate with metafiction. In *The Broom of the System*, Wallace shows Lenore Beadsman struggling with the belief instilled by her grandmother that "life is words and nothing else" (119). In *Three Farmers*, Powers explores how the twentieth "century has become *about* itself . . . Art takes itself as both subject and content" (83). In *The Twenty-Seventh City*, Franzen similarly presents a younger generation that is preoccupied with self-consciousness whether in their daily affairs—Luisa's actions are staged for "the audience she often felt behind her" (*TS* 47)—or in their artistic expressions—Duane's photography is designed to ensure that "nobody gets the idea they're looking at anything but a picture." He wants his work to suggest an "implied photographer" (*TS* 63). Beyond such references, Franzen does not quite succumb to Kennedy's temptation, but *The Twenty-Seventh City* is a novel about novels, poems, and other stories that self-consciously presents a layered network of intertextual references. As I noted in Chapter 1, Franzen described his early work to Donald Antrim as an attempt to create "a conversation with the literary figures of [his] parents' generation. The great sixties and seventies Postmoderns" (73). There are certainly hints of this dialogue in several of his first novel's smart asides, such as the moment early in the book when postmodern allusion gets confused with peer-group politics as Luisa and Duane talk:

"What are you, paranoid or something?"
"Yeah. Paranoid." He leaned back in the seat, reached out the open window, and adjusted the extra mirror. "My life's gotten kind of weird lately . . . Do you know Thomas Pynchon?"
"No," Luisa said. "Do you know Stacy Montefusco?" (*TS* 55)

Such fragments allow Franzen to dramatize his literary heritage while he also stresses how little impact critically-admired postmodernism made on the general public. But, like the frames surrounding his first novel, Franzen's claim that the novel predominantly engages with his postmodern predecessors is only partly accurate: *The Twenty-Seventh City* certainly establishes a dialogue with earlier literature, but the range of this dialogue goes well beyond an engagement with literary postmodernism.

In filling their novels with information, Franzen's postmodern predecessors often gestured—as I noted earlier—toward the encyclopedia as a model for their data collection. Extending outward from the encyclopedia toward vaster data storehouses, *Gravity's Rainbow* suggests the museum as an analogue of a reader's experience of its vast and diverse knowledge. Pynchon imagines "some very extensive museum, a place of many levels, and new wings that generate like living tissue—though if it all does grow toward some end shape, those who are here inside can't see it" (537). Franzen, himself, has often flirted with such large analogues for the novel. In an interview following his essay on Gaddis, he described *Ulysses* as a "big, chilly Old World cathedral stuffed with iconography" ("Having Difficulty"), and in "Why Bother?" he imagines literary America as a "once-great city that had been gutted and drained by white flight and superhighways," though "visiting readers could still pay weekend visits to certain well-policed cultural monuments—the temple of Toni Morrison, the orchestra of John Updike" (*A* 62). Reversing the trope of literature as city, *The Twenty-Seventh City* presents the city as a literary landscape, a kind of museum or cathedral to earlier works that the reader and the characters pass through. At the level of plot, this is apparent in the kernel story of a woman (in this case, Barbara Probst) being abducted by an Indian, which replays the earliest stories that arose in this frontier town. As Sandweiss notes, even years after St. Louis resembled "anything like a frontier village," a nineteenth-century memoirist such as Anne Lucas Hunt could fear that "the Indians might carry [her] off" from the city's streets (Sandweiss xxvii; Hunt 271). That the Indians in Franzen's novel are invading America from the subcontinent, as opposed to the Native Americans being plagued by invading Europeans, is presumably a historical joke on Franzen's part. At the same time, the local details of the modern cityscape are haunted by the literary past. The novel's first page, for example, reminds the reader of the origin of the novel, by identifying the "*Cervantes* Convention center" (*TS* 5, emphasis mine). Similarly, when the action shuttles past the Mississippi of Twain's novels, the connection is reinforced by boats named "*Huck Finn* and *Tom Sawyer*" (*TS* 493–4). But the most sustained and important intertextual linkages in this literary landscape are undoubtedly to St. Louis native T. S. Eliot and his epic poem of spiritual despair, *The Waste Land* (1922).[6]

The parallels between the two works are multiple. Both works share formal similarities, making use of a mosaic of viewpoints. Both also present time as layered: the mixture of contemporary and historical voices in Eliot's poem suggests, as he was to write in "Burnt Norton," that "all time is eternally present" (171). Franzen, similarly, takes pains in his novel to illuminate the echoes of the past submerged in the present through his literary allusions and by casting modern St. Louis in a historical perspective that reveals its lands as a former "hunting ground for the Cahokia people, native Americans leading lives which bore . . . little connection with the subsequent Caucasian experience" (*TS* 154). A constellation of other minor references emphasize the connections between the two works: like Eliot, Franzen includes in his novel "scattered Tarot cards" (*TS* 177), allusions to *Oedipus* (*TS* 224, 363), an emphasis on rituals (St. Louis's Veiled Prophet is particularly relevant here), and allusions to "the voices of the dead" (*TS* 272). Franzen is even more explicit when he names Jammu's mother "Shanti," just one letter removed from the famous triple incantation that ends Eliot's poem.[7] But beyond these similarities, Franzen has clearly, and carefully, embedded a number of more extended allusions to Eliot's poem in his first novel. The most significant of these are revealed by *The Twenty-Seventh City*'s chronology.

The Waste Land begins by insisting that "April is the cruelest month," but Eliot soon cuts away from the image of budding lilacs to build up a picture of the arid, broken earth that precedes the rites of spring. Franzen has mapped out the temporal coordinates of his narrative to parallel the movement of the dead land into spring. After a short summary of earlier events, Franzen's narrative begins at the decline of the year, in September, when the St. Louis of the mid-1980s that he dissects is "a city gone dead," massed around "the dry river" (*TS* 201, 203). The city's "air smells like tar" (*TS* 254), and as characters walk over "the dried mud, a maze of cracks, sent up dust plumes as they crossed it" (*TS* 160). Echoing the voices of the desiccated waste land Franzen succinctly notes: "The land needed rain" (*TS* 160). As the narrative progresses, however, several key incidents arc toward a climax in April—the Indian investors seeking to engineer a real estate panic in St. Louis plan to sell out in April (*TS* 83), while Barbara Probst is killed in the same month. The most important of these events, however, is the election concerning St. Louis's political boundaries, which occupies the political center of the book. But while "the Land was dry" (*TS* 158) earlier in the novel, the end of March brings "humid, changing weather" (*TS* 447), and as in Eliot's poem April begins with spring rain.

The timing of this rain in relation to the novel's plot reinforces the parallels between the two works and merits further examination. The April election is framed as a confrontation between two opposing figureheads: Jammu, the politically ambitious police chief, and Martin Probst, the talismanic chairman of Municipal Growth. Encoded in the characters' names are clues to the symbolic roles they are set to play in this contest: Jammu shares her name with the state of Jammu and Kashmir, a region that Ved Mehta—one of Franzen's sources for information about India in the novel[8]—describes as a heavily disputed territory characterized by an "explosive mixture of religion and politics" (126). Her name, then, is synonymous with disputes over land, and she stands for political instability in the novel. Probst's name, by contrast, is Germanic, recalling *der Probst*, the provost of a cathedral chapter.[9] He initially seems to stand for stability and tradition, but the religious overtones to his name are not accidental because Probst also seems set to play the quasi-sacred role of King of the Wood or Fisher King in this novel. In Eliot's source text, Jessie Weston's *From Ritual to Romance* (1920), the King is ailing, and his decline is inextricably linked to his land. Weston explains: "[the King's] infirmity, for some mysterious and unexplained reason, reacts disastrously upon his kingdom . . . depriving it of vegetation" (20). As the crucial figure in Franzen's "City of symbols" (*TS* 393), Probst similarly detects a connection between his malaise and the troubles in the city. "What if he was the city?" he asks himself, "more than centrally located: the thing itself? . . . he was sick, and the city was sick on the inside too" (*TS* 216–17).[10] His position as representative of the city is further cemented as he is selected to play the symbolic role of Veiled Prophet of Khorassan. Created in the nineteenth century by the city's elite businessmen, the Veiled Prophet is intended to represent the power of the city's leaders—in a history of the ritual, Thomas M. Spencer reports that the Prophet was meant to "preside and be recognized as infallible" (3)— so Probst's election records his anointment as figurative ruler of the city.

Fertility is an important component of the Fisher King's (and, for that matter, the Veiled Prophet's)[11] role. Weston notes that "the loss of virility in the [King] brings about a suspension of the reproductive processes of Nature" (23). The sterility of the Waste Land can only be alleviated by restoring the King's potency. In Franzen's novel, Probst has been unmanned (prior to being kidnapped, his wife has had an affair), but when he kisses Jammu for the first time on the first day of April (*TS* 449), the novel's microclimate almost immediately registers a change, and the spring rains come. By 6 p.m. on the same day "rain pelted steadily" upon the city (*TS* 453), and the rains continue through the elections held on 2 April. The price of fertility in many vegetation rituals (particularly those discussed by James Frazer, whose research for *The Golden Bough* provided the foundation for Weston's study) is often the killing of the king, and so the narrative logic of *The Twenty-Seventh City* seems to move toward Probst's inevitable death. Franzen hints at the influence of fertility myths when he observes that "Spring was . . . the time of year when great men died" (*TS* 481), while a later news report warns the reader that "*Public life required that popular figures sometimes play the sacrificial victim*" (*TS* 509). Despite all these hints Probst does not die to the save the land, though—as in *Strong Motion*—a woman is shot instead. But while the template of the fertility ritual is invoked, the fate of the natural world in Franzen's novel is entwined with Eliot's life and work according to a more personal algorithm.

The invisible poet

The elaborate pattern of links to Eliot's poem establish what Franzen calls "a hidden symmetry" (*TS* 354) in his cityscape, but despite their abundance it is precisely the hidden nature of the references and allusions that requires further examination. While many writers and their works are named in the novel—the list includes Isaac Asimov, Thomas Pynchon, Jane Austen, Jean-Paul Sartre, William Shakespeare, Edmund Spenser, Herman Melville, Dostoevsky, and Heinrich Heine—Eliot does not receive even a single mention. This seems even more peculiar given that Franzen takes the trouble to include a lesson on twentieth-century American poetry at a local St. Louis school in the novel. Summarizing a century of poetry, the teacher explains:

William Carlos Williams was a doctor. He lived all his life in Paterson, New Jersey. As we go on, we'll find that it's not unusual for American poets to

have other full-time professions. Many have been teachers. Wallace
Stevens, who's perhaps our greatest poet of this century, a very hard poet,
worked for an insurance company. He was a vice president when he died.
Sylvia Plath, whom I'm sure you've all heard of, was a mother and a
housewife . . . Amy Lowell and Ezra Pound, who were both profound
influences on Williams . . . (*TS* 99)

The lesson is interrupted in midsentence, but that Eliot is not named in a class that directs its attention onto the poets rather than the poetry may seem appropriate. But his omission here is more directly linked to the fact that his memory had been gradually obscured in St. Louis. In 1923, Eliot noted that a solitary letter from Edna McCourt had been the "first intimation that I have had that my work is known" in St. Louis (554), and even in later decades he scarcely achieved greater recognition in his hometown. For all the city's statues of celebrated citizens, by the time Franzen wrote his novel, there was, as Timothy Goeglein notes, "no memorial, no garden, no library, no museum, no bronze bust, no marker, nothing that would tell the world it was the birthplace and childhood home of the greatest poet and literary critic of the modern era" (64). In fact, Franzen seems to have been aware that by the 1980s Eliot's birthplace 2635 Locust Street had been destroyed and replaced by a parking lot in 1973.[12] As Franzen writes in *The Twenty-Seventh City*, "History lives or dies in buildings," and the building of Eliot's birth was gone (*TS* 154).

The fate of Eliot in St. Louis provides the model for the destruction of nature in the novel. While aridity was the bane of Eliot's waste land, now, as Franzen notes, "the problem was concrete" (*TS* 105). The novel dates the turning point as "the seventies"—the decade the parking lot appeared on Locust Street—which "became the Era of the Parking Lot, as acres of asphalt replaced half-vacant office buildings downtown" (*TS* 25–6). But by the mid-1980s concrete and asphalt have spread beyond downtown. In the suburb of Webster Groves Probst's gardener Mohnwirbel no longer seems to tend to nature, but instead is to be found "rak[ing] concrete" (*TS* 87). Mohnwirbel's name suggests the German for vortex—*Wirbel*—and like a vortex drawing everything into its center, the concrete he rakes becomes one of the central images of the book. Stadiums are simply "tiers of concrete" (*TS* 123), at parties people talk of "concrete piles" (*TS* 91), and Probst's dreams are nightmares where concrete consumes everything:

> The concrete was like gluey oatmeal . . . Probst was running across the freshly poured foundation at Westhaven. He was following a trail of

footprints, trying to catch the man who'd made them. (Was it the sub contractor?) A skin of rainwater covered the concrete, mirroring the blue sky, but the sky wasn't blue; it was the color of concrete. A purple bird flew across it, heckling and jeckling in its spiny tongue. Probst ran on and came to the crest of a concrete hill overlooking a concrete valley . . . The footprints tugged Probst downwards. As he approached he saw that Jack had sunk into the concrete up to his waist, and that his eyes were crusted over with blood. They were cracked, swollen sockets. The eyeballs had been pecked out. Probst stopped, and Jack said, "Martin?" in a voice ragged with fear. Probst couldn't speak. (*TS* 143)

Nature—the sky, the hill, the valley—are concreted over, and Probst's friend Jack, a sunken modern Tiresias, is paralyzed by concrete. But unlike Eliot's waste land, where the thunder speaks and it is possible at last to fish, in Franzen's concrete waste land the future suggests no respite from concrete and asphalt, no resurgence for the nature world. As the plot unfolds "City government people" pass through, "pointing at future parking lots" (*TS* 256). In Franzen's dark novel the Era of the Parking Lot shows no sign of ending.

Beyond the waste land

To a certain extent, this mosaic of allusions to Eliot does suggest ways in which Franzen's relationship to his postmodern predecessors might be elaborated. After all, embedding allusions to Eliot in their novels was a regular practice for elder postmodernists. For example, in his first novel, *V.* (1963), Thomas Pynchon has a character complain that "T. S. Eliot ruined us all" (308) while William Gaddis planned to incorporate every line of *Four Quartets* into his massive novel, *The Recognitions*, and later succinctly described Eliot as "our finest poet of the century" in his 1994 novel, *A Frolic of His Own* (40). But equally, there are parallels to his post-postmodern contemporaries, too. In *The Broom of the System*, Wallace shares Franzen's understanding of how an individual in a city is part of lots of larger stories, too—as Wallace put it, an individual's story is part of "a larger narrative system of which this piece was only a part" (*Broom* 336)—while he also carries on an extended dialogue with an earlier writer.[13] But like *The Twenty-Seventh City*, Wallace's first novel also connects the 1970s and the idea of waste lands, when he has his 1970s city planners announce that "we need a wasteland . . . a point of savage reference . . . a blasted region" (54).

Franzen's vision of the modern world suffocated by asphalt and concrete is, however, shared more explicitly by Powers and Vollmann in their later works. In *The Gold Bug Variations*, Powers sees the spread of bituminous asphalt as an index of humanity's resistance to the complexity of nature, and he questions "why . . . we want to revoke the contract [with nature], scatter it like a nuisance cobweb, simplify it with asphalt" (325). In a similar vein, Vollmann has attempted in his ambitious *Seven Dreams* series to trace the history of America, from its first discovery through to "the present when everything is sort of concreted over" ("Interview" 12). Despite the heavy framework of literary reference, the ecological dimension to Franzen's intertextual dialogue is indicative of post-postmodernism's attempt to use allusion to direct attention toward the "real" world outside the book. This fascination with the ecosystem in his first book is not, however, an isolated exploration and his warnings about the destruction of nature provide one of many connections between *The Twenty-Seventh City* and *Strong Motion*. In Franzen's second novel, however, his ecological speculations are complicated by his fascination with ecofeminism and chaos theory.

Chapter 4

Midnight in the System Rooms
Strong Motion

> *Earthquake technology enables man to give back to the earth . . . It's an act of sacrificial love. We give back. The earth takes and is greener.*
> Don DeLillo, Great Jones Street *(77–8)*

If *The Twenty-Seventh City*'s vision is of St. Louis as a concrete waste land, then *Strong Motion*, which is both a development and a careful condensation of Franzen's methods, extends the network of allusions not just to Eliot's poem, but to his life as well. *Strong Motion* shares *The Waste Land*'s fascination with "Phoenician Deities," and opens with its protagonist, Louis Holland, "walking in distant wastelands" (*SM* 52, 14), but the geography of Franzen's novel also retraces Eliot's footsteps. Just as Eliot left St. Louis for Massachusetts in the first decade of the twentieth century, so *Strong Motion* parallels this movement by leaving St. Louis to shuttle between Harvard and nearby Somerville in "the last decade of the twentieth century" (*SM* 468–9). But while both Eliot and Franzen left America in the years following their time at Harvard, Franzen's novel about the Boston area seems to owe some of its obsessions to another American émigré. At the end of *Strong Motion*, Louis discovers that "his mood of patience and suspended judgment made him an ideal reader" of Henry James (*SM* 499), and Franzen's novel sometimes seems to be engaged in a dialogue with his cosmopolitan predecessor's thoughts about Boston and the novel.

In 1898, James argued that one of the weaknesses of the American novel was its failure to engage with the impact of business upon contemporary life and insisted that "the typical American figure is above all that 'business man' whom the novelist and the dramatist have scarce yet seriously touched" ("The Question" 202).[1] Franzen explicitly attempts to correct this oversight of earlier American writers in his second book's account of "people . . . in the business districts" (*SM* 468), though his dark portrayal of American business is also entangled with another Jamesian exploration. In *Strong Motion*, Louis is particularly fascinated by James's novel "*The Bostonians*" (*SM* 499), which seems appropriate given the geography of both books[2] and given the motivation that underpins James's novel. In his notebooks, James explains that he wanted "to write a very *American* tale, a tale very characteristic of our social conditions, and I asked myself what was the most salient and peculiar point in our social life. The answer was: the situation of women, the decline of the sentiment of sex, the agitation on their behalf" (47). While Franzen takes on James's instruction to address the role of business in American life, his study of the impact of the business world upon the planet bleeds into an examination of "the situation of women" that anatomizes the foundations of ecofeminism. In this investigation, Franzen discovers that the same "eternal feminists" who populated James's book are now marching in prochoice rallies (*SM* 499).

Narrative parallels

There are a number of small overlaps between *The Bostonians* and *Strong Motion*. For instance, just as James's Miss Birdseye tries "to persuade herself that taste was only frivolity in the disguise of knowledge" (57), so Renée Seitchek finds "it a huge strain to be responsible for [her] tastes" in the face of "these experts who're all trying to be more knowledgeable than each other" (*SM* 171). But while the plot of *Strong Motion* might be thought of as a distant conversation with James replacing the earlier books fascination with Eliot, Franzen's first two novels are also linked by structural similarities and plot overlaps. *Strong Motion*'s exploration of unexpected seismological disturbances, for example, can be located in the mediascape of Franzen's first novel, where Barbara Probst's radio announces a show featuring "Dr. Ernest Quitschak, a seismologist who's going to tell us . . . the next big earthquake . . . could happen any—day—now, right here in Missouri" (*TS* 93).[3] In their initial structures, too, there are similarities between the first two novels, as in both books Franzen follows an opening chapter that introduces one of the central characters, with a second chapter that views urban decline in a national context. *The Twenty-Seventh City*'s second chapter begins:

> In 1870 St. Louis was America's Fourth City. It was a booming rail center, the country's leading inland port, a wholesaler for half a continent. Only New York, Philadelphia and Brooklyn had larger populations. (*TS* 24)

Moving in parallel, *Strong Motion* begins its second chapter by remarking that:

> Like Rome, Somerville was built on seven hills. . . . Earlier in the century Somerville had been the most densely populated city in the country, a demographic feat achieved by spacing the streets narrowly and dispensing with parks and front lawns. (*SM* 22)

This technique of opening with the germ of a character-based story, before cutting in the second chapter to a broader urban canvas, probably has its roots in Maj Sjöwall and Per Wahlöö's Martin Beck stories, though as I'll also argue in this chapter, the tendency to view the world through a long lens is very much at the core of *Strong Motion*'s investigations.[4]

The novel's panoramic lens is also evident in another connection between Franzen's first two books, which takes place at the level of language. While his first novel takes the city of *St. Louis* as its focus, the city's name is echoed in the second book's protagonist, *Louis* Holland. *Louis* is also just a one-letter variation from *Luisa*, the youthful focus of *The Twenty-Seventh City*, but *Holland* suggests "whole land," the holistic perspective toward nature that underwrites the novel's ecological vision of "the whole earth" (*SM* 83). At the same time, the etymology of *Holland* (*holt* [wood] + *lant* [land]) introduces the symbol of the tree, which echoes through the text as part of this ecological vision, from Franzen's initial description of Eileen as having "the limbs of a willow tree" (*SM* 3), through the movie "*Maple-tree Girl*" (*SM* 229), to the idyllic precolonial vision of an America that was "all trees and no fences" (*SM* 376).

As these connections to *The Twenty-Seventh City* suggest, Franzen's fascination with names is important to *Strong Motion*. In an ironic juxtaposition that recalls his play with the name *Barbara* in the earlier novel, for example, Melanie Holland shares her name with Saint Melanie of Rome. But while the fifth-century saint gave all her money to charity, Franzen's twentieth-century equivalent is desperately trying to hoard as much money as she can. On a deeper level, however, in this novel's preoccupation with "the letters of the English alphabet" (*SM* 229), characters' names often subtly encode their relationships. Just as Franzen introduces Louis's sister, Eileen, as a "faithful . . . image of her mother," Melanie (*SM* 3), so their names reinforce this connection, since *Melanie* includes all but one of the letters in Eileen's name.[5] A similar alphabetical game underpins several relationships in the book. Louis's fluctuation, for example, between two prospective partners—Renée and Lauren—can be abstracted to initials that produce either a symbiotic L[eft] and R[ight], like two hands clapping, or a self-absorbed L[eft] and L[eft]. Equally, there's an alphabetical code at stake in one of the novel's central oppositions, the standoff between science and religion embodied by the seismologist, Renée Seitchek, and the Protestant minister, Philip Stites. Although these two characters are divided over the question of abortion, Franzen spends much of Chapter 10 stressing the connection and mutual fascination that exists between the two. Their initials underline these links. Alphabetically, the only difference between the initials PS and RS is one letter, the letter Q, just as the only difference between the characters is a Q, or question: science or religion?

But while there are intimate and extensive connections between *The Twenty-Seventh City* and *Strong Motion*, there are significant differences, too. Although *Strong Motion* represents a notable artistic advance upon the first novel, at the same time the later book represents a deliberate narrowing of focus matched with a corresponding broadening of the novel's implications. This initial move toward contraction can, again, be considered in terms of Franzen's post-postmodern contemporaries, Powers and Wallace.

After Powers's journey "through the century's spectrum" in *Three Farmers on Their Way to a Dance*, he returned to America in his second novel (299). While his first book had balanced its intellectual excursions with narratives set on different continents that all, in some way, referred back to the global crisis of the First World War, *Prisoner's Dilemma* (1988) is preoccupied with the somewhat smaller scale hidden in that "condensed sign language, the secret code of family" (13). But while the "crisis of family" (19) provides much of the foreground of this novel, Powers's focus on the microcosm is enlarged by his sense of how the small can impact upon the large through his allusions to Edward Lorenz's pioneering work with weather systems. In *Prisoner's Dilemma*, Artie Hobson provides a neat summary of Lorenz's most famous concept (which laid the foundations for chaos theory), when he "recalled the Butterfly Effect, that model of random motion describing how a butterfly flapping its wings in Peking propagates an unpredictable chain reaction of air currents, ultimately altering tomorrow's weather in Duluth" (94). Demonstrating how small causes can produce disproportionately large effects, Powers's novel is informed about the ways that scientists have abandoned linear forms in favor of "falling . . . into randomness" and uncertainty (149).

Although the term *contraction* can only be relative when applied to Wallace's first three works, his second book, *Girl with Curious Hair*, is a collection of (mostly) short stories that acknowledges the need for smaller scales because "limitations of space and patience" are a "constant and defining limitation, these quick and distracting days" (357). But while Wallace, like Powers, moves to a reduced scale in his second book, his stories are also about connecting the small with the large, recording the conflicts as people come into contact with "large-scale systems" such as the advertising industry, political systems, and the nexus of interests that drive television (155). These conflicts allow Wallace to reveal (as he wrote in a short story published 2 years after *Girl with Curious Hair*) how the individual has a "role in the interplay of forces probably beyond the comprehension of everything and everyone involved" ("Order" 94).

A similar movement toward condensation is evident in Franzen's second novel. While in *The Twenty-Seventh City* Franzen's family plot was entangled in the many stories swarming in the labyrinth of St. Louis, and relayed through a carefully distancing narrative lens, in *Strong Motion* his focus from the very first paragraph onward is much more consistently centered upon the volatile dynamics of the Holland family. Again, like Powers and Wallace, Franzen's story is also interested in the individual's butterfly-like interaction with "large-scale systems." But while I explore the chaotics of Franzen's text in some detail below, it is worth mentioning, first, that in parallel with *Strong Motion*'s more curtailed focus, Franzen's second novel also articulates its message with greater directness. As Franzen explains, "instead of sending my bombs in a Jiffy-Pak mailer of irony and understatement, as I had with *The Twenty-Seventh City*, I'd come out throwing rhetorical Molotov cocktails" in *Strong Motion* (*A* 62–3). Amongst the clearest products of this revised rhetorical strategy are *Strong Motion*'s constant attacks upon the media, attacks that place Franzen squarely in the American grain.

In 1838, James Fenimore Cooper warned that the media in America "would seem to be expressly devised by the great agent of mischief, to depress and destroy all that is good and to elevate and advance all that is evil in the nation" (*American Democrat* 455). That Cooper was suspicious of America's emerging media systems seems consistent with his novels' preference for the natural "earth fattened by the decayed vegetation of centuries, and black with loam" over an increasingly urbanized America, where "the towns grow, and new streets spring up, and the whole face of the earth undergoes change" (*Pathfinder* 36, 100). But beyond Cooper, suspicion of the media has, at times, sent writers such as Salinger, DeLillo, Pynchon, and Gaddis into hiding. Franzen is certainly a product of the influence of these writers, but his travels in Europe add a Germanic twist. In *The Discomfort Zone*, Franzen recalls his exposure to the work of Austrian satirist, Karl Kraus, and Kraus's hatred of the press, in particular, is distilled in almost pure form into the mediascape of *Strong Motion*. "What syphilis has spared,"

Kraus complained, "the media will ravage," and in his disgust at the stupidity of the press and its alliance with business interests, Kraus launched his own independent magazine, *Die Fackel* (*The Torch*) in 1899 (47). By contrast, the media in Franzen's book seem, at first, to be little more than amoral and a bit bloodthirsty. After Rita Kernaghan dies, for example, Franzen reports that "neither the *Globe* nor the *Herald* could quite hide its delight at having a death . . . to justify big headlines" (*SM* 26). However, as the reports of this death begin to filter out, Franzen slowly reveals the stupidity of the media: in the *Globe*'s report, the title of Rita's book "*Princess Itaray*" is mangled and transformed into "*Princess of Italy*" (*SM* 12, 27), while Melanie Holland is incorrectly listed as a resident of Cleveland, rather than Evanston. The major vehicle for Franzen's attack on the media, however, is Alec Bressler, who, like Kraus, attempts to run an independent media outlet, though Bressler is clearly a target for a fair amount of Franzen's satire.[6] After all, while Bressler wants to remove any discussion of the news from his broadcasts, Franzen carefully undermines this ambition by naming his station WSNE, an obvious anagram of *news*. Nevertheless, Bressler's attacks on the media carry much of the novel's argument against the press: "isn't it the responsibility also of every sinking person in the country to say to networks and noosepapers: You are my enemy now. You betrayed me. You are not really on my side. You are on side of money" (*SM* 99). Franzen's attempt to render a bad foreign accent produces some pregnant puns, here (*noose/ news, sinking/ thinking*), but the real importance of Bressler's outburst is that two pages later Franzen coolly confirms his assertions with a neat illustration of the way money interests provide a foundation for the media:

> "There's no man in this world that wakes up in the morning but by the grace of our Lord"
> The television's response to this avowal was a perfume ad. (*SM* 101)

Such attacks on the media, of course, also find their counterparts in James's *The Bostonians*, with its critique of journalism and "the great arts of publicity" (139). But alongside such attacks, one of the other "rhetorical Molotov cocktails" that Franzen is clearly throwing in *Strong Motion* concerns the connection between the irresponsibility of male sexuality and industrial waste practices. The foundations of this examination initially betray significant affinities with ecofeminist criticism.

Shortly before *Strong Motion* was published, ecofeminists such as Karen Warren argued that both the domination of women by men and the domination of the natural world by humans were conceptually linked by a shared "logic of domination" (129). When applied to the earth, "this logic always makes use of premises about morally significant differences between human beings and the rest of nature, along with a premise that asserts that these differences allow human beings to dominate nonhumans" (Davion 10). When extrapolated to consider the "situation of women," an equivalent logic can be seen to operate ensuring that masculine power is, as Franzen writes, "structurally guaranteed" (*SM* 263).

In its broad thematic arcs, Franzen's novel seems to explore how this common logic of domination functions. For example, the rise of Sweeting-Aldren—the company that most consistently fulfils the biblical injunction to "fill the earth and subdue it" (*SM* 376, Gen. 1:28) in the novel—coincides with "the golden hours for the patriarchy" (*SM* 392). While industry is connected to patriarchy, so the female body is insistently linked to the natural world. Near the end of the book, for instance, Louis imagines how he can make Renée's "belly convulse like a hillside in the throes of a disaster" (*SM* 496). Probably the most graphic expressions of the logic of domination, however, afflict Louis when he sleeps. Shortly after Louis reads about a chemical spill of "greenish effluent" leeching out of property owned by Sweeting-Aldren (*SM* 92), he dreams of his mother being penetrated by her grandfather, a man who had millions invested in the early rise of the company. But while the dream merges masculinity and industry, so the language carefully connects the waste to the earthquakes, prefiguring a link the characters haven't established yet:

> She was still perched on a chair, the hem of her yellow dress still raised almost to her hips. But now there was only one man in the room . . . Catching sight of Louis, he at once turned away and did something to his pants, adjusted something in front. This was when Louis realized that the entire room was slick with semen, greenish white semen deep enough to cover the soles of his shoes, and he woke up *quaking* violently. (*SM* 93, emphasis mine)

There are clearly strong affinities, here, between the ecofeminist position on the subjection of women and nature and Franzen's vision in the novel. Yet, the very neatness of the dualities outlined by ecofeminism seem to present too linear an equation for Franzen, and his novel ultimately complicates this model through his use of chaos theory and the systemic form of *Strong Motion*.

The narrative system

As Franzen has observed, *Strong Motion* is a "systems novel of conspiracy and apocalypse" (*A* 247), and as such it represents perhaps his most impressive and polished artistic achievement. The term *Systems Novel* was coined by Tom LeClair to describe the work of DeLillo and his contemporaries, and the body of thought underlying this designation was the systems theory that derives from the work of Ludwig von Bertalanffy. An Austrian biologist, Bertalanffy attempted to replace the mechanistic approach to living systems with a mathematical and biological approach that worked from both the "top down" and the "bottom up," stressing reciprocal relationships between the two. In this new epistemology, the emphasis was on open rather than closed systems; dynamic, reciprocal relationships rather than separate static components, and so on. The classic systems novelists, for LeClair, were writers who attempted to replicate the systems understanding of the world rather than the crude mechanistic model of cause and effect that we find in a traditional novel. These writers comprised a sophisticated strand of scientifically informed contemporary fiction that "use[d] postmodern techniques to model the dense and tangled relations of modern history, politics, and science" ("The Systems Novel" 40).

Like his scientifically informed postmodern predecessors, Franzen selected his scientific sources for *Strong Motion* carefully, and for the most part they are written into the novel. Franzen notes, for example, that "the classic example" of induced seismicity "was in the early sixties, at the Rocky Mountain Arsenal, outside Denver" (*SM* 158), which directs the reader's attention to a series of articles, dating from November 1962, by David M. Evans positing "a direct relationship between . . . earthquakes and contaminated waste-water being injected into a 12,045-foot disposal well at the Rocky Mountain Arsenal" (11). Similarly, Franzen identifies the "*Atlantic Monthly*" issue with "THE ORIGIN OF PETROLEUM. February 1986" on the cover about "the scientist Renée had mentioned, the one named Gold" (*SM* 369), which very specifically directs the reader to an essay by David Osborne about "an astrophysicist at Cornell University named Thomas Gold" (Osborne 39). Franzen's fidelity to his scientific sources, in fact, was evidently so impressive that it persuaded two geophysicists authoring a report on real induced seismic activity to include his novel amongst 20 real earthquake sequences, though they lament that "no injection data (volume or pressures) were available in [*Strong Motion*], although it seems probable from the novel that injection volumes were substantial" (Davis and Frohlich 213). Scientific life evidently draws on art.

But aside from his specific sources, evidence of systems thinking is certainly tangible in all Franzen's novels. In *The Twenty-Seventh City* Buzz Wismer, who models "meteorological fields" and runs a "systems check on himself" (*TS* 158, 353), is the focus of systems thinking, while *The Corrections*, as I argue in Chapter 5, criticizes the tendency of both people and corporations to create closed systems in their lives. But *Strong Motion* has the most extensive systems angle, and in Franzen's career-long conversation with postmodernism, it marks the moment where his practice is least divided because it overlaps most strongly with the work of his postmodern ancestors Don DeLillo, William Gaddis, Thomas Pynchon, and Robert Coover.

Strong Motion's systems orientation is encoded in the book's title. The novel's plot is not really concerned with the phenomenon of "strong motion," the large amplitude ground shaking that occurs near an epicenter. Instead, the seismological principle that underlies the narrative is induced seismicity, which Franzen glosses as what "happens after you've been pumping lots of liquid underground, and basically it's as if the rock down there gets slippery from all the extra liquid" and triggers an earthquake (*SM* 158). But Franzen refers to strong motion in the title of his novel because it represents an area of study where different systems interconnect to produce a complex knot of uncertainty. As Renée explains: "you can make recordings of strong motion, though unfortunately everything's so complicated by the local geological context that it's hard to extract much information about the earthquake itself" (*SM* 184). Two of the novel's governing themes, then, are introduced by the title—systemic interconnections and uncertainty—and the four named parts of the book introduce some of the impersonal systems that contain Franzen's characters.

The novel's first section is titled "Default Gender" and several meanings cluster around this phrase. Default gender identifies not only the benefits that arise from being male in a male-oriented society—the hidden privileges that result from "belonging to the default gender" (*SM* 263)—but it also signals the tendency to posit male agency behind actions. Renée explains this when she notes that she assigns a masculine identity to "an animal without gender . . . Default gender: male" (*SM* 208). Yet, despite her ability to analyze this tendency, in an irony that she is not aware of, Franzen shows that knowledge does not allow her to step outside of the system, as she assigns the default gender to scientists when she assumes that a scientist named A. F. Krasner must be male, only for Franzen to later reveal that the *A* is for Anna (*SM* 159, 371). In systems terms, however, "Default Gender" also reveals that the controlling system of this section will be biology or the tendency of characters to default to behavior dictated by gender. Louis, for example, is introduced in terms of stereotypically masculine behavior throughout this section—his tendency to fight, his urge to act in a "protective" manner when another male is near his sister (*SM* 9)—and, critically, his stereotypically male drive to procreate shapes "Default Gender." The first part of the book begins when, shortly after Christmas in 1989, Louis discovers that Lauren Bowles has rejected him to marry the grandly named Emmett Andrew Osterlitz of Beaumont. Spurned by his prospective mate, Louis immediately seeks to flee Texas and moves to New England in March. After a chance meeting with Renée on a beach, Louis begins to pursue her in much the same manner that the dog Louis meets on the same beach follows him. But falling in love with the intelligent Renée is an effort compared to lusting after the passionate but uninformed Lauren. While Louis's mind has to "train . . . itself to appreciate Renée" (*SM* 214), Lauren, whose name is an anagram of *unreal*, represents a simple male fantasy of sexual magnetism, so she need do little more than express an interest in seeing him to persuade him to abandon the period of nearly 2 months that he has devoted to building a relationship with Renée.[7] All Louis wants with Lauren is to fulfill a simple biological equation, "to be her man" (*SM* 220). "Default Gender," then, ends with a lesson in the ways that biology controls behavior, the lesson that Renée learns later in the book: sooner or later "men inevitably remained true to their gender" (*SM* 263).

The novel's second section, "I ♥ Life," introduces a second system that Franzen's characters are caught within: the political system. The slogan "I ♥ Life" echoes through the book and is always associated with the politics of reproduction (*SM* 101, 317, 344). The phrase appears at public demonstrations calling for an end to abortions, but the love of life is mingled with threat and violence at these demonstrations. Of course, the dictates of male biology also suggested violence, and in much the same way that masculinity shaped the first section, political protests appear to shape the second part of the book, since the section climaxes with Renée addressing the protestors and (at least initially) appearing to suffer the consequences of challenging this system. The movement from the biological system of part one to the political system of part two—like the parallactic shifts in *The Twenty-Seventh City*—introduces several changes in scale: the focus moves from the personal to the public, and the kind of pain endured shifts from the emotional to the physical. Both of these kinds of pain have been inflicted upon Renée, underlining—as Bob

Holland will explain—that when the final accounts are drawn up for these systems "it's usually the women who pay" (*SM* 407).

"Argilla Road" is the third and shortest section of the novel and is dominated by history. Composed of information that largely originates from history professor, Bob Holland, "Argilla Road" traces the emergence of the modern corporation back to foundational texts of Western religion and philosophy and introduces a further jump in scale.[8] If the movement of the first two sections was from the individual to the public, the third section now shows people merely as "pawns in the grip of history" (*SM* 387) and outlines how Louis is a product of "ineluctable heredity" (*SM* 388). But, if the previous two sections have climaxed with a woman being made a victim of a system, then the third section marks a shift in this progression, as it comes to a close with a woman refusing to acknowledge her responsibility to history, as Anna Krasner denies her links to her past with Sweeting-Aldren.

The last section of the book, titled "Living in the Black," introduces economics as a controlling system. At this point, literal money is exchanged (Renée receives donations totaling about $19,000, and burns a check for $600,000), the narrative debts are tallied as characters begin to be measured against a putative "absolute standard of goodness" (*SM* 423), and Franzen affirms that we are all "indebted to the earth" (*SM* 382).

Temporal form

Before outlining how the individual structures and systemic interactions of these four parts of the novel relate to systems theory, I would like to briefly consider the significance of *Strong Motion*'s structure against what Joseph Frank calls the "spatial form" practiced by Franzen's postmodern and modern predecessors. In "Spatial Form in Modern Literature" (1963), Frank defines a mode of ordering literary works that breaks with the belief that we understand narrative through a linear temporal sequence. Rather than experiencing literature as a form "composed of a succession of words proceeding through time" (6), modernist writers, Frank argued, were attempting to order their works spatially, after the techniques of the plastic arts. In a work exhibiting spatial form, such as Joyce's *Ulysses*, we see a novel composed from a series of scattered cross-references that do not necessarily cohere when the novel is apprehended in linear sequence, but rather relate "to each other independently of the time sequence of the narrative" (16). This structure means that "a knowledge of the whole is essential to the understanding of any part" (19), so to appreciate any single scene in *Ulysses* a reader must reconstruct the sense of that scene by assembling "fragments, sometimes hundreds of pages apart, scattered through the book" (18).

Frank's examples are primarily drawn from high modernism—Proust, Joyce, Eliot, and Pound—but these structural techniques are part of modernism's bequest to postmodernism. Though the juxtapositions of Don DeLillo's *Libra* (1988), for instance, are much less radical than Joyce's, his novel nevertheless offers a clear example of spatial form in the post-modern novel. In a scene late in the book, DeLillo sets the reader in Lee Harvey Oswald's scattered consciousness:

> He has proof of his subscriptions to left-wing journals. He has the court summons describing the incident that led to his arrest.
> The revolution must be a school of unfettered thought.
> Rain-slick streets.
> Aerospace is the coming thing, with courses at night in economic theory. (335)

Considered in linear sequence, this passage makes limited sense. Considered in terms of the spatial arrangement of the entire novel, however, DeLillo's passage is much easier to decode. Oswald's reflection on "the revolution," for example, can be understood by connecting this fragment to a scene 156 pages earlier, when this phrase is identified as a quotation from Castro (179). Recognizing this echo makes sense, here, because Oswald is thinking of going to Cuba. "Rain-slick streets" recasts a kind of mantra that appears 289 pages earlier in a violent fantasy Oswald has as a boy in New Orleans (46). Apprehended spatially, then, the juxtaposition of these two phrases implies a continuum between his violent youth and his violent adulthood. The reference to "Aerospace" is from the preceding page, and reminds the reader that the cover story Oswald gives his wife for his move to Cuba is that he is "looking for work in the aerospace industry" (334). But the courses in "economic theory" represent a second form of long-term yearning, which Oswald will repeat 81 pages later when he is in prison (416). Piecing this last sentence together with the preceding fragments, the reader gets a sense of two different hopes—one deceitful, one idealistic—for a better life that might result from the move to Cuba.

While some post-postmodern works continue to experiment with this kind of spatial form—Wallace's *Infinite Jest*, for example, absolutely depends upon the reader piecing together scattered fragments—*Strong Motion* represents a radical break with this practice. Instead of arranging his novels spatially, Franzen's structure places *increased* stress on the temporal experience of reading one of his novels in *linear* sequence. This mode of structuring, which might be called *temporal form*, relies upon Franzen setting out his chronology so that the temporal sequence of the book imitates the events of the plot. A radical fusion of formalist and contentist impulses, temporal form is at its most extreme in *The Corrections*, but it can also be detected in *Strong Motion*, where Franzen has arranged his narrative system, so that the chronology of each of the four sections is dictated by the logic of earthquakes.

Each of the first three parts of the book moves toward a kind of climax, a building up of narrative pressure and suspense that causes a rift from which implications ripple outward to impact upon other characters: Louis abandons Renée; Renée is shot; Bob perceives the family history underlying the swarm of earthquakes. Just as the epicenter of an earthquake throws waves outward from it, so the climaxes at the end of each section function as small narrative earthquakes, that blow the narrative lens back into a past that precedes the climax of the end of the preceding part. From section to section the novel does not proceed in a linear fashion; instead it moves toward a climax, is knocked back in time by that climax, and then proceeds toward the present again from a different temporal location. Represented graphically, the chronological structure of the contemporary action in the book would look something like Figure 4.1.

Viewed like this, we see "time folded back on itself" (*SM* 339), as the temporal arrangement of this story about earthquakes imitates the fallout

PART ONE

| End of March/ Early April, 1990: Louis arrives in New England and contacts Elaine | June 7: Louis collects his things from Renée's apartment, and sees Howard's car there |

PART TWO

| Summer 1989: Renée and Howard meet at her parents' house | June 21, 1990: Renée has her abortion and is shot |

PART THREE

c. June 10, 1990 – June 11
Bob and Louis talk in Evanston

PART FOUR

| c. June 4 Elaine and Peter holiday in Côte d'Azur | Late April 1991 Louis and Elaine discuss having a baby |

FIGURE 4.1 Temporal form in *Strong Motion*.

from an earthquake. But Franzen's experiments with temporal form also shape the internal dynamics of these sections. In Chapters 3 and 4, which have been arranged so they occupy the center of part one, Franzen parallels the geological layers of the earth by splitting the focus of each episode between different layers of time: one recounts his present day infatuation with Renée, the other documents his earlier obsession with Lauren. In this structure, we see an earlier layer of Louis's life being gradually wrenched up to penetrate the surface of his present day existence. The long historical perspective of "Argilla Road" is similarly designed to parallel layers of geological strata, with the structure of this episode representing what Franzen calls some "deep and destabilizing drilling into the past" (personal correspondence). But while it is useful to isolate these components to identify their chronological structure and significance—and I return to the idea of temporal form in the next chapter—the larger logic of the book is an argument about the impossibility of reducing any complicated phenomenon to its component parts. The influence of chaos theory is important here.

One of the key concepts of chaos theory is the phenomenon of so-called self-similarity, which derives from Benoit Mandelbrot's critique of Euclidean geometry. Examining the presence of irregular forms in nature, Mandelbrot found formal overlaps that could be described as examples of "recursive symmetry." N. Katherine Hayles explains: "a figure or system displays recursive symmetry when the same general form is repeated across many different length scales, as though the forms were being progressively enlarged or diminished" ("Introduction" 10). This principle clearly informs Franzen's novel. Just as the logic of earthquakes dictates the structure of the novel, so at the level of consciousness, our sense of the present is prey to "upheavals and subsidences . . . occurring in the landscape of . . . memory" (*SM* 180), at the level of embodiment, a scarred female body resembles "the San Andreas Fault" (*SM* 496), and at the level of human interaction, sex can be seen as "a re-creation of strong motion" (*SM* 166).

But while *Strong Motion* replicates Mandelbrot's recursive symmetries, it also employs the nonlinear conception of cause and effect that characterizes Lorenz's butterfly effect. The classical doctrine of scientific discovery was founded upon the Laplacian principle that the components of a process could be considered as part of a closed system, where each discrete unit could be isolated and analyzed to identify a linear flow of cause and effect. Taken to its logical endpoint, this viewpoint is underpinned by the optimistic belief that the natural world can ultimately be explained by reducing it to its component parts. By contrast, chaos theory envisions every action to take place within an open system that is inherently dynamic because such systems have to be conceived, as Anthony Wilden explains, not in isolation as "a unilinear sequence of causes and effects," but like other systems "simulating life," which are "necessarily in communication with another 'system' or 'environment'" (96, 36). The dynamic complexity of an open system, however, means that small causes can "jump . . . the track of the ordinary" and produce disproportionately large effects (*SM* 456). Such unpredictable interactions produce what Ilya Prigogine calls "an extraordinary complexity" that contributed to the "end of certainty" within classical science (41).

In the "spreading chaos" of Franzen's novel (*SM* 456), uncertainty and nonlinear chains of causality are everywhere. Like Lorenz's butterfly, some of these instances involve small initial actions prompting large responses. Renée's appearance on television, for example, while ostensibly an attempt to discuss earthquakes gets entangled in a debate about reproductive rights and results in her receiving an enormous amount of telephone calls and letters. Science, clearly, cannot exist isolated from larger communicative systems. But the novel's clearest demonstration of nonlinear causality arrives near the end of the book, when Franzen undermines the reader's expectations by revealing that the evil capitalists at Sweeting-Aldren have not, in a simplistic sense, 'caused' the major earthquake on June 24: "a Sweeting-Aldren injection well could . . . not have caused the earthquake; at most it could have destabilized the fault, or provided a general instability with a path of least resistance. But the entire subject of rupture propagation was not at all well understood" (*SM* 476).

It is at this point that Franzen's interest in Chaos theory begins to intersect with, and complicate, the ecofeminist dimension of his text. Although ecofeminism outlines a duality, where mankind's domination of the earth directly maps on to masculine domination of the feminine, Franzen's understanding of chaotic interactions makes him reluctant to reduce such complicated relationships to this kind of linear algorithm. Despite the novel's evident sympathies with ecofeminism, then, Franzen is concerned with revealing how much more complicated issues of gender and ecology are. In the microcosm of the Holland family, for example, Franzen reverses gender expectations and shows that it is Melanie and Eileen who support the system of capitalist exploitation because they seek its economic rewards, while both Bob and Louis attempt to opt out of the system, however illusory that attempt may be. Rather than present the linear dualities of a closed system, then, *Strong Motion*'s tentacular reach judges the wider open system that creates the conditions for domination, whether it is based upon gender, economics, or ecology.

Internal chaos

As a seismologist, Renée is well aware of the impossibility of reducing the natural world to a closed system where everything can be explained. In her professional life, she recognizes in theory that "the science of earthquakes is a science of uncertainties" (*SM* 211) that can never be reduced to its orderly, discrete components. Yet, Renée's personal life, by contrast, has been explicitly driven by an attempt to live her life within a closed system. Renée is obsessed by order and cannot withstand the taint of chaos that emerges in open systems. Her apartment on Pleasant Avenue, as Louis discovers, embodies the zeal for isolation and closure that rules her life: "It was a bare, clean place. There was nothing on the kitchen counter but a radio/cassette player, nothing in the dish rack . . . everything about the place made him feel intrusive, as though even his footsteps might disturb things" (*SM* 132). Her home is like a monk's cell, purged of worldly contamination, and her research is similarly abstract. When Louis asks her if she has been to any of the islands whose geology she studies, Renée explains that her work tends to isolate her in the system rooms: "I thought geophysics would get me outdoors . . . Six years later I've hardly left this room" (*SM* 186). The list-making instinct at the heart of her character is indicative of this "orderly Renée" (*SM* 175) who can even enjoy music only in a "hermetic way" (*SM* 168).[9]

As Renée's relationship with Louis approaches crisis point, he criticizes her desire to remain isolated, complaining that "the only way you can stay exemplary is to stay by yourself" (*SM* 193), and after they split up, she responds by restoring her home to its earlier pristine condition: "she swept the whole apartment and washed . . . eventually she got the apartment as clean and bare as it was the night she first slept with Louis Holland" (*SM* 340). But for all Louis's criticisms, his life is almost equally hermetic. The novel begins by introducing Louis as a denizen of a "world where you were by yourself" (*SM* 4), and, indeed, he describes himself to Renée (in phrasing that parallels her object of study) as "an island. An island" (*SM* 187). Like Renée, his apartment reveals his desire for isolation—he has taken a room in a two-bedroom apartment because the student leasing the other room has promised him that "our paths will never cross" (*SM* 23)—and he seems to love baseball because it's a system that reduces complex interlocking forces (players, climate, umpire, managers, coaches, etc.) to produce the certainty of "knowledge as clean and permanent . . . as a box score" (*SM* 490).[10]

These characters seem to believe that isolation produces certainty. Yet while Louis spends much of the novel trying to avoid circulating with the rest of the world—when not sealed in his own apartment, Louis locks himself in a room in the Bowles's house, and then does the same in Eileen's house—both his story and Renée's are stories about having to engage with the chaotic interactions of the world's "circulatory systems" (*SM* 45). But while embracing "internal chaos" can be destructive in this novel (*SM* 472), Louis and Renée have to reach what chaos theorist Roger Lewin calls "the edge of chaos," a region of optimized efficiency. Lewin explains: "As you leave ordered territory and enter the region of chaos you traverse maximum computational capacity, maximum information manipulation" (qtd. in Hermanson "Chaos" 43). In the context of their need to reach the boundary between too strict order and unruly chaos, it is significant that Franzen first brings these two characters together on a beach, where the rigidity of the land merges with the turbulence of the Atlantic Ocean. The productive boundary between chaos and order is further symbolized when into Renée's orderly apartment is introduced a manila folder of earthquake files, which is thrown into a space next to her refrigerator on May 10. Acting on "something like superstition" (*SM* 175), Renée leaves it there for 15 days. During this period, Renée and Louis begin to make progress (both emotionally and intellectually) but after these 15 days, their openness begins to recede. On May 26, Renée gives Louis an apartment key, offering to make him a permanent fixture with her private world. This seems like a positive gesture, but rather than indicating their openness to the rest of the world, it indicates their plan to create a two-person "closed system" (*SM* 393). Shortly after this, on June 1, Renée and Louis go to dine with Peter and Eileen, but—again—they are not going to see them in the hope of some genuine reciprocity. Instead, they hope to take information away from them about the Stoorhuys family and keep it to themselves. The real irony of this failure of openness is revealed toward the end of the book when Peter explains to Louis that "all you had to do was tell me, and none of this would have happened" (*SM* 447). Had Louis and Renée made the small gesture of sharing their information with him, the large consequence of Renée being shot would not have taken place.

The fabric of life

While the plot and structure of *Strong Motion* illustrate the chaotic interactions between microcosm and macrocosm, so Franzen also complicates our understanding of the individual life within the systems that contain it, by revealing "how deeply" the individual is "immersed in the world" (*SM* 350). As Renée recovers after her abortion, she detects "action" taking place "within three . . . frames of reference" (*SM* 349) and, in fact, throughout the novel Franzen's narrative technique is to set the scale of the individual human life against at least two others frames of reference. One way that he does this is through the arrangement of his chapters. At the end of Chapter 9, for example, Franzen provides a climax that focuses on the illogical decisions that can be a product of human emotion, as Melanie, "a lady who's obviously not all there" at this point (*SM* 296), is pushed to desperation by Renée's financial demands. The emotional peak of this chapter, however, is carefully placed to contrast sharply with the impersonality of the start of Chapter 10, which begins at "midnight in the system rooms" (*SM* 298). Just as Franzen had imagined in one of his student publications, how the act of ordering in a restaurant might be reduced to a series of "loops and subroutines" ("Fresh Frozen" B5), so Chapter 10 offers the life of an American through the lines of a computer program. This objective account of a world unfiltered by human perception—a kind of late-century update of one of Virginia Woolf's many attempts to "describe the world seen without a self" (*The Waves* 221)—leads Franzen to argue that, stripped of what philosophers of mind (after Joseph Levine) call *qualia*, the subjective qualities that color our introspective existences, the "average American intelligence can now be simulated by a program running to 11,000 lines" (*SM* 302). An extract from this program reveals that modern existence can be reduced to two basic desires—the urges to gratify bodily functions and to seek consumer gratification—but the irony of this reductive gesture is that the hysterical Melanie is conceived throughout the book in terms of these two desires. The apparent act of reduction serves to highlight how some of Franzen's characters have purged their lives of anything but greed and need.

Following the impersonality of the system rooms, Franzen provides a third scale through which to view the world in Chapter 11. In this section, the narrative is focalized through the mind of a raccoon. This shift to the animal scale might seem to be distant from human concerns, but just as the objectivity of the system's room replicated Melanie's mindset, so the raccoon also sheds light on Franzen's characters. Franzen explains that by "never mating, never interacting with his own kind in any way," this reclusive raccoon "almost ceased to have a nature" (*SM* 339). His existence, then, is a warning to Louis and Renée about their tendency to live as if life were a closed system, and Franzen highlights the connection between Renée and the raccoon by ending his section with both woman and animal staring at the same passing train.

The tripartite hierarchy of computer system–human–animal outlined through these juxtapositions stresses not just how individual characters are deeply bound into the "whole fabric of life" (*SM* 381), but also how modern existence is reducing subjectivity to the narrowed parameters of a computer program. Another three scales, past–present–future, are also evident in the unusual technique Franzen employs to describe his characters, a technique that partially recalls Proust. In the earlier novel, when Marcel describes his friend Robert de Saint-Loup, he sees in his face a map of his genealogy:

> when I looked at him closely I could see to what extent the vigorous bone structure of his triangular face must have been modeled on that of his ancestors, a face designed rather for an ardent bowman than for a sensitive man of letters. Beneath the delicate skin the bold construction, the feudal architecture were apparent. (2: 460)

In a similar fashion Franzen, near the start of the book, describes Peter's face as "one of those urban faces that had been reconceived so many times that the skin, like a piece of paper smudged and abraded by multiple erasures, had lost its capacity to hold a clear image" (*SM* 6). At first, this seems to simply be one of the ways that Franzen attempts to slight those allied with the forces of business, and yet as the book progresses, the idea of facial palimpsests recurs. Shortly after this scene, Louis detects "a conceivable middle-aged Eileen suddenly beginning to show through" her face, "like old wallpaper beneath a coat of new paint" (*SM* 11). Later he describes faces at a party as "urban palimpsest faces" (*SM* 124), and after he sees a picture of a young Renée he suddenly begins to see "things about her that until now her manner had concealed . . . she struck him as younger" (*SM* 153).

Operating consistently throughout the book, this method of description is one of the ways that Franzen reinforces his themes at the level of the individual sentence. On one level, the idea of a face being composed of layers prompts a comparison between human life and "geological life" (*SM* 182). Just as the sedimentary portions of the earth's crust are made up of stratified levels laid down over time, so the faces of Franzen's characters are not static, but products of a similar kind of temporal layering, where the past (or the future) is never totally obscured by the present, but can be detected by a careful examination of facial topography. But this contrast between individual and geological scales is also supplemented by a consideration of evolutionary scales. When Louis sees Renée's mother late in the book, he insists that "he was looking at Renée who had aged twenty-five years" (*SM* 438). What Louis, of course, sees in her face is the imprint of genetic inheritance, and the idea of the individual carrying visible signs of genetic connection is the idea that fundamentally animates Franzen's prose on a page-by-page basis. But just as the second chapter of the novel cannot view Somerville, without considering it in the light of its long evolution, so Franzen cannot describe his characters without stressing their own long evolution—and hence their kinship—from lower animals. From the opening description of Rita Kernaghan's "kitty-cat face" (*SM* 10), through the "snake-like contractions" of Mr. Aldren's hand under the dress of a woman with a "dark mane" of hair (*SM* 188), there are too many instances of this technique to document.[11] But Franzen does not only describe humans as if they were similar to animals, but his narrative voice also describes animals in comparison to animals: his raccoon, for example, has "shoulders like a cat" and extends "an arm like a monkey" (*SM* 209, cf. 337). The long chain of comparisons and similarities at different scales is all a function of the novel's larger argument about the need for connection. His story about Louis and Renée's need to connect is paralleled by prose that reveals how deeply humanity is embedded in an ecological chain. The greedy capitalists of Franzen's novel try to set themselves up as masters of this ecology. By contrast Louis and Renée try to hide from the world, just as Eddie Hobson's does in *Prisoner's Dilemma* within his imaginary "magic kingdom World World" (185). As *Strong Motion* reveals, however, both strategies are mistakenly predicated on the belief that an individual can be separated from the swirling interconnected systems that surround the self. Donald Worster reaffirms this point in *Nature's Economy* (1994), arguing that "the idea of man's autarchy can only be a delusion" but at the same time "a kind of schizoid withdrawal into a make-believe world" is also impossible (333). Though the chronology of the novel moves toward the millennium, the ecological underpinnings of the novel circle back to the past and Darwin's recognition that humanity is inextricably entangled with "plants and animals" in a "web of complex relations" (124–5).

Chapter 5

Millennial Fictions
The Corrections

Families are pretty crazy when you see them close up.
Paula Fox, Western Wind *(111)*

With its intimation of imminent ecological disaster, the closing pages of *Strong Motion* cast the reader apocalyptically forward toward the end of "the twentieth century" (*SM* 469). Nine years later, Franzen is still looking at "the Next Millennium" (*C* 170), but while *The Corrections* revises the systemic approach of the earlier book, his third novel—from its opening invocation to "the whole northern religion of things coming to an end" onward (*C* 3)—much more explicitly sets its eschatological vision within the cultural and literary context of a millennial America that fascinated the postmodern novelist.

Shortly before he died in 1985, Barth's "ideal postmodernist" Italo Calvino began a final work in which he meditated on the approaching millennium (*Friday Book* 203). His manuscript drew on ideas he had been increasingly obsessed with in his last years—the multiple forms of fiction, the future of literature—but Calvino chose to begin by intertwining the fate of the novel with the close of the millennium. "It has been," he wrote, "the millennium of the book, in that it has seen the object we call a book take on the form now familiar to us. Perhaps it is a sign of our millennium's end that we frequently wonder what will happen to literature and books in the so-called postindustrial era of technology" (1). That Calvino had begun to speculate about the millennium a full 15 years before century's end hints at the magnetic lure the event held for writers in general. But American writers, in particular, have always had a heightened sensitivity for millenarianism. Perhaps because America was conceived, as Douglas Robinson argues in *American Apocalypses* (1985), as "the Western site of the millennium," intimations of the millennium can be detected in the works of many classic American writers (xi). In Herman Melville's *White-Jacket* (1850), for example, he reflects critically on the maxims that preachers hope will bring "about a Millennium" (324); in Nathaniel Hawthorne's *The Blithedale Romance* (1852), the narrator remarks that their utopian community has begun the journey "towards the millennium of love" (24); while in 1846 Edgar Allan Poe questioned when we may "be warranted in looking for the millennium" (*Essays* 1386). But, as the twentieth century drew to a close the American novelist's fascination with the millennium began to fluoresce. In a typically self-conscious reference to his place in history, John Barth took the approaching millennium as the theme of his postmillennial novel *Coming Soon!!!*, which revolves around one narrator's plan for an "end-of-millennium novel" (143). Earlier still, DeLillo evidently read Norman Cohn's classic study *The Pursuit of the Millennium* (1957),[1] and this account of millenarian movements surely shaped his fascination with "millennial hysteria" in *Mao II* (80), as well as his survey of the last decades of the twentieth century in *Underworld* (1997). In DeLillo's big novel everything is marked by "the sheen of Last Things," and as the book moves toward its conclusion, DeLillo even glosses the coming of the Last Days, announcing that: "on the last day Our Lord will come to judge everyone who has ever lived in this world" (577, 717).

The twilight of the twentieth century, however, did not just affect older writers. The millennium casts its shadow over the work of Franzen and his post-postmodern contemporaries, too, and—like Calvino—their sense of its approach often seems to shade into anxious speculation about the future of the novel. Though Wallace mocked older writers' fascination with the millennium,[2] he described his massive novel, *Infinite Jest*, as an attempt to capture "what it's like to live in America around the millennium" ("Salon Interview") and evidently wrote "millennium" on the title page of the first draft of the book (Moore). While his essays ponder the fate of fiction in the age of television, *Infinite Jest*, itself, is preoccupied with the years 2009–10, charting the painful emergence of a "whole new millennial era" (620) and his fascination with the millennium carried over into his short fiction collection, *Oblivion* (2004), where the final story traces the lead-up to "the true millennium" (285). A similar fascination with century's end runs through many of Richard Powers's novels. Like DeLillo, Powers has confessed to a fascination with Cohn's *The Pursuit of the Millennium*,[3] and his 1998 novel *Gain* features Adventists, while *Operation Wandering Soul* (1993) even includes a mini essay arguing that "Millenarianism is born in the longing for confederation and the fear of collapse, in the desire to know where the world is going, in the need for closure" (122).

Throughout the 1990s Franzen famously worried—as Calvino predicted—about the end of books in an era of electronic entertainment. *The Corrections* also shares Wallace's fascination with the space between eras, while the desperate need for closure that Powers ascribes to millenarianism neatly encapsulates the thematic and narrative energy of Franzen's third novel. But Franzen's novel is more specifically shadowed by other millennial imagery—not least the sense of a disintegrating social structure—which permeates, in particular, its early stages and structure. Although the New York of Franzen's novel is layered with traces of early religions—Chip's doorman shares the name Zoroaster with the Persian prophet (*C* 21), while the late day of the midtown pier evokes "twilight by the Styx" (*C* 130)— there seem to be stronger hints of John of Patmos's Book of Revelation. On the most superficial level, the risen Christ of the last days is the lamb of God, and this is obviously echoed in the family name *Lambert* and on the several occasions (heavy with hints of self-consumption) where lamb is presented as a meal (*C* 34, 83, 162, 421). St. John promises that as the last days approach, Jesus "cometh with clouds" (Rev. 1:7), and he hears the words of God "as of a trumpet" (Rev. 1:11). Alfred and Enid, appropriately, arrive in New York on a cloudy day, and when Enid boasts to her friends about her less-than-holy son, her voice is a "trumpet" (*C* 17), an instrument that is also widely associated with her offspring (*C* 158, 352). More suggestively, St. John announces that "He that overcometh, the same shall be clothed in white raiment" (Rev. 3.5), and the crowd of passengers who board the *Gunnar Myrdal*—attempting, in the case of Alfred, to overcome age and infirmity—are clothed in "white raiment" (*C* 130).

The book as a whole, of course, moves toward "Chip's great revelation" (*C* 530), and the overall structure of this movement recalls some of Revelation's numerology. The book of Revelation is famously patterned around the supposedly mystic number seven—there are seven churches, seven seals, seven angels, and seven last plagues. Moving in parallel, *The Corrections* is divided into seven sections, while the book opens with Alfred reflecting on "seven decades of life" (*C* 10), and he retires "seven weeks short of a full year" (*C* 152). One of the seven angels and churches is "the angel of the church in Philadelphia" (Rev. 3:7) and when the novel switches its focus to Philadelphia, the reader discovers that Gary's chapter is punctuated by seven numbered headlines. At this point of multiple overlaps between Revelation and *The Corrections*, however, Franzen carefully breaks the association between the two. The headlines in Gary's story are provided by a presentation from the Axon corporation, and the seventh of these fractures the religious atmosphere, insisting, "NO, IT'S NOT A BOOK OF THE BIBLE!" (*C* 198).

While this scene hints at a contrast between religion and the chemical promises that offer spiritual sustenance in the modern world—Axon's pharmacological fixes for the physiology of the brain—in the larger context of *The Corrections* it betrays Franzen's divided attitude toward the millenarianism that fascinated both his postmodern ancestors and his immediate contemporaries. As the novel simultaneously invokes and undermines millennial longing, so it simultaneously rejects and accepts the legacy of the postmodern novel. But to set Franzen's millennial reckoning of his postmodern inheritance in context, it's helpful to circle back to his fascination with the list.

A millennial correction

Near the start of *The Corrections*, the failing writer Chip Lambert filters his old books, deciding which texts he can sell to fund his fading sexual entanglement with Julia Vrais:

> he purged the Marxists from his bookshelves . . . Jürgen Habermas's *Reason and the Rationalization of Society*, which he'd found too difficult to read, let alone annotate, was in mint condition . . . But Jürgen Habermas didn't have Julia's long, cool, pear-tree limbs, Theodor Adorno didn't have Julia's grapy smell of lecherous pliability, Fred Jameson didn't have Julia's artful tongue . . . [he] sold his feminists, his formalists, his structuralists, his poststructuralists, his Freudians, and his queers . . . he piled his Foucault and Greenblatt and hooks and Poovey into shopping bags and sold them all. (*C* 92)

Although the emphasis has shifted slightly (these books are sold, rather than simply thrown away), Franzen is clearly recasting, here, the scene in *Strong Motion* where Renée discards her unwanted books. Both the character profiles and the psychological well springs behind lists overlap— Chip and Renée are both academics who have fraught relations with their mothers and both resort to their books as if they might provide some kind of solution to crises in their personal lives. But unlike the scattered list of books that Renée produces, the parameters of Chip's catalogue are recognizably narrower, his list easier to parse. Instead of the rich plurality of

Renée's list, all the members of Chip's book list are obviously representatives of academic criticism. In E. M. Forster's terms, this is a flat, rather than round, mode of characterization. Instead of providing an index of the hidden depths and the surprisingly various passions of a character, Chip's books make it easy to see one type of writing that Franzen thinks should be rejected in favor of sensuous existence. The academic theorizing of Chip's books, he suggests, falls miserably short of the fleshy pleasures of touching Julia.

I've tried to argue throughout this study that references and allusions to books are one key to understanding Franzen's shifting aesthetic preoccupations, and the narrowed field of Chip's list at first seems to be indicative of the resolution that Franzen arrived at in the 9 years between his second and third novels. This resolution appears to be predicated upon overcoming the aesthetic division that characterizes his early work in favor of a more conventional kind of novel that relies upon a more unified thematic attack. Franzen's own comments about *The Corrections* seem to support this conclusion. "I was . . . looking," he told Donald Antrim, "for a counterpoint to the relative abstraction of the cultural or political or linguistic preoccupations that drove the previous generation of big novels . . . a correction towards more traditional and humane motives for a novel" (77). In its loose outlines, *The Corrections* does deal with his most limited and conventional artistic material. As LeClair noted, Franzen "does not historicize beyond one American generation" ("Shortfall" 4) in this book, the major action of the novel takes only 3 months, and, unlike *Strong Motion* with its long narrative perspective and complex ecological speculations, Franzen's third book works on the smaller scale of the "family ecosystem" (*C* 176). But the move toward a more traditional surface for his third novel is not as one dimensional as most readers of the novel suggest. In *Late Postmodernism*, for example, Jeremy Green provides a neat summary of the widely held view that Franzen's third book is a retreat from postmodern complexity. At the start of Franzen's career, Green explains, Franzen "tried to align himself" with a "postmodernist literary tradition" (10), but while his third novel retains the notion of paranoid connections from his predecessors work, Franzen's new approach "places the novel firmly in the realist lineage" (106). This overview is persuasive, but in this chapter I'd like to concentrate on questions of narrative structure and representation of character, to argue that the apparently conservative retreat in *The Corrections* is balanced by a corresponding move toward more extended language games and toward a more extended intertextual dialogue with Franzen's post-modern predecessors. If this third book represents the emergence of post-postmodern proper in Franzen's work—and it is probably too early to tell—then it illustrates the continued imaginative hold of Gaddis and DeLillo, in particular, upon this new movement. But because *The Corrections* took so long for Franzen to complete, and because for much of that time he was formulating his (sometimes misleading) ideas in public by writing about other peoples' novels, I spend somewhat more time at the start of this chapter excavating both the development of Franzen's novel and its initial intertextual dialogues.

The evolution of *The Corrections*

Although there is a 9-year gap between *Strong Motion* and *The Corrections*, the DNA of Franzen's third novel lies latent in his first two books. Franzen began working on *The Corrections* before *Strong Motion* had been published, and he selected his title a year later, in 1993. But for all this initial momentum, he returned to *The Twenty-Seventh City* to help create *The Corrections'* geography, generational drama, and even its minor characters. Chuck and Bea Meisner, for example, are relocated from *The Twenty-Seventh City* to provide the focus for Lambert envy in the later book, while the presence of a frustrated mother and wife preoccupied with "the whole matrix of Christmases" in the first novel suggests a trial run for Enid Lambert (*TS* 262). Similarly, just as St. Louis's Eliot connection framed *The Twenty-Seventh City*, so the imagined territory of Midwestern St. Jude, which provides one of *The Corrections'* geographic poles, is connected to St. Louis because of its literary resonance. St. Jude is, as Franzen acknowledges, "a St. Louis-like place" ("In the Mind's Eye" G1), but the two are subtly linked because Franzen and Eliot's fellow St. Louis native, Tennessee Williams, apparently spent his final years with a small shrine to St. Jude, patron saint of hopeless causes (Spoto 328). Williams also seems to have shared Franzen's sense of the city's destruction of nature—in his memoirs he renames the city "St. Pollution" (220)—but, if *The Corrections* shares a Midwestern setting with Franzen's first novel, the narrative friction that provides the novel's engine comes from a contrast between "uncool midwestern dreams" (*SM* 263) and the sophistication of the Eastern seaboard that provides a backdrop to *Strong Motion*. *The Corrections* draws from *Strong Motion* its sibling rivalry, its collegiate setting, and its account of the tentacular reach of multinational companies, while it also hints at the "ecodisaster" (*C* 34) threatened more explicitly in the earlier books. The geography and themes of *The Corrections*, then, are close to a synthesis of Franzen's first two novels, and, as such, it both significantly converges with and diverges from the parallel works by

Franzen's post-postmodern contemporaries: Powers's *The Gold Bug Variations* and Wallace's *Infinite Jest.*

Powers and Wallace's third novels are each longer than their author's two previous books, are each interspersed with references to the millennium, and—in terms of critical attention at least—they each represent the high watermark in their author's body of work. In these works (as I noted in Chapter 1), Powers and Wallace seem to most clearly imitate their postmodern ancestors' encyclopedic masterpieces, and there are a number of formal parallels between their efforts. For all the branching narrative offshoots, both writers construct their novels around two central intersecting narratives and both employ plots dense with mathematical references that rely upon the new sciences of chaos and complexity. With such a weight of nonliterary material, both Powers and Wallace seem to accept Thomas Pynchon's contention that we have now "come to live among flows of data more vast than anything the world has seen before" ("Is it O.K." 1), and so both novels are centered around characters who are defined by their relationship to data. Powers's novel takes the twentieth century's "reservoir of naked data" as its backdrop and places at the center of the book Stuart Ressler, a once-promising molecular biologist, who is distinguished by the "perfect recall" of his memory (514, 422). *Infinite Jest*'s "elegant complexity" is similarly based around an obsession with "data retrieval," and this obsession partly stems from Hal Incandenza (one of two central characters), who, Wallace tells the reader, "tested out at Whatever's Beyond Eidetic" (322, 317).

Although Chip Lambert has "nearly eidetic" recall of his breast-obsessed script, *The Academy Purple* (*C* 534), his encounters with data are rarely a focus of *The Corrections*. Yet, in his early drafts of the novel, Franzen seems to have begun a work of greater complexity, which, like *Infinite Jest* and *The Gold Bug Variations*, would conceive of its characters in terms of their relation to bodies of data. Between 1992 and 1998, he planned a massive novel, with a labyrinthine extrinsic plot somewhat like his first two books, yet this work was designed to be "bigger, more encompassing, more universal, speaking to *everything* in the culture" ("Making the Corrections" 31). A fragment from this manuscript was published under the title "How He Came to Be Nowhere" in 1996, and though there are hints at the edges of the work of the obsessions that would characterize *The Corrections*,[4] this draft seems to have more in common with the data explorations of Powers and Wallace than with Franzen's published novel. There is no sign of the Lambert family, here, or their small-town envies and intrafamilial friction. Instead the pivotal character is Andy Aberant, whose parents are dead, and who has three sisters "excellent though substantially overweight Christian women with many children, all of whom reside in Texas" (113). Aberant is a pathological liar who is being subjected to a polygraph test by an FBI special agent, and whose failings are presumably to be traced (in a gesture that recalls Powers's novel's fascination with "gene transfer" [411]) to biological inheritance, since his father bears the pregnant name *Gene Aberant*. But while Andy cannot match Ressler and Incandenza's mnemonic feats, he, too, is to be understood in terms of encyclopedic knowledge. Franzen writes: "Andy . . . came into the world needing people to believe that he knew everything," but "he had the breadth and depth of knowledge of a card catalog. He was full of data which often proved not very reliable" (122–3).

"How He Came to Be Nowhere" was intended to serve as the first chapter of Franzen's third novel, and was part of the 200-page manuscript that he sold to Farrar, Strauss, and Giroux in 1996. Aberant features in two more fragments from this draft: in "Somewhere North of Wilmington" Andy's investigations into different kinds of fraud perpetrated by Jimmy Passafaro at a Teamsters Mausoleum are recounted, and in "At the Party for the Artist with No Last Name," Andy's experiment with Virtual Reality later on the day of his polygraph test are described. A striking feature of these later extracts is that while "How He Came to Be Nowhere" is a third-person narrative, both of the later fragments are narrated in the first person by Aberant. It's notable, too, that both *Gold Bug* and *Infinite Jest* mix first- and third-person narration, and Franzen seems to have experimented with a blend of third- and first-person narration even after he had apparently discarded all but 20 pages of the 200 pages promised to Farrar, Strauss, and Giroux in 1997.[5] But while Aberant's adventures were sprawling through complex fraud cases and new recreational technologies, Franzen had conceived of the Lambert family quite early on, perhaps as a kind of counterpoint to Andy's activities. Franzen had begun to imagine Chip Lambert in Spring 1992, when he was still teaching at Swarthmore,[6] and as early as summer 1992 a character called Denise Passafaro exists in the early drafts of the novel alongside a character named Robin. The coexistence of the Lamberts and Andy Aberant is also clear because in the same year that "How He Came to Be Nowhere" appeared, Franzen published "Chez Lambert," which introduces Alfred and Enid in a sketch that is very close to the "St. Jude" chapter of the published novel. In the 1996 Farrar, Strauss, and Giroux draft, "Chez Lambert" was to have been the second chapter of *The Corrections*, and Keith Gessen has argued that the differences between this extract and the opening of *The Corrections* indicate a shift away from the language and scientific preoccupations "favored by Thomas Pynchon and his many progeny" (34).[7] And yet, what is striking about the evolution of *The Corrections* is that Franzen's movement away from the kind of "encyclopedia of the Information Age" that Powers and Wallace produced (Powers, *Galatea* 215), is not so much a rejection of either his earlier plans for the book or of his dialogue with his postmodern predecessors.

One of his earliest ideas for the book, for example, was a sketch of a father who murders squirrels ("This Year's Great"). The draft containing this scene was evidently abandoned, though the paragraph detailing the capture of a squirrel remains in the final volume (*C* 128–9), and the persistence of this scene hints at one of the keys to understanding the gradual development of *The Corrections*. Although Franzen seems to have radically recast the novel on several occasions and reports that he threw out "thousands" of pages in the process ("Jonathan Franzen's Big Book" 20), judging from Franzen's comments about the book's development, *The Corrections* as we now have it seems to be a kind of palimpsest. Although much of the earlier drafts seem to have been erased, their bones are still visible beneath the skin of the finished novel. The earliest version of the novel, for example, is described by Franzen as having an "incredibly elaborate plot, involving prisons and insider trading and racial street warfare in Philadelphia and orphans and the Catholic Worker" ("Making the Corrections" 31). Though elements of this version of the novel have clearly been dropped, in the story of Robin Passafaro's family of "troublemakers and true believers" (*C* 339), the reader finds Catholicism, an orphan, and street violence in Philadelphia. The framework of the insider trading narrative is nested in Gary's dealings with the Axon corporation, while the thematic relevance of prisons resonates through the book from the land owned by Connecticut State Department of Corrections that lurks at the edges of Chip's story at D— College (*C* 34) to the young Gary Lambert's popsicle prison (*C* 271–2).[8] Just as these early drafts of the novel continue to be visible beneath the surface of the published book, so the engagement with postmodernism, which Gessen identifies as being removed from the surface of the novel, persists in a kind of subterranean dialogue into the final version of the book. Here, again, is a point of connection between Franzen and his contemporaries.

Post-postmodern anxieties

The titles of Powers and Wallace's third novels both allude to earlier literary works—Powers draws on Poe; Wallace, of course, on Shakespeare—and both books, like *The Corrections*, are in different ways about coming to terms with the death of a father figure. As I suggested in Chapter 1, this fascination with dead ancestors preoccupies the post-postmodern generation, but in Wallace and Franzen's novels, the relationship to the dead father is by extension a dialogue with artistic father figures, a shift that is self-consciously underlined by allusions to Harold Bloom's theories of influence. First sketched out in his study *Yeats* (1970), and then elaborated in more detail in the series of books beginning with *The Anxiety of Influence* (1973), Bloom's oracular theories are less concerned with source study and the transmission of images between poets, than with the psychodynamics of agonistic poetic succession. For Bloom, a poem comes into being as a reading of an earlier poem, a reading that is necessarily anxious because Bloom conceives of a poet's relation to his precursor as an oedipal struggle for canonical survival. The various stages of this agonistic relation are worked out through six esoterically named revisionary ratios, and the whole process is broadly analogous to Freud's "family romance."[9] While *Infinite Jest* refers to "Professor H. Bloom's turgid studies of artistic *influenza*" and quotes from *The Anxiety of Influence* on "*clinamen* and *tessera*" (1077n366),[10] his long novel seems to carry on a complex coded dialogue with his literary ancestors, James Joyce and Don DeLillo. Franzen, by contrast, is more subtle in his allusion to Bloom,[11] but more forthright in his identification of his key literary precursors: William Gaddis and Don DeLillo.

Franzen acknowledged DeLillo's importance to the development of *The Corrections* in his widely quoted *Harper's* essay (where he reveals that he wrote to DeLillo "in distress" about the future of the novel [*A* 95]), but he made his filial relation explicit in a later interview when he described DeLillo as a "sort of dad-like" figure who he believed he had begun to overcome ("Esquire Conversation"). DeLillo's long novel *Underworld* (1997) is important, here, because Franzen read the manuscript of *Underworld* in Mexico in 1996, and *The Corrections* clearly shares significant affinities with DeLillo's book: both alternate viewpoints and gradually move backward in time to shed light on current behavior; both have significant affinities in terms of their fascination with networks of connections and their interest in structures of the brain. But while I explore parallels between *The Corrections* and *Underworld* later in this chapter, I'd like to suggest here that the skeleton plot of Franzen's novel seems to enact what Harold Bloom would call a *clinamen* upon DeLillo's earlier novel, *White Noise* (1985).

The first of Bloom's revisionary ratios, a clinamen is a poetic misreading or corrective movement that "implies that the precursor . . . went accurately up to a certain point, but then should have swerved, precisely in the direction that the new" work takes (14). There is something of this in *The Corrections'* adaptation of *White Noise*'s plot. The narrative foundations of DeLillo's novel clearly overlap with Franzen's novel—its fascination with "the miscellaneous swarming air of families" (5–6), its college setting, its critique of consumer culture, and its characters who believe in the restorative power of lists.[12] But beyond this, the larger framework of DeLillo's plot—recounting a parent who is increasingly suffering from memory lapses, a mother who is secretly taking mood-altering drugs, and a child who begins to police that drug taking—is obviously also recreated in *The Corrections*. But while the progress of DeLillo's narrative is to take from these familial tensions and move outward from the family toward ecological catastrophes and elaborate murder plots, Franzen corrects this movement and redirects his narrative energy deeper into the heart of the family. This "kind of traditional stuff," the emotional family narrative that Franzen said he could not find elsewhere in DeLillo, is superimposed onto the foundations outlined in DeLillo's earlier novel ("Esquire Conversation").

Yet, while DeLillo is a crucial influence upon *The Corrections*, Franzen's novel establishes a much fuller, and more complex, intertextual dialogue with the work of William Gaddis, whom Franzen also described as a kind of father figure (*A* 265). Like the allusive titles *The Gold Bug Variations* and *Infinite Jest*, the title of Franzen's third novel is also a coded allusion, referring in this instance to Gaddis's first novel, *The Recognitions*. There are several overlaps between the two novels. Both books critique those who are unable to "distinguish the false from the authentic" (*C* 258), and as critics often note, Chip's email address is "exprof@gaddisfly.com" (*C* 431). Similarly, near the beginning of the novel, Chip resembles Gaddis's money-obsessed writer Otto Pivner: Chip's complaint, while taking a cab ride in New York, that "without money he was hardly a man" (*C* 105) recalls Pivner's observation that "a man does feel castrated in New York without money" (150–1). But while there are also connections to Gaddis's *JR* (1975),[13] shortly after Franzen completed *The Corrections*, he published "Mr. Difficult," an essay on Gaddis's work that accused him of betraying his readers in his later novels.

As I outlined in Chapter 2, "Mr. Difficult" outlines two conflicting models of literary appreciation, but both models exist mainly to provide Franzen with a kind of stick with which to beat Gaddis. Gaddis, for Franzen, "frankly endorsed Status and disdained Contract" (*A* 242), and he presents a lengthy critique of his work that climaxes in an attack on Gaddis's *A Frolic of His Own* as an example of "the particular corrosiveness of literary postmodernism" (*A* 265). Yet, when read alongside *The Corrections*, I'd like to suggest that essay and novel attempt something akin to what Harold Bloom calls *tessera* upon Gaddis's fourth novel. In Bloom's model, the tessera is an act of completion and antithesis, which represents the later writer's "attempt to persuade himself (and us) that the precursor's Word would be worn out if not redeemed as a newly fulfilled and enlarged Word of the ephebe" (67). Considered in Bloom's terms, *The Corrections* seems to attempt such an act of revisionary renewal by closely following the laundry list of faults that Franzen evidently perceived in Gaddis's last novel.

In "Mr. Difficult," for example, *A Frolic of His Own* is criticized for having "a very large child" as its central character: "the selfish, unreasonable, self-pitying, incapable, insatiable Oscar . . . a suffering artist who (ha ha!) happens to have little talent . . . His long play about the Civil War is obviously and unfunnily bad" (*A* 265). Yet in criticizing this central narrative situation, consciously or unconsciously, Franzen is (minus the Civil War reference) describing the kernel of his own novel. How else can Chip Lambert—a 39-year-old man who dresses (and acts) like a teenager—be described other than as a "very large child"? How else to describe his behavior, talents, and his sexual appetites other than as "selfish, unreasonable, self-pitying, incapable" and "insatiable"? Yet, the more these characters are compared, the more the parallels accumulate: both Chip and Oscar are simultaneously repulsed and seduced by American commerce. Both are estranged from their fathers, but move toward something of a reconciliation with fathers who die at the end of each novel. Both are writers and, indeed, both could be described as "a suffering artist who . . . happens to have little talent." Crucially, however, there is a significant overlap in the realization that both come to concerning their "literary" works' relationship to the movies. Both their works are largely written as self-vindications, but as Chip scrambles toward an exit from Franzen's somewhat-cartoonish Lithuania, he realizes suddenly why his self-indulgent screenplay has been such a failure: "All of a sudden he understood why nobody, including himself, had ever liked his screenplay: he'd written a thriller where he should have written a farce" (*C* 534). This epiphany marks one of the climaxes of Chip's story, but in allowing his character this recognition, Franzen is actually rewriting Oscar's recognition of the limitations of *his* self-justifying script at the end of *Frolic*: "No, no I cast myself a hundred years too early didn't I, with those tragic heroics . . . when it was farce all the time" (557).

The broad arc of Chip's story in *The Corrections*, then, significantly recasts Oscar Crease's story. And when the reader realizes that Orfic, the shadowy company that controls much of the action in *The Corrections*, is only one letter away from being an anagram of *Frolic*—and anagrams abound in Franzen's novel—the fraught subterranean dialogue *The Corrections* carries on with Gaddis's work becomes much clearer. Rather than entirely rejecting Gaddis's example, the correction that Franzen's novel proposes is a subtle attempt to (in Bloom's words) "retain [Gaddis's] terms but to mean them in another sense" (14). It is an attempt to renew the outline of Gaddis's postmodern novel by correcting its perceived failings as a contract novel.

If Franzen's essays in the 1990s signaled what turned out to be only a partial refutation of Gaddis's work, then they less equivocally record his admiration for Paula Fox's novel, *Desperate Characters* (1970).[14] A slim, realist story of Otto and Sophie Bentwood's dissolving marriage that unfolds over 4 days in 1968, Fox's novella is more or less the polar opposite of a novel such as *The Recognitions*, but it evidently helped Franzen conceive of several elements of his novel. The New York of Fox's novel, where anger and social unrest are on the rise and there is "refuse everywhere" on the streets (13) is recognizably the New York of Franzen's novel, where "doormen in this neighborhood hosed the sidewalks twice a day, and sanitation trucks with brushes . . . scoured the streets three times a week . . . in New York City you never had to go far to find filth and rage. A nearby street sign seemed to read *Filth Avenue*" (*C* 102). Equally, alongside this gloomy texture of cities in decline, Franzen shares Fox's fascination with food and excretion, but he more subtly takes care to make his New York protagonist about the same age as Fox's Otto Bentwood.[15] Chip is 39 at the start of the novel, whereas Otto is just over 40, and this near-parallel seems to be intended to illustrate the difference between America in the late 1990s and life in the late 1960s. While 40-year-old Otto is prematurely aged and yearns for a former century, Chip wears clothes that he is "too old for" and craves girls who are "college age" (*C* 15). This disparity between the two similarly aged men in different decades seems to be Franzen's commentary on a millennial America, where "the whole country's been handed over to kids and you never have to stop being a kid" ("Only Correct"). Beyond this intertextual dialogue, Green has argued that *Desperate Characters* also "provides a structural model for *The Corrections*," because each section of the book is a "novella, modeled to some extent on *Desperate Characters*, [that] follows the protagonist through a brief period of crisis to the brink of major, even catastrophic, change" (97, 105). This is certainly a useful way to conceptualize the relationship between the two books, but the actual structure of *The Corrections* is somewhat more nuanced than Green's summary suggests, both in terms of the individual chronological structures of the sections and the way that each section interacts with the rest of the book. It's useful, here to return to the idea of spatial and temporal form outlined in the last chapter.

Narrative strategies (I): Narrative corrections and temporal form

Drawing together the disparate stories of the three Lambert children, the broad chronological structure of *The Corrections* resembles the tangled spool of Christmas lights that Alfred struggles with, toward the end of the novel: "He couldn't follow the three constituent wires through all their twists and braidings. The circuit was semiparallel in some complex way he didn't see the point of" (*C* 460). Alfred, here, functions as an analogue for the reader. Although he has conceived of his children in series—Gary first, followed 4 years later by Chip, and Denise a further 7 years later—their biographies, as they are recast in the novel, are presented in messy parallel, with the arcs of their lives obscured by Franzen's carefully scattered chronology.

This parallel structure is not immediately obvious at the start of the novel, which opens in neat linear fashion with a sketch of Thursday September 30, in St. Jude. The second part of the book, "The Failure," shifts to New York, but presents the Saturday immediately following the opening scene, and (at least initially) continues the story of Alfred and Enid. But even though on four occasions Franzen fractures this story, to insert a lengthy analepsis filling in his backstory, the events of Saturday, October 2, in New York are presented in series, progressively moving toward Chip's flight and Denise's farewell to Alfred and Enid. The third part of the novel, devoted to Gary, starts on a Sunday night, but this is not the Sunday following the events of the Saturday in the previous chapter. The terms of the novel's chronology have shifted. Gary's story pulls the narrative lens back in time, to begin on Sunday, September 12, and then proceeds through to Tuesday, October 5. But this narrative only briefly intersects with the events of the preceding story—on Sunday, October 3, Denise calls Gary to recount Saturday's action (*C* 202), and then meets him on Monday with further details (*C* 213). Otherwise, Gary's story is in parallel, layered over the top of the preceding narrative, and this is largely true of the other later episodes: following the end of "The Failure" we need to wait until page 239 to pick up Alfred and Enid's adventures after their departure from New York; page 423 before we learn what happens to Denise after she meets Gary; and page 429 to hear from Chip in Lithuania. In the intervening pages, Franzen circles back and forth in time, weaving the stories of his characters' lives together. Although it is impossible to precisely locate the temporal coordinates of each story,[16]

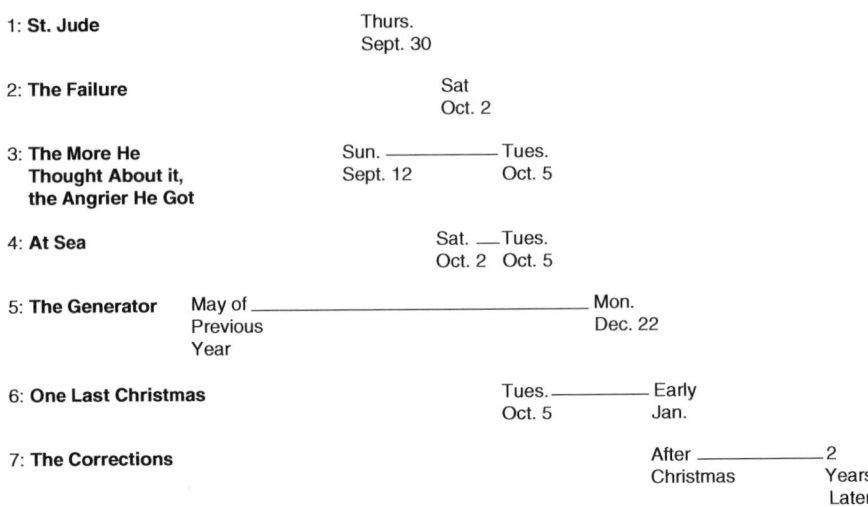

FIGURE 5.1 Skeleton Chronology of *The Corrections*.

if the many embedded flashbacks—the most crucial of which interrupt parts four and five—are overlooked, the broad outlines of the contemporary action looks something like Figure 5.1.

It's clear from this outline that only two of the episodes have the narrow timeline of Fox's novella, and that while the basic story of Alfred's decline requires just a little over three complete months to unfold, to set his demise against the total family constellation requires Franzen to circle backward and forward across a 3-year period. This process of narrative layering can occasionally be disorientating, and a reader might end up feeling like Alfred, when he cannot see the point of his lights' parallel circuitry. But the parallel arrangement alerts the reader to the parallels in the children's lives by setting past and present acts alongside each other: both Gary and Chip consciously conceive of themselves as correcting their father's choices, but while one does so in terms of financial aggression, the other seeks a correction in terms of gender roles; similarly both Denise and Chip lose their jobs for sexual indiscretions, but while Denise is attracted to older men, Chip is fascinated by younger women. As I'll argue later in this chapter, this structure also helps illuminate Franzen's treatment of selfhood, but underpinning his presentation of these sprawling parallel stories, and helping the reader to navigate the book, are narrative strategies that operate consistently throughout the book and help to explain the mechanics of his narrative. The first strategy that Franzen employs might be described as the process of "narrative corrections." Franzen introduces this technique early in "The Failure," when Enid begins to question the way her son smells:

> "Does anybody smell fish, though?'
> "We're near the ocean," Chip said.
> "No, it's you." Enid leaned and buried her face in Chip's leather sleeve. "Your jacket smells *strongly* of fish"
> He wrenched free of her. "Mother. Please." (*C* 19)

When the reader first encounters this scene, it seems designed to provide little more than local color, fleshing out the fraught dynamics of the Lambert family—we see the seeds of dispute emerge within moments of their meeting, and Enid is immediately sketched as an overpowering, meddling, maternal figure. Seventy-five pages later, however, it becomes clear that there is more to this smell of fish, when Franzen reveals that the previous day Chip stole a filet of salmon by sliding it under his sweater and into his pants (*C* 94). The discussion about the fish that initially seemed incidental is revealed to have a causal connection, and the smell reveals something about Chip, rather than Enid. Franzen has led the reader toward one assumption, only to insert a later scene that forces a correction of their initial supposition.

There are many other examples where Franzen uses his narrative to correct the angle of the reader's line of sight. In the central example, for instance, when Alfred wanders into a bathroom aboard the cruise ship and encounters a man with "blue cheeks" who taunts him, his vision seems nothing more than a symptom of his increasing dementia, an impression that is strengthened by the scurrying turd he notices at the same time (*C* 330). The extra information that Franzen offers, explaining that the blue-cheeked man is "the man from signals" who "came from the distant past" (*C* 331), doesn't do much to fix this scene within the context of the rest of the novel, though readers with long memories might link it to the oblique observation that "the betrayal had begun in Signals" from the second part of the book (*C* 68). The initial impression of Alfred's craziness is gradually corrected, however, as 24 pages later Franzen introduces Don Armour as a man "whose cheeks, closely shaved, were nearly as blue and glaucous as a plum" (*C* 354). Then—in case any reader had missed the link—nearly 200 pages later his importance to the core of the narrative is cemented when Alfred explains to Denise that the "Fellow with the blue cheeks" has left evidence of his fling with Denise in the basement of their St. Jude home

(*C* 518). By doing this, Franzen corrects our view of Alfred as an old man whose manias are scattered and incoherent, and reveals the lucid thread of an obsession that has tormented him for 15 years.

Franzen's technique, here, is a diluted example of Frank's spatial form and it works on a basic level to build suspense and reward careful reading. On another level, however, it is significant as one of the ways that Franzen attempts to marry form and content. Just as the stories are *about* the characters correcting their views, so the form of the narrative imitates that procedure, implicating the reader in the book's critique by revealing the readers' tendency to make premature judgments from partial data. Yet, while the spatial form of these narrative corrections gives the book as a whole its overarching unity, on the microlevel Franzen experiments with the temporal form developed in *Strong Motion*. Critics have described the novel as displaying only "loose organization" (Green 107), but as Franzen told Jessica Murphy, shortly after the novel was published, "the part of me that is somewhat formally obsessed and writes for insiders—for other writers—wanted to be able to say that each of the [five] sections has its own distinctive, chronological structure," and these structures are intimately linked to the temporal arrangement of the text ("Mainstream and Meaningful").

In its entirety *The Corrections* seems to plot a straightforward movement, beginning with Alfred and ending with Enid, but in each of the five major sections of the novel, Franzen arranges the larger story to stress homologies between its form and content. In the first instance, "The Failure" is a looping narrative since it begins and ends at different airports. The geography of this "loop of time" (*C* 451) introduces the flight motif that recurs around Chip and other characters (especially Robin Passafaro, whose bird name suggests flight), while the looping structure prefigures the larger movement of the novel, as the Lambert children ultimately circle back to their family home to confront (however imperfectly, in Gary's case) their pasts. Within the "great circle" of this first section (*C* 535), however, Franzen uses line breaks to split his narrative into 10 separate sections. These divisions create an appropriately fragmented framework for a character whose life is as scattered as Chip's. But while not all of these narrative particles directly concern him, the fragments that do tell his story are carefully arranged. After an 18-page sketch that establishes the chronological setting as Saturday October 2 (*C* 15–32), Franzen dips back to 6 years earlier, to fill in the backstory moving from Chip's appointment at D— College up to his Thanksgiving day argument with Melissa, roughly 2 years before

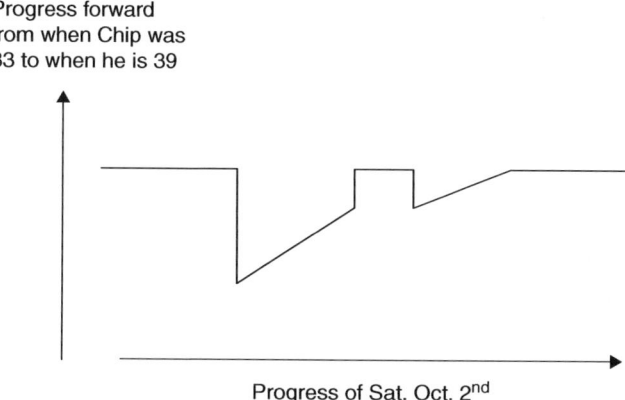

FIGURE 5.2 Chronological structure of "The failure".

the contemporary action. This analepsis takes 31 pages, but the movement is rapid, hurrying back to the present (*C* 32–62). Following this section, "The Failure" hovers in Chip's apartment, with Alfred, Denise, and Enid who "wonder . . . where Chip had gone" (*C* 68). As if to answer this question, the narrative picks up the story of Chip's affair with Melissa 2 months after Thanksgiving and surges forward to October 1, when Chip stole the salmon (*C* 76–98). Represented graphically, then, Chip's story looks something like Figure 5.2.

Just as the story of "The Failure" is one of Chip's past coming back to haunt him (the return of his parents, his earlier lies about the *Wall Street Journal*, and so on), so the temporal form of this section imitates that story. The structure is one of the past rapidly thrusting up into the "present day" of the novel, and while it serves to establish the importance of intimate exchanges between the past and the present in the novel as a whole, as the first major section of the book it also seems to be designed to create momentum, propelling the reader (like Chip) further into the novel.

After this fragmented forward movement, "The More He Thought About it, the Angrier He Got" represents a tangible shift in the texture of the narrative, a renegotiation of the terms of Franzen's story. Like Ted Roth later in the book, who refuses "to live in the past" (*C* 305), the temporal form of this section reflects Gary's desire to live aggressively in the present. In fact, the sustaining list that Gary derives from his wife, his "All-Time Caroline Ten," begins by asserting his freedom from his genetic past: "You're nothing at all like your father," she tells him (*C* 182). To emphasize the forced immediacy of Gary's life, Franzen employs an analepsis on only two brief occasions, and unlike the excavations of the past in Chip's narrative, neither of these excursions acknowledges a past beyond the year of the present action.[17] But as the temporal layout of this section imitates the ahistorical thrust of Gary's will, this section is also structured to replicate his fragile internal state. Unlike the 10-part structure of "The Failure," Gary's story is only divided into two sections (pivoting on page 185), presumably to imitate Gary's divided self, torn between loyalty to his mother and to his wife. This division is stressed by the fact that the first half of the chapter ends with a putative break with Caroline ("We're going to split up over a trip to St. Jude!" [*C* 185]), and the second half with a paranoid glance toward Enid ("she knew that he'd betrayed her" [*C* 235]), and Franzen underlines the connection between these two women through their names (the first three letters of Enid are reversed at the end of Caroline). But for all the competing psychological pressures these women exert, Gary is also prey to a "too-annihilating will to specialness" (*C* 195) and the narrative technique of this section imitates this aspect of his character, too, by ensuring that—unlike all the other major sections of the novel—the narrative voice in this part of the book reflects only Gary's concerns and viewpoint.

Because Franzen intended the novel's fourth section to represent "the center of the novel" ("Making the Corrections" 32), as we move beyond Gary's section there are a web of verbal echoes linking "At Sea" back to earlier parts of the book. "The Failure" opens by shrouding Alfred in prescient aquatic imagery—he is "paddling" and lunging like "a man floundering in water" (*C* 15)—while Gary's section likens the *Narnia* chronicles to "a luxury cruise" (*C* 168), and extends the aquatic motif by imagining the brain to be an "inner-sea world . . . kelpy ganglia and squidlike neurons and eellike capillaries . . . flash by" (*C* 187). The climax at the heart of this section, and the book itself, is, of course, Alfred's fall into the cold waters of the North Atlantic (it is, then, a *Fall* cruise in two senses), so falling provides the controlling idea behind the temporal form of this section. "At Sea" begins with just five short paragraphs on "flotation's terrors" (*C* 239), before it drops 32 years into the past and stays there for 40 pages. In stark contrast, however, to the steps into the past in "The Failure," which arc upward into the present, this long account hangs free of the contemporary narrative threatening that the story "could sink" into the past "and by sinking disappear" (*C* 239). Even when the drop into the past is interrupted, the past's spell is broken only by a different kind of dropping: the talking turd that awakens Alfred "with a jolt" (*C* 28). When Alfred literally falls, at the end of "At Sea," the connection between his fall from the ship and the narrative's drop into the past is affirmed by the fact that he reflects upon his children's youth as he falls.

This dramatic climax is followed by "The Generator," which introduces a different chronological structure, though one that's dimensions significantly parallel Chip's earlier story. There is a notable change of pace in this, the fifth section of the book, and, typically, the shift can be traced to one of Franzen's encounters with another book. While he was working on *The Corrections*, Franzen read Stendhal's *The Red and the Black* (1830)—a novel that shares "The Generator's" interest in adultery—and having been struck by Stendhal's minute attention to detail in rendering the affair between Julien Sorel and Louise de Rênal, he sought to replicate Stendhal's sudden decrease in pace and careful exploration of charged quotidian moments in *The Corrections'* only extended love story. While the major contemporary action of "At Sea" unfolds over just 4 days, the equivalent action in "The Generator" requires a longer time frame than any of the other sections, unfurling over approximately 19 months from the day Brian hires Denise. This story is itself framed by a genealogy of Robin Passafaro that reaches back to her grandfather and uncles. Within this long lens, however, the structure of "The Generator" parallels "The Failure" in two ways. First, the story of Denise's tangled affair with Robin and Brian is interrupted by significant shifts back to Denise's past (*C* 350–74, 374–81), and as in Chip's story these installments are angled to surge back toward the present. Second, "The Generator" is linked to "The Failure," because just as Chip's story included an analepsis that filled in Denise's story (*C* 117–26), so "The Generator" concludes by picking up Chip's story once again.

Finally, "One Last Christmas" is divided by line breaks into six sections, the first five of which recount the run up to Christmas day, with the concluding segment detailing Alfred's drug holiday. Recapitulating the rest of the book and rounding off the earlier stories, each of the first five sections begins with a sentence addressing one of the major characters: Alfred (*C* 459), Enid (*C* 464), Gary (*C* 481), Denise (*C* 499) and Chip (*C* 530). In this structure, Denise is pivotal as Franzen reveals her to be the agent of both the family's current disintegration and its (partial) future rehabilitation: Franzen permits Denise to discover that her affair with Don Armour has instigated the chain of events that controlled Alfred's manias and prompted Enid's money worries, while she also goes on, with Chip's help, to prompt the family's slow reinte-gration. Bringing together the disparate stories into one section, "One Last Christmas" articulates the novel's final accounting and prepares to shuttle the reader out of the book and into the telescoped panorama of the narrative's final section.

Narrative strategies (II): Narrative connections

Alongside this dual-leveled fusion of form and content, one of *The Corrections'* other underlying narrative procedures is to insist upon a high degree of connectivity between its component parts. In *The Corrections* details from individual stories consistently fold back into other stories, recycling characters, products, and phrases, to create a densely connected society, and reviewers typically identified this aspect of Franzen's novel as part of the legacy of DeLillo's *Underworld*. James Wood, for example, describes *The Corrections* as a descendant of *Underworld*'s fascination with representing "the interconnectedness of American society," while Adam Begley classified Franzen as a member of "the everything-is-connected school of fiction" and particularly linked the novel's tendency to connect "wildly disparate strands" to *Underworld*'s influence (10). This comparison helps to illuminate part of the philosophy that underlies Franzen's assemblage of narrative connections.

Underworld's belief that "everything is connected" (825)[18] provides DeLillo's long narrative with its principal mode of organization, but it is also responsible for the dense texture of paranoia that hangs over the novel's excavation of millennial life. In *Underworld*'s America nothing takes place in a vacuum, and even soft drinks can be implicated in the military industrial complex through a sinister web of connections. In his study, *American Magic and Dread* (2000), Mark Osteen explains one such chain of connections by examining references to orange:

> Chuckie Wainwright's plane "Long Tall Sally" drops Agent Orange on the jungles of Vietnam; during his stint in Vietnam, Matt remarks that the drums of Agent Orange resemble "cans of frozen Minute Maid"; a few years earlier, one of the elder Wainwright's clients was Minute Maid orange juice. In 1974, as Klara watches Sergei Eisenstein's long-lost film *Unterwelt*, she recognizes the soundtrack as Prokofiev's overture for the opera *Love for Three Oranges*, and during her work to transform "Long Tall Sally" into an artwork she wears an orange T-shirt. Near the end of the novel . . . [a] billboard is selling Minute Maid orange juice. (215)

DeLillo's carefully structured novel, then, maps out a disturbing interpenetration of consumerism and combat, creating what David Cowart calls "a textual nexus, linking virtually all of the novel's themes and motifs" (192). None of these connections are explicit, rather they seem to be subterranean pipelines that hint at the dark side to capitalism and prompt confusion and awe in his characters when they glimpse the vertiginous scale of the systems that seem to surround them. In the novel, Matt Shay summarizes such feelings when he asks: "how can you tell the difference between orange juice and agent orange if the same massive system connects them at levels outside your comprehension?" (465). There is something of this paranoid sense of the omnipresence of the modern corporation operating in Franzen's novel. On a relatively basic level, Franzen connects together two Pennsylvanian families—Gary Lambert's and Ted Roth's—with the world of the Uzbek upper middle class, and the Lithuanian criminal warlord, Gitanas Misevičius by giving them all the same car: a Ford Stomper (*C* 200, 325, 530). This connection works on two levels. First, by reminding his reader that "sport-utility vehicles" are the "workhorses of the warlord class" (*C* 452), Franzen evidently means to connect the aggression inherent in Gary's materialist life to the open violence of Misevičius's Lithuania, underlining "the broad similarities between black-market Lithuania and free-market America" (*C* 441). Second, by having characters in North America, Northern Europe, and West Central Asia own the same car, Franzen highlights the flattening of local and national cultures in a global economy dominated by multinational companies, and the threatening name points to the aggressive nature of this flattening process.

The story of Alfred's employer, Midland Pacific, however, involves a more complicated textual nexus. The disintegration of Midland Pacific (and, as a consequence, of the Lambert family) begins 15 years before the novel's opening scene, in the early 80s when Hillard and Chauncy Wroth cast their acquisitive gaze over the company. The Wroths are greed personified and have "no discernible desires or interests apart from making money" (*C* 69). As the novel progresses, the story of Orfic Midland (as the company is renamed) and of the Wroths is told in fragments, but the circulation of both money and the company in this novel's economy tends to create the vicious circles of a closed system. In a heavily ironic gesture, for example, the money-hungry Wroths eventually have to sell the company after losing money in, of all places, a gold mine (*C* 152), losing money over money, in effect. But no character is entrapped by the ever decreasing circles of the world of finance more than Chip Lambert. Not only does Chip take money from a Lithuanian criminal warlord only to lose that money to other Lithuanian criminal warlords at the end of the novel, but the arc of his story is tightly prescribed by the development of Midland Pacific.

As an assistant professor at D— College, Chip styles his life in opposition to the power of big corporations teaching a course entitled "Consuming Narratives" that reveals "how to criticize mass culture" and the advertising campaigns of multinational corporations (*C* 40). Yet, in a gesture that coolly undermines Chip's academic theorizing, Franzen reveals that the building where Chip teaches is named "Wroth Hall" (*C* 44), presumably after the entrepreneurs of greed who bought his father's company. Ironically, then, he is only able to critique consumerism through the fiat of consumerism, and his course on consuming narratives is itself a narrative of consumption, as higher education is swallowed by big business. But even off campus, Chip is unable to escape the influence of Orfic. In "The Failure," for example, Chip attempts to flee his parents and the story of their financial woe that stems from the Wroth's takeover of Midland Pacific. Yet, as he escapes them and tries to make changes in his own life, Franzen shows him calling the film producer he has struggled to woo only to be cut off by a payphone: "the phone went dead, the wasted quarters clanking in its gut. The text on its faceplate had Baby Bell coloration, but it read: ORFIC TELECOM, **3 MINUTES 25 ¢,** EACH ADDT. MIN. 40 ¢." (*C* 104). Even as Chip tries to escape the fate of his family, his story remorselessly circles back to the company that underlies the deeper troubles buried in his family's history. The company, then, acts as one of the "different kind of prison[s]" that holds Chip (*C* 134).

Orfic turns up elsewhere in the book, too: liquidating a port in the largest industrial area in Lithuania (*C* 112), being bulk purchased for CenTrust by Gary (*C* 152–3), being owned by Norwegian and Swedish tourists (*C* 324). But the tendency of corporations to create closed systems is replicated on a smaller scale, in the case of the mergers-and-acquisitions specialists who carry the appropriately violent pun name, Bragg Knuter & Speigh. Together with Axon, this company tries to persuade Alfred to sell a patent, employs Chip as a flexitime proofreader, sells shares to Gary, and negotiates neurological treatment schemes with Denise (*C* 72, 87, 188, 204–9). Creating an incredibly claustrophobic world, these companies exercise the kind of ubiquity that helps structure DeLillo's *Underworld*.

But where Franzen crucially diverges from DeLillo's example is in his treatment of the connections between characters. For example, when Denise listens to Jerry Schwarz explain that a band called the Nomatics died "when Tom Paquette quit" (*C* 424), it's peculiar that she should be involved in a discussion in Pennsylvania concerning the father of Melissa Paquette, the student from Chip's Connecticut College who he has an affair with in "The Failure." But, significantly, this connection—and the many similar links between characters elsewhere in the book—is not a symptom of the omnipresence of corporate control, but rather an indication of one of two traits that Franzen wants to tell us about his characters, and also—implicitly—about his conception of the so-called social novel.

On a basic level, Franzen has established many interconnections between the Lamberts as a way of demonstrating how behavior is internalized and repeated in the matrix of the family. For instance, although the scenes are temporally separated by about 32 years, both Gary and Alfred are confronted by the St. Jude Museum of Transport, and both, for different reasons, are infuriated by the relationship people who go to such places have to knowledge. Alfred is disgusted by the engineering ignorance of the museum's visitors ("people didn't understand the first goddamned thing about running a railroad" [*C* 256]), while Gary hates their naivety ("filling their misshapen heads with facts. As if facts were going to save them!" [*C* 175]). Despite Gary's attempts to distance himself from his family past in general, and his father in particular, their parallel connection and reaction to the museum reveals the inescapability of his inheritance, a fact that Franzen humorously underlines by making it a museum (i.e., an archive of the past) that prompts this connection. In light of this, it becomes clear that Franzen is enjoying a joke at Gary's expense, when he reveals that one of his favorite songs is "Time after Time" (*C* 179).

On a more complex level, however, Franzen wants to communicate to the reader something about the world that his characters have made for themselves. While aboard the cruise ship, the *Gunnar Myrdal*, Enid observes that "it's a small world" (*C* 326), and—with Denise unwittingly talking about the father of one of Chip's students, Ted and Sylvia Roth visiting Denise's restaurant, and Chip dating Denise's college friend, Julia Vrais before going to work for Julia's husband—this belief seems to be justified. These characters circulate, incestuously, within a closed system. But the shrinking world that these characters inhabit is not a true reflection of the world, as Franzen subtly intimates through the name he selects for their cruise ship. The Swedish economist, Gunnar Myrdal is most famous for his enormous work, *An American Dilemma: The Negro Problem and Modern Democracy* (1944), a study of race relations that argued that American democracy had failed to extend its ideals to its African American population. Just as Franzen sees the logic of a closed system's vicious circle operating between both American corporations and his characters, so Myrdal identifies the mechanism of the "vicious circle" underlying the problem of race relations: "White prejudice and discrimination keep the Negro low in standards of living, health, education, manners and morals. This, in its turn, gives support to white prejudice. White prejudice and Negro standards thus mutually 'cause' each other" (75). It's feasible to identify something similar to the circular logic that Myrdal sees at the heart of race relations when the turd confronts Alfred aboard the *Gunnar Myrdal* (according to the turd, for a jail to fulfill its function, it needs to have a "Negro in it" [*C* 284]) but by giving the cruise ship such a suggestive name, Franzen is really wrestling with two major themes. First, the *Gunnar Myrdal* is Franzen's way of subtly critiquing the tendency of his white, middle-class characters to isolate themselves within their own narrow racial and economic strata. Their world is shrinking simply because of their refusal to engage with other social echelons. Second, this network of connections between characters is a direct consequence of, or a commentary upon, Franzen's theorizing about the novel's relationship to society during the late century.

Throughout "Why Bother?" Franzen lamented the demise of the broad-canvassed novel that maintained "maximum diversity and contrast packed into a single exciting experience," and concluded with a vision of fiction that was concerned with America only as "a nation of independently empowered tribes" (*A* 80, 96). But whether or not this partitioning of American experience "is a good thing or a bad thing," Franzen explains, "tragic realists offer no opinion. They simply represent it" (*A* 97). The incestuous connections between characters aboard the Gunnar Myrdal offer Franzen one such opportunity to represent the social dimension of an atomized America, but the cruise ship also lets him explore the literary consequences of such division. The Nobel Prize provides the key to this exploration.

The idea of the Nobel Prize is hinted at insistently during "At Sea." Enid stares at letters on a frosted glass door, waiting for them to form into words "No. Bel. Nob-ell. No Bell" [*C* 314]), and while aboard the *Gunnar Myrdal*, the aging couples discuss previous winners of "the Nobel Prize" (*C* 295). Since Myrdal won the Nobel Prize for economics in 1974, it is peculiar that during the conversation none of the characters think to make this connection.[19] Instead their discussion is purely literary, paying no attention to the world outside of the arts. It is surely relevant, then, that their failure to make this link implicitly poses one of the key questions that Franzen explored in "Why Bother?": What is the relationship between literature and the social world that surrounds it? Just as the cruise ship raises this question, it also seems to resolve it. While the ship is named after Gunnar Myrdal, it also contains a reading room named after "Knut Hamsun" (*C* 294). As the author of *Hunger* (1890), Hamsun is, of course, relevant to the novel's overall fascination with food, but as a writer who consistently supported Hitler throughout the Second World War, he is significant here because he permits Franzen to pose questions about literature's relation to the social world that surrounds it. If a reader, like Per Nygren, read books purely because they have won a literary prize, should that reader also be aware of the world that surrounds that literature, in case they are unwittingly admiring the work of a Nazi sympathizer? What difference does an author's political convictions make to society's estimate of their worth? *The Corrections*, then, does not, as many readers have argued, retreat "from the challenge of the politically engaged and genuinely exploratory social novel" to seek refuge in the narrower confines of "individual crises" (Green 188) as much as it rehearses the question of what will happen if American society fragments into small incestuous units, and (in parallel) what will happen if literature becomes concerned with such a small portion of the world, aside from the larger social and political currents that shape the contemporary world. But if Franzen does not simply abandon his investigation into the social world's relation to the individual in favor of simple character studies, then it is also true that his exploration of character in *The Corrections* is a good deal more complex than has previously been recognized. As always, Franzen's investigation into identity is heavily tied into a dialogue with his postmodern predecessors and their fascination with metafictional games.

Fictions of the self

While the reaction against postmodern metafiction in the 1990s centered upon its tendency toward literary self-absorption, some major strands of self-referring fiction were moving well beyond the literary to draw widely from the sciences. John Barth is probably the writer who has most frequently been accused of this kind of textual self-absorption, but in actual fact his metafictional devices consistently suggest interdisciplinary frameworks. As early as 1966, Barth had outlined the risk of "dismaying . . . [the] poor humanist" (xxvii) by including a sophisticated computer as the putative author of *Giles Goat-Boy*, but in the middle of the 1990s he patterned a metafictional story collection, *On With the Story*, around ideas drawn from quantum physics. Taking an epigraph from Heisenberg, Barth worked an extended parallel between quantum physics' uncertainty principle and the ontological uncertainty surrounding his text, and complained "if only life were as simple as theoretical physics" (104).[20] But perhaps his most significant interpenetration of metafiction and scientific research is presented by Barth's attempt to respond to new theories of selfhood derived from neuroscience and the materialist philosophy of mind.

Throughout the 1990s, Barth's books linked the fiction-making process to research into the working procedures of consciousness. In *Coming Soon!!!*, for example, Barth explains that "we're *never* not Making It All Up . . . in its need to sort out the instreaming flood of sense-data, human consciousness has evolved into a nonstop Scenario Machine or Ficting Factory, all of us the ongoing authors of the Stories-in-Progress of Our Lives" (17).[21] His stories about story-telling, then, become parallels to the mechanisms the brain uses to create a sense of self, and, as Barth acknowledges, this conception of how the mind works is largely derived from Daniel Dennett's *Consciousness Explained* (1991).[22] Seeking to critique Cartesian dualism and the extravagant Freudian "hypothesis of an internal dream playwright composing therapeutic dream plays for the benefit of the ego," Dennett proposed what he called the "Multiple Drafts" model of consciousness (14). According to this theory, there is no single center of consciousness, but instead "all varieties of thought or mental activity—are accomplished in the brain by parallel, multitrack processes of interpretation . . . of sensory inputs" (111). The acts of interpretation performed by these distributed processing units upon sensory data are likened by Dennett to the act of "editorial revision" (111), and their endpoint is a draft that corresponds to what we think of as our identity. The brain is, then, a kind of narrative machine creating a story of existence, though this story—and by extension selfhood, too—is far from stable. Instead the "fragmentary drafts of 'narrative'" are short lived, as different drafts are promoted "in swift succession" (254). What passes for our sense of self, is actually a succession of multiple drafts. Dennett's self, then, is continually in flux, and as sensory data prompts changes to crackle across the neural web, so the self rewrites itself.

There are, of course, similarly fluid conceptions of self-creation from much earlier in literature and philosophy. In *The Red and the Black*, for example, Stendhal describes Julien as he sets "about designing himself a completely new persona" when he enters the seminary at Besançon (193). But Dennett's conception of consciousness, with its extended parallels to the writing process, has fascinated novelists, and it provides another connection between aging postmodernists such as Barth, and his younger, scientifically informed progeny. Richard Powers, for example, has explained that he understands "*narrative* in the broader sense . . . to include the whole process of fabulation, inference, and situational tale-spinning that consciousness uses to situate itself and make a continuity out of the interruptive fragments of perception. I am interested in this wider process of explanatory story-making in all my books" ("An Interview" 14–15). There are significant overlaps between this conception of narrative and Dennett's theories, and the editorial revisions that consciousness makes to stitch together a sense of self clearly provides the foundation for *The Echo Maker*, where Powers's neurologist explains: "consciousness works by telling a story, one that is whole continuous, and stable. When that story breaks, consciousness rewrites it. Each revised draft claims to be the original" (185).[23]

Although in Franzen's first two novels such speculations play a secondary role, subordinate to the dictates of story, he frequently explores the idea that identity is unstable, little more than a story we tell ourselves about ourselves. In *The Twenty-Seventh City*, for instance, the process is externalized. Martin Probst assures himself that the story he has told himself about his moral rectitude is correct, by matching it to the stories others tell about him: "If he had any doubts about whether he was a stickler when it came to ethics, he only had to open the newspaper. There they said it: Martin Probst is a stickler when it comes to ethics" (*TS* 377). Their story matches his story, therefore it must be correct. But while he was working on *The Corrections*, Franzen read Steven Pinker's *How the Mind Works* (1997), which summarizes Dennett's theory of the self as "a large collection of partly finished drafts" (143–4) and the entire structure of *The Corrections* is designed to reveal how each of the characters is in the process of fabulating themselves.

Denise, who "told herself a story" and tried to "recognize herself in it" (*C* 499–500), and who is sufficiently self-conscious to be able to detect different drafts of her identity ("a Version 3.2 or a Version 4.0" [*C* 422]), is the most explicit example of this technique. But *The Corrections* is, at its core, an encyclopedia of the twenty-first century self, a theater Franzen has designed to bring the different conceptions of selfhood his characters draft to explain themselves to themselves into conflict. The drama is initiated by the first words that Alfred speaks on Thursday, September 30: "I am—" (*C* 11). His unfinished sentence intimates that the attempt to articulate one's sense of self is a tentative, provisional quest that may ultimately prove elusive. But as the book progresses, each character in turn completes that sentence in their own way. The novel presents the reader, first, with Chip's Foucauldian self, where subjectivity is shaped by institutional power structures. This is followed by Gary's materialist account of identity, where chemicals in the brain mold mood and behavior, which in turn is set against Caroline's world of self-help psychology. The accumulation of conflicting explanations of selfhood continues as the novel progresses—through Schopenhauer and sentimental selves—with the mode of self-conception shifting according to whose consciousness filters the narrative perspective. These drafts of the self are tested and (depending upon the character) rewritten within each story, but the critical aspect of this process is that instead of explicitly privileging one formulation of self, Franzen stresses that these explanations of identity are separate fictions of the self, no more than stories that his characters tell to explain their behavior to themselves.

The novel's parallel structure throws these competing stories about the self into particularly sharp relief. In two scenes separated by more than a 100 pages, for example, Franzen presents essentially the same situation— a father walks into his son's room—that prompts basically the same response—a feeling of sadness shades into reflection about the self. What changes is the mode of interpretation. First, Franzen has Gary wander into Caleb's room:

> Gary let his gaze drift into corners of the boy's room that he ordinarily took care not to look at. Neglected in piles, like the loot in a thief's apartment, was new photographic and computer and video equipment . . . Such a riot of luxury in the lair of an eleven-year-old! Various chemicals that molecular floodgates had been holding back all afternoon burst loose and flooded Gary's neural pathways. A cascade of reactions initiated by Factor 6 relaxed his tear valves. (*C* 156)

As the narrative burrows further into the past, Franzen presents a parallel scene as Alfred wanders into the young Gary's room and sees a model of an electric chair that Gary has made out of Popsicle sticks:

> He found himself susceptible . . . to the pathos of Gary's impulse to fashion an object and seek his father's approval . . . [and] to the impossibility of squaring this crude object with the precise mental picture of an electric chair that he had formed at the dinner table . . . maybe *every* "real" thing in the world was as shabbily protean, underneath, as this electric chair. Maybe his mind was even now doing to the seemingly real hardwood floor on which he knelt exactly what it had done, hours earlier, to the unseen chair. Maybe a floor became truly a floor only in his mental reconstruction of it. (*C* 272)

In order to make the parallel as suggestive as possible, Franzen has taken care to make Gary the same age in the second scene as Caleb is in the first,[24] but the chains of reflection that the two fathers engage in after seeing their sons' rooms are principally designed to illuminate the way they're drafting their identities and worlds according to their obsessions. Gary's response is couched in the language of materialist theories of the mind, explaining his rising sorrow in terms of the matter of the brain, the balance of chemicals coursing through his synapses. There is, then, some word play involved here. Franzen has introduced Gary as a "strict materialist" (*C* 139), but this classification denotes two separates strands of his character. He *is* a materialist in the common sense of the word, inasmuch as he places a high value on possessions. But he is also a materialist in a philosophical sense, because he is obsessed with the material basis of consciousness. Franzen is playing with the dual meaning of *materialism* in this scene, then, because one type of materialism prompts the other. The mass of material possessions facilitates a conception of the mind based upon its material structure.

Gary's reductionist conception of consciousness stems from Pinker, who describes the mind as a naturally-selected neural computer in *How the Mind Works*, and this view is parodied by Franzen when Gary is accused of treating his father like "some worn-out old machine" (*C* 211). But when Alfred walks into Gary's room—in the parallel scene—the pitch of self examination has recognizably changed from the earlier materialist view. Alfred's sadness becomes manifest as a Schopenhauerian sadness about the world. His musings derive from Schopenhauer's conception of a reality that is mediated by the act of consciousness, which transforms the "thing-in-itself" into a "representation," a somewhat-romantic delusion designed to blind us to the real mechanics of the world. But Franzen contrasts these two approaches to selfhood not because the novel is heavily invested in exploring any friction between materialism and Schopenhauerian will. Instead, these two scenes are simply illustrations of how two characters have found explanations of human behavior that allow them to remain (relatively) psychically intact in an inhospitable world. Were other characters to encounter this identical situation, they would similarly filter the scene through their own theory of how people work—Chip might reflect on the shaping influence of the family as institutional power structure; Enid might refer to some sentimental conception of love.

This variation makes the stakes involved in the novel's exploration of character much more complicated than any kind of binary opposition (such as Schopenhauer vs. materialism) can adequately capture.[25] In fact, while many reviewers described the book as a simple resurrection of the novel of character, *The Corrections*—by drawing on Dennett to show different characters articulating different, and sometimes fluid, drafts of selfhood—is actually arranged to formulate the question of what foundation a novel of character might actually be based upon?[26] The flow of chemicals in the brain? The blind drives of the will? The influence of pop psychology? Each of these ideas is rehearsed and introduced as a possibility, but not explicitly privileged because, correctly understood, this mass of theories about character simply comprises the superstructure of the novel. The substructure, or deep heart, of the book involves two underlying grids that further complicate Franzen's representation of character.

While Dennett's multiple drafts model provides one framework for Franzen to bring different explanations of selfhood into conflict, another theory of how the mind works outlines one of the novel's larger underlying grids. Underpinning Dennett's system is a second model that, in many of its manifestations, is less concerned with the isolated characters themselves, than with the world in which they move and the ways in which they overlap.

Perhaps unsurprisingly, given *Strong Motion*'s interest in recursive symmetry, Franzen's early novels frequently identify analogues between the self and more visible structures and this bleeds into a larger American obsession with the relationship between architectural structures and the mind. Just as Hawthorne's *The House of the Seven Gables* (1851) opens by imagining the Pyncheon house as resembling a "human countenance" (5), and Edgar Allan Poe's "Fall of the House of Usher" begins with a building whose "eye-like windows" and "barely perceptible fissure" (138) suggest a model of a schizophrenic human mind, so *The Twenty-Seventh City* presents "the faces of . . . buildings" and reflects upon a correspondence of "dwellings to dwellers, of structure and humanity" (*TS* 231). In *The Corrections*, this correspondence is amplified in the description of Midland Pacific's headquarters:

> The brain of the Midland Pacific, the temple of its soul, was a Depression-era limestone office building with rounded rooftop crenellations like the edges of a skimpy waffle. Higher-order consciousness had its cortical seat in the boardroom and executive dining room on the sixteenth floor and in the offices of the more abstract departments (Operations, Legal, Public Relations) whose vice presidents were on fifteen. Down at reptile-brain bottom of the building were billing, payroll, personnel, and data storage. In between were mid-level skill functions such as Engineering, which encompassed bridges, track buildings, and signals. (*C* 351)

The tripartite division of the brain that Franzen maps onto this building—providing a vertical hierarchy of reptilian brain, midbrain, and cerebral cortex—follows the research of neuroscientist Paul D. MacLean, who used this three-way division as the foundation for his theory of the "Triune Brain." Though in some ways an attempt to scientize Freud, MacLean's model is fundamentally built around evolutionary action. At the base of the brain is the brain stem, which evolved millions of years ago and which because of its primitive functions (the generation of fear responses, in particular) and its resemblance to "the brain of a salamander or a rattlesnake" (Restak 136),

MacLean termed the reptilian brain. Above this—and evolving after the reptilian brain—is the midbrain. Devoted to the generation of emotions, the sophistication of the midbrain is roughly equivalent to the brain of most mammals. At the top is the youngest component of the brain, the sophisticated cerebral cortex, the seat of language skills and abstract problem-solving abilities, and its characteristic response to the world is a rational one.

Like Franzen, MacLean compared this structure to architectural forms—he likens it to a "building to which wings and superstructure have been added" (8)—but the major thrust of his theory was that humanity was catastrophically at war with itself because the evolution of the brain built the more sophisticated cerebral structures on top of (rather than in place of) the earlier and more primitive neural components of the brain. The co-existence of these three brains introduces an internal division into the self because dictates of the different brains inevitably conflicted with each other, and this interplay is complicated by the fact that (unlike the cortex) the reptilian brain and the midbrain are nonverbal. This creates what MacLean calls a "schizophysiology": we "look at ourselves and the world through the eyes of three quite different mentalities," but only one of these has the power of speech (MacLean qtd. in Sagan 55).

In a general overview of localization theory, Anne Harrington notes that MacLean's "dramatic idea of a built in 'schizophysiology' in the human nervous system made a considerable impression in . . . the 1960s and 1970s" (215), and it seems to have significantly influenced novelists such as DeLillo, Powers, and Wallace. Franzen may have derived the model from DeLillo or from Pinker, who summarizes the theory in *How the Mind Works* as "an evolutionary palimpsest of three layers" (370). But whatever his source, its larger significance to *The Corrections* revolves around the way MacLean's vertical division of the brain—which is made explicit in Franzen's description of Midland Pacific's headquarters—is implicitly evoked by descriptions of houses and characters elsewhere in the novel. Franzen spatializes neurology in *The Corrections* so that, as in his earlier books, the suburban "landscape recapitulates personality" (*TS* 264).

While the Midland Pacific building provides a graphic key to MacLean's research, Franzen withdraws from the corporation to the domestic scale through the rest of the novel. This is particularly clear in terms of Chip's transformation at the end of the novel. As things go slowly wrong in Lithuania, Chip infuriates his sister because his actions betray a coldly intellectual response to his family, as when he announces that "parents have an overwhelming Darwinian hard-wired genetic stake in their children's welfare. But children, it seems to me, have no corresponding debt to their parents" (*C* 432). It is surely significant, here, that even as Chip relies on cortical abstraction to reason away any emotional connection to his family, Franzen carefully undermines him by framing his refusal in terms that invoke both the Darwinian evolution and the architecture of the brain that underpin MacLean's model. In terms of the triune brain, Chip is relying purely on the cortex, but his language is rich with reminders of "another world below" (*C* 239), the parts of the brain he has isolated himself from. This abstract, cortical isolation is revised, however, when Chip returns to St. Jude, and an echo back to the triune Midland Pacific building is suggested as Chip notes that "the house felt more like a body . . . than like a building" (*C* 538). Within the house, Chip showers and detects that "his brain in the shower was piscine or amphibian, registering impressions, reacting to the moment. He wasn't far from terror" (*C* 538).[27] Clearly at this point, Chip is descending from the proud intellectual illusions of the cortex that have secured his isolation from his family, toward a recognition of the lower structures of the brain. Though the fear-dominated reptilian chassis is close, Chip is overcoming the schizophysiology of his brain by replacing cold abstract cerebration with a connection to the emotional impulses of the centrally located midbrain, balanced between the upper and lower levels. In doing so, this cerebral descent acts as a prelude to the discovery of an empathetic relationship to the rest of his family that marks the novel's conclusion.

Yet Chip's earlier tendency to intellectualize existence is clearly presented as a characteristic of the Lambert males throughout the book. Just as Chip appeals to Darwin in writing to his sister, Alfred and Gary—as I've noted—appeal to Schopenhauer and materialism, respectively. But while Chip seems to overcome the divisions inherent in his cerebral architecture, others are less successful. Shortly after Chip locates the midbrain and is reintegrated into the family, Gary leaves "in his most rational mode," thus affirming the isolation of cortical reason from the emotional midbrain (*C* 543). But Gary and Alfred's relationship to the triune brain is more complicated than simple cortical isolation and can be keyed to a more general meditation that suggests how MacLean's model might be transposed to the suburbs:

> Whether anybody was home meant everything to a house. It was more than a major fact: it was the only fact.
> The family was the house's soul.
> The waking mind was like the light in a house.
> The soul was like the gopher in his hole.
> Consciousness was to brain as family was to house. (*C* 267)

Despite the ways that Alfred and Gary intellectualize the conditions of their lives, their spatial relationship to their homes follows this algorithm, suggesting ways that their level of consciousness might be related to the triune architecture of the brain.

Franzen makes it clear early in the book that the Lambert household stands as a microcosm for America, and that this microcosm revolves around its basement: "and so in the house of the Lamberts, as in St. Jude, as in the country as a whole, life came to be lived underground" (*C* 10). On a straightforward level, the underworld of the house is Alfred's world, and in this schematic it parallels the reptilian brain, so in the basement Alfred reacts to primitive impulses—urinating in coffee cans, contemplating violence. In a maneuver that underlines the deeper unity between Alfred and Gary—despite their conflicting understanding of the self—Franzen parallels Alfred's confinement in the basement by replicating "the solitary father's depression in a basement" (*C* 169) in Gary's life. Like Alfred, Gary hides himself in the basement to escape conflicts with his family, and like Alfred his behavior is driven by more primitive impulses as he masturbates over his laptop. Of course, Alfred and Gary also engage in more elevated acts in their respective basements—after all, Alfred's lab is located in his basement—but the point here is not simply the cognitive sophistication of the act, but its underlying motives. Both Gary and Alfred resort to their basements as part of their efforts to assert a basic selfish urge, a kind of reptilian self-preservation. They want to assert the primacy of their imperial selves, and to refuse to recognize the care of others, a fact Franzen makes explicit when Alfred broods in the basement, insisting "though he was cold to her it seemed unfair that she was cold in turn to him" (*C* 264). A snapshot of the Lambert family, which moves from the father to encompass the wider dynamics of the family, underlines this interpretation: "Maybe the futile light in a house with three people separately absorbed in the basement and only one upstairs . . . was like the mind of a depressed person" (*C* 267).

In this graphic model of the triune brain, Franzen uses the divided family to map the divided self. With only one isolated emotional figure in the midlevel of house and consciousness and everyone else isolated in the basement, the reptilian brain, he suggests, is in charge. At the same time, however, this layout insistently connects insular self-absorption to the reptilian brain. This association of selfishness with reptilian dictates parallels his later connection between the cortex and intellectual selfishness. Both polarities, Franzen suggests, isolate the self and a connection to the emotional midbrain is necessary to overcome the divisions in the self.

This complex layering of theories drawn from MacLean and Dennett makes it clear that the psychological substrate of Franzen's novel is not predicated upon some crude binary opposition. Even as Gary's mechanistic materialist conception of the brain is challenged within the story, the triune brain insistently underpins the larger action of the novel, and Dennett's multiple drafts provide an avenue for multiple characters to test the limits of their conception of selfhood. As in so many other areas, Franzen's attitude toward neuroscience in his novels is evidently marked by division. But there is also a second grid that underlies the novel's conception of character, and this grid illuminates another aspect of Franzen's divided attitude toward postmodernism.

In the cage

In his essay about William Gaddis, Franzen sets up a misleading dialectic where postmodernism is the antithesis of character-based fiction:

> If Robert Coover's *Public Burning* and Pynchon's *Crying of Lot 49* moved me, it was mainly because I liked Coover's character Richard Nixon and Pynchon's Oedipa Maas. But postmodern fiction wasn't supposed to be about sympathetic characters. Characters, properly speaking, weren't even supposed to exist. Characters were feeble, suspect constructs. (*A* 247)

It's difficult to see, from this, where the idea that postmodern fiction does not focus upon characters comes from, and the difficulty persists not just because the two examples of postmodernism he draws on here are defined, for him, in terms of character. Most of the essay, in fact, discusses Gaddis's work in terms of its characters—his experience of reading *The Recognitions* is one of "following Wyatt's pilgrimage" (*A* 245); he describes *JR* as a story about "an eleven-year-old Long Island schoolboy named JR Vansant" (*A* 255). But if Gaddis, Coover, and Pynchon do not embody this ideal of characterless fiction, William H. Gass, who Franzen accuses of "sophistry" in the same essay (*A* 260), might be a more likely target of Franzen's ire.

In his influential essay collection, *Fiction and the Figures of Life* (1970), Gass attacks misconceptions that he feels lie at the root of our experience of fiction, and several of these concern the notion of character. Gass stresses the fact that books are made out of language and urges the reader not to mistake a linguistic construct for a mysterious reality: "although no one wonders, of a painted peach, whether the tree it grew on was watered properly, we are happily witness, week after week, to further examination of Hamlet or Madame Bovary, quite as if they were real" (31). Similarly, in "The Concept of Character in Fiction," he argues that although we expect everyday language to refer beyond itself, novelistic language must not draw attention away from itself. So, while in real life the name Nicholas Nickleby ought to refer to a real figure with that name, in a novel the same name must not suggest "a real Nickleby," living "just beyond the page" (54). This confinement of literary characters to their purely linguistic existence provides one of the grids that underlies *The Corrections*.

A character, Gass insists, is "a proper name" not a person (44), but DeLillo suggests a further refinement, noting that "'character' in English not only means someone in a story but a mark or a symbol . . . like a letter of the alphabet" (*The Names* 10). Although reviewers such as James Wood greeted *The Corrections* as a return to conventional notions of characterization after the reductive linguistic games of DeLillo and Gass,[28] Franzen's characters are actually meant to be both "someone in a story" and "letter[s] of the alphabet" in the linguistic games Franzen plays. For example, subjecting the Lambert family to the process of "alphabetical . . . sorting" that Denise undertakes at Midpac (*C* 353), a significant pattern begins to emerge. Laid out in order, *A*lfred, *C*hip, *D*enise, *E*nid, and *G*ary, suggest a pattern that, rather than undermining the story, actually recapitulates the family dynamic that *The Corrections* explores. Beginning with the Alpha-father, Franzen appears to have laid out a neat set of A, B, Cs to demonstrate the flow of patriarchal power. On closer examination, however, it becomes clear that Franzen has deliberately fractured this scheme, so that the two father figures in the family—Alfred, and Gary (who, like Alfred has three children)—are isolated from the rest of their family. This schematic basically encodes one of the stories that Franzen is telling in his novel: the structure of the family has changed, and the patriarch is now in exile, separated from his children.

Embedded within this A–C–D–E–G framework, however, is also a neat schematic of the family's relationships. Just as *A* is next to *C*, so Chip is the character who is closest to Alfred's affections, as Denise observes, "if there was anybody in the world whom Alfred did love purely for his own sake, it was Chip" (*C* 523). In parallel, *G* is next to *E*, because (after himself) Gary cares most about his mother. Denise, of course, lies in the center of this arrangement, just as throughout the book she functions as either an agent of division for, or the binding glue that brings unity to, the family as a whole. Taken together, these first letters of the family members' names also offer a pertinent anagram: *CAGED*. This is another of the techniques Franzen uses to stress that familial inheritance is a kind of prison for these characters, and the inescapability of the family unit is reinscribed a further level down, in the names of the female characters. The letters for Enid's name are embedded within Denise, but just as Denise insists upon how different she is from her mother, it is significant that Denise is an anagram of *denies*.

Enid is a key name in other contexts, too. It is surely significant that, when Chip runs from his mother in "The Failure," his steps lead toward another mother figure, whose first name is only one letter removed from Enid's: Eden Procuro. Eden's name fits with the other biblical resonances at the start of this millennial fiction, but as a substitute mother-figure (who Chip seems to believe will resolve all his problems, if only she'd pay attention to him) Eden has a pregnant name in other respects. Chip goes to Eden to satisfy several desires—he needs money and he need's Julia's body—so it's appropriate that Eden is an anagram of *need*. The overlap of money and sexual desire is appropriate, here, because Procuro also suggests *procure*, a verb normally used in connection with prostitution. The dark side to Eden's business, however, is also nested in her last name, which contains a near anagram of *corrupt*.

Enid is also connected to the novel's fascination with food. *The Corrections* features one character who is a chef, is filled with references to food, and Franzen told Donald Antrim that most of his characters "are hungry people" (77). It is appropriate, then, that if you spell the name of the overpowering mother backward, you come up with *dine*.[29] But what does Enid dine upon? Well, the first obvious conclusion would be her appropriately named son, Chip. Aside from his snack-food name, Chip also has "butter-yellow hair" (*C* 15) and used to teach a class about consumption. As a secondary option—and surely just as delicious—there is Chip's girlfriend Julia Vrais, who Franzen tells us is "chocolate-haired" (*C* 27). Given the strong linguistic hints of cannibalization, Denise's fears late in the book that her family might have "eaten her alive if she hadn't run away" (*C* 499) do not seem so far fetched.

Franzen has encoded many more puns and anagrams throughout the book. Gary Lambert, for example, can be rearranged to produce such appropriate derivates as *rage, germ*, and *brat*. But the most personal of these encrypted messages reveals some of the biographical roots of the novel. Chip's full name—Charles—shares four letters with Alfred and Lambert—*E, A, R, L*—spelling out the name of both Shakespeare's mad King Lear, and the name of Franzen's father. Like Wallace's Shakespeare-suffused

Infinite Jest, then, Franzen's novel is partly intended to be "a long encomium to the dead father" (Wallace, Interview with David Wiley).

How to end a post-postmodern novel

"Conclusions," George Eliot observed in a letter in 1857, "are the weak points of most authors, but some of the fault lies in the very nature of a conclusion, which is at best a negation" (324). The conclusion of *The Corrections*, which takes just 6 pages to cover more than 2 years—in the course of which Alfred dies, Chip gets married and has two children, and Denise gets a new job—may at first seem to be a negation of the rest of the book. While 560 pages have been devoted to minutely chronicling 3 months, the contracted ending with its tidy conclusion recalls Henry James's satiric pronouncement on the end of the nineteenth-century novel, with its "distribution at the last of prizes, pensions, husbands, wives, babies, millions, appended paragraphs, and cheerful remarks" ("The Art of Fiction" 190). Yet, the neatness of the summary ending to Franzen's novel is not without its difficult loose ends. The fact that the narrative voice sits so close to Enid's consciousness as she unravels a list of Alfred's faults in these final moments seems to sit awkwardly in relation to the rest of the book. The alternating perspectives of the novel's body seem to have been designed to confirm Proust's remark that "the truth is so variable for each of us, that other people have difficulty in recognizing what it is" (5: 13),[30] and each individual narrative has been carefully arranged to qualify and challenge the "truths" discovered by any individual perspective. After this parallactic movement, it is difficult to accept the authority of one character's summary of such important material. Even after Enid has completed her marital economy, it is hard to get a steady reading of the tone of the novel's last sentence: "She was seventy-five and she was going to make some changes in her life" (*C* 566). The note of optimism struck by the last ten words is so deeply qualified by the first four words that pathos seems to fall into irony.

These discordant notes in the final pages of *The Corrections* introduce a note of uncertainty into what initially appears to be a very neat summation. But even taking this disharmony into account, the end of *The Corrections* is a substantial shift from the open ending that is so often considered typical of the modernist and postmodernist novel. Indeed, it is striking to consider how many of Franzen's postmodern predecessors ended their major works not just with open-ended uncertainty, but actually with an unfinished sentence: *Gravity's Rainbow* ends in midsentence, on the brink of a nuclear winter; at the end of Gaddis's *JR*, the disembodied voice of JR Vansant trails off into an ellipsis, waiting for an answer that never comes, while Coover's *The Adventures of Lucky Pierre* concludes in the middle of a sentence that is moving toward either Pierre's orgasm or death, perhaps both. I would hesitate to suggest that such a movement toward closure is essentially characteristic of the post-postmodern novel, but a survey of Franzen's endings and a comparison to the end of works by Richard Powers does suggest an interesting development.[31]

Franzen's earliest work, *The Twenty-Seventh City*, concludes with not just uncertainty, but with that classic postmodern trademark, linguistic uncertainty: as Balwan Singh filters back into the Indian subcontinent, Franzen describes him as "He jumped, turned in midair, and landed seated, looking back into the empty western sky as the lorry carried him east to set him free among the other thirty million Indians named Singh" (*TS* 517). In this neatly poised sentence, Franzen's narrative lens slowly widens from its focus on a Midwestern American city, to take in the world outside America. But even as the lens widens, he freezes his character between the two poles of his novel—the *east* and *west* of the sentence stand for the Eastern and Western cultures Franzen has contrasted. Nevertheless, as the sentence maps its coordinates back onto the rest of the book, there is no hint of what will happen to Singh next, no sense of how the story may continue. We end, instead, with a signifier whose range of potential signifieds is helplessly broad.

Something similar is suggested by the last sentences of *Strong Motion*, which describes Louis Holland as "He walked away from her, over the crest of the bridge and down the other side . . . 'Nothing's wrong. I swear to you. I just have to walk now. Walk with me, come on. We have to keep walking'" (*SM* 508). Like the end of Franzen's first novel, this conclusion also emphasizes motion and recapitulates important themes established earlier in the book. The motion over the bridge indicates connection and recalls Alec Bressler's earlier advice about not alienating other people ("why burn the bridges?" he tells Louis, who, at the end, is mending his bridge toward Renée [*SM* 87]), while the fact that the book ends with the two characters walking into wider world reaffirms the novel's argument about the need for open circulation, rather than the claustrophobia of a closed system. The scale of this scene is recognizably smaller than Singh's passage into the subcontinent, but the movement of the individual into the larger world is the same. At the same time, there are fewer questions left (Sweeting-Aldren, the ostensible villains of the book, have already been widely identified as guilty, though Franzen carefully qualifies that assessment), and though some important questions are left hanging, they are principally personal matters: will Renée and Louis have a baby, as has been intimated in the earlier conversation? Will Melanie return to Bob?

But while the movement of the three endings of Franzen's novels is consistently toward smaller scales and increased closure, it is notable that all these endings remain at the same ontological level. A valuable contrast to the conclusions of Powers's first three novels is pertinent here. In each of his first three books, Powers bases his novel upon a relatively traditional foundation and then relies upon the conventions of realism until the final pages, when he consistently introduces a metafictional element into his work. At the end of *Three Farmers*, the narrator P—reveals the book to be "*my* account" (336), at the end of *Prisoner's Dilemma* Powers momentarily drops the story of the Hobson family to discuss his own family and reveals how writing fiction could be a way "to make some sense of the loss" of his own father (345), and the closing pages of *Gold Bug* reveal that the novel the reader has just read has been a product of two of the character's stitching together their respective stories. By constructing his novels along a realist plane, before suddenly introducing a metafictional element, Powers attempts a synthesis of two apparently opposed modes of rendering the world: the supposedly realist and the self-reflexive. This post-postmodern fusion of forms is intended to have a twofold effect. The realist dimension to his novels is designed to elicit the traditional effects of fiction—understanding, empathy with another's perspective—while the metafictional element hopes to draw the reader's attention outside the book, to recognize the way her own life story is constructed and narrated. The appeal of such a novel where realism shades into metafiction, resides, as Powers argues in "Being and Seeming," in its ability:

> to interrupt our imaginary continuities and put us head to head with a maker who is not us. Story is a denuding, laying the reader bare, and the force of that denuding lies not in our entering into a perfect representation, but in our coming back out. It lies in that moment . . . when we come to remember how finely narrated is the life outside this constructed frame, a story needing only some other minds' pale analogies to resensitize us to everything in it that we've grown habituated to. (17)

For Powers, then, fiction is, as he writes in *Prisoner's Dilemma*, "a place to hide out in long enough to learn how to come back" (345), and the crucial element is the reemergence from the restorative imaginative space that metafiction prompts. Although Franzen does not insist upon a metafictional element at the end of *The Corrections*, he does share Powers's vision of a book as a kind of haven from the world. Near the end of *Strong Motion*, Franzen prompts Louis to recognize that a person can be "consoled by literature" (*SM* 499), and in interviews he has described how a novel can be "an alternate, imagined world in which, for the duration of the project, [the reader] can take daily refuge" ("A Difficult Haven" 12). At the same time, Franzen has, like Powers, clearly taken care in *The Corrections*, more than in any of his other books, to periodically fracture the illusion he works to create, effectively prompting the same kind of return to the world that Powers achieves through self-reference. In "The Failure," for example, the willfully obscured names (D—College, W—Corporation, etc.) serve not to heighten the realistic elements of the book, but rather self-consciously draw attention to the book's artifice. Following a similar technique, Franzen sometimes deliberately fractures the realistic plane by inserting implausibly childish names such as "Mayor Goode" of "Nicetown" (*C* 342).

The ending of Franzen's novels, and (to a lesser extent) the ending of Powers's early novels, do suggest that this branch of post-postmodernism represents a gradual, qualified return to more conventional methods of closure. At the same time, however, the careful puncturing of the illusions of realism stresses their continued affinities to postmodernism. If, as both critics and writers suggest, postmodernism came to an end just before the millennium that shadows so much of this generation's work, it is still very early to be trying to take stock of the movements that are gradually emerging in its wake. Equally, after just three novels it is still rather early to try to graph the arc of Franzen's career. Nevertheless, these first three novels—like Powers and Wallace's early work—suggest not a rejection of postmodernism, but a gradual correction.

Notes

Preface

[1] In early 2002, Charles B. Harris introduced a special issue of the *American Book Review* by exploring the continued vitality of an earlier generation of postmodernists (Barth, Federman), alongside the emergence of "another generation of novelists whose fiction, while bearing clear family resemblances, has staked out new directions of its own" ("PoMo's Wake" 1). Robert L. McLaughlin's 2004 essay, "Post-Postmodern Discontent," suggests that a number of writers who came to prominence in the late 1980s have been "responding to the perceived dead end of postmodernism, a dead end that has been reached because of postmodernism's detachment from the social world and immersion in a world of nonreferential language" (55). Significantly, both writers consider Franzen an important figure in the slow movement beyond postmodernism.

[2] Aside from the Great-American-Novel rhetoric that surrounded Franzen's third novel, Laura Shapiro described Franzen's first book as "downright revolutionary" in *Newsweek* (59), while in *Esquire*, Sven Birkerts heralded *The Corrections* for its "swooping lyrical intensity" ("Novel" 71). Obviously I'm not suggesting that these aren't noteworthy books, but the inflated descriptions do more to obscure the real value of Franzen's work. *The Twenty-Seventh City* is not notable for its revolutionary qualities, and—in spite of Birkerts customary intelligence—it's hard to imagine just what *swooping* lyrical intensity might be.

[3] The *Review of Contemporary Fiction* has devoted special issues to both writers (in 1998 Powers shared an issue's focus with Rikki Ducornet; in 1993 a "Young Writers" issue concentrated on Wallace, William T. Vollmann, and Susan Daitch); books elucidating their fiction include Joseph Dewey's *Understanding Richard Powers* (2002), Marshall Boswell's *Understanding David Foster Wallace* (2003), and my *David Foster Wallace's Infinite Jest: A Reader's Guide* (2003).

[4] In the *British Medical Journal*, Richard Smith quoted *The Corrections* in an essay on spending on health and the arts, while David V. Forrest and Lucien J. Côté discussed the same novel in the *Journal of the American Academy of Psychoanalysis and Dynamic Psychiatry*, where they examine Alfred and Enid's deterioration.

[5] Because so little has been written on Franzen, I inevitably refer on multiple occasions to the small body of secondary literature devoted to his fiction. At times, this must give the impression that I'm persistently disagreeing with other critics, but this is misleading. Often I admire the earlier work on Franzen, and my repeated reference to other studies is simply a product of the (so far) limited availability of critical studies of his fiction.

6. For discussions of the Oprah affair, see Ribbat, "Handling the Media" (2002); Rooney, *Reading with Oprah* (2005); Green, *Late Postmodernism* (2005); Ozick, *The Din in the Head* (2006); Fitzpatrick, *The Anxiety of Obsolescence* (2006); and Annesley, "Market Corrections" (2006).
7. Robert Rebein, for example, has attempted to glibly smooth the finer distinctions of Franzen's relationship to postmodernism with a reductive formula that asserts that Franzen "said 'no' to Po-Mo" (201).

Chapter 1

1. The date of the first use of the term *postmodern* (or its derivatives) in English is the subject of a small critical industry in itself. In adopting the dates in this chapter, I follow Fred R. Shapiro's "Prehistory of *Postmodern*" (2001). If the field is expanded beyond English, the situation becomes even more complex, and in *The Origins of Postmodernity* (1998), Perry Anderson identifies the use of the Spanish *postmodernismo* in 1934, in the work of Federico de Onís, who employed the term "to describe a conservative reflux within modernism itself" (4).
2. This ground has been widely covered by other histories of postmodernism, and it is not my aim to reductively or simplistically reproduce such work here. Brief examples of this tendency to construct postmodernism as a subversion of modernism might draw on Leslie Fiedler's famous argument that after the elitism of modernism, "a closing of the gap between elite and mass culture [was] precisely the function of the novel now" (336). Equally, critics such as Ihab Hassan and William V. Spanos argued that the postmodern writer was now drawn to existentialism rather than modernism, with Spanos identifying a tradition "not in the 'anti-Aristotelian' line that goes back from the Concrete poets to Proust, Joyce, Mallarmé, Gautier, and Pater, but in the 'anti-Aristotelian' line that looks back from Beckett, Ionesco, and the Sartre of *Nausea*" (39).
3. Modernist critics such as Harry Levin, in "What was Modernism?," and Robert Martin Adams, in (again) "What was Modernism?," were particularly vocal in framing the literature after modernism in terms of a withdrawal from the formal perfections of modernism. Levin suggested that the new writers were intimidated by the richness and scale of modernist achievement, and had consequently settled for disappointing "traditional form[s], *more or less well made*" (272, emphasis mine). Robert Martin Adams similarly felt that these new works lacked formal distinction, and he attacked postmodernism as "a blank spot on our cultural map, to be filled with *amorphous*, nondescript creatures" (30, emphasis mine).
4. Tom LeClair's *The Art of Excess* (1989) draws on such diverse fields as cybernetics, anthropology, and nonlinear mathematics to argue that his chosen postmodern novelists direct readers toward "global and cultural wholes" rather than chaotic fragments (27). N. Katherine Hayles's works *The Cosmic Web* (1984) and *Chaos Bound* (1990) similarly explored the way that scientific research might elucidate the works of postmodern writers such as Pynchon, Borges, and Lessing. More recently, Joseph M. Conte's *Design and Debris* (2002) and Joseph Tabbi's *Cognitive Fictions* (2002) have carried on such explorations.

[5] In an interview with Susana Pajares Tosca, Coover locates the origins of the novel in 1969. He does, however, give a more detailed account of the book's early stages in "The Public Burning Log 1966–77," in which Coover records that while living in England in 1970 he launched "a new work about a pornographic film hero, with a working title of *Winter*." By the end of that year he notes that "the first of the nine projected *Winter* 'reels' is completed. As 'research,' we take in the 'First Annual Wet Dream Festival' in Amsterdam in November, a kind of pornfilm love-in." In an entry for 1971 he writes that "The second 'reel' of what I am now calling *Lucky Pierre* is completed in a rough draft and most of the third, each reel being the length of a short novel" (87).

[6] I discuss Levin above, but in *A Homemade World* (1975), the usually so perspicacious Hugh Kenner argued that despite the superficial resemblance between such postmodern works as *The Recognitions* and *Gravity's Rainbow* and the modernist masterpieces that "solicit[ed] our note cards" (211), the "world of American modernism terminates," Kenner argued, "not in climactic masterworks but in an anticlimactic 'age of transition'" (xviii). In its modern guise, the belief that there are no postmodern masterpieces emerges in much diluted form in Michael André Bernstein's "Making Modernist Masterpieces" (1998). Without reference to a single example from postmodernism, Bernstein asserts that while the drive to create "a new kind of encyclopedic masterpiece" (5) was a key characteristic of modernism, postmodernism "counters assertions of the masterpiece's universality with an insistence that every work explicitly acknowledge its own historicity and partiality. At its most radical, postmodernism throws into doubt the category of genius" that a masterpiece depends upon (12). I discuss the encyclopedic novel as a postmodern genre more fully in my essay, "The Collapse of Everything." In *The Art of Excess*, LeClair terms such works novels of excess.

[7] Steiner's essay is, as this quotation suggests, rather idiosyncratic and is surprisingly marred by errors such as her misuse of the term "category mistake" (435).

[8] My title, here, is partially borrowed from the title of Lawrence Norfolk's review of David Foster Wallace in the *Times Literary Supplement*.

[9] McCaffery first put together a volume on Avant-Pop in 1993, when Black Ice published *Avant-Pop: Fiction for a Daydream Nation*, but I discuss only his later volume above because McCaffery's introduction to *After Yesterday's Crash* serves as something like a real manifesto for Avant-Pop, whereas Avant-Pop has no equivalent programmatic statement. *Avant-Pop* has not been a widely adopted term, but its value has been explored by Peter Schneck in "Pop Goes the Novel." Schneck finds elements of McCaffery's construction of Avant-Pop "remarkably reductive" (67), but he locates in Avant-Pop and Susan Sontag's work a common "mixture of frustration and fascination with the postmodern self-image of literature" (73).

[10] Though a full development of this idea is beyond the scope of this chapter, it is worth mentioning that a significant subgenre of male postmodernism in the 1990s was the development of books by aging male writers about aging male writers: to add to Barth's *Coming Soon!!!*, there are at least William Gaddis's *A Frolic of His Own* (1994), Don DeLillo's *Mao II* (1991), William Gass's *The Tunnel* (1995), David Markson's *Reader's Block* (1996), and—at the end of the century—Joseph Heller's *Portrait of an Artist, as an Old Man* (2000).

11. Barth has also considered "what Post-Postmodernism, if any, lies around the next corner" in his essay collection, *Further Fridays* (124, cf. 120, 310).
12. Apart from reworking the same thematic material (i.e., what happens after, and what are the effects of, postmodernism), Wallace highlighted the congruence of the two works by at times employing identical phrasing. In "Westward," for example, the writer Mark Nechtr is described as a "born watcher" (248); 4 years later Wallace began his *Review of Contemporary Fiction* essay by describing writers generally as "born watchers" (151).
13. As a further indication of postmodernism's desire to spiral criticism back into fiction, note that Jameson's phrase "the end of this or that" is incorporated in Barth's discussion in "The End: An Introduction" ("the end of this, the end of that") quoted earlier in this chapter. If 1991 marked a growing disaffection with self-reference, Jameson's study, of course, signaled a new wave of interest in a different strand of postmodernism.
14. Wallace's big novel, *Infinite Jest* (1996), had been accompanied by a widely reprinted photograph of Wallace in which, sure enough, he had a scruffy beard and a bandana.
15. See Wallace's *Infinite Jest* (333) and Powers's *The Gold Bug Variations*, where the relationship between map and territory is filtered through Lewis Carroll (88).
16. Franzen also includes William T. Vollmann as one of his classmates, here, but while I discuss his first novel in Chapter 3, I do not consider his work as a whole in comparison to Franzen's because Vollmann's incredibly prolific output makes a comparison with Franzen's three novels, and two books of nonfiction, fairly futile.
17. I use the phrase "apparently," here, because I have been unable to locate the source from which Newman quotes Bellamy. When I became frustrated by my inability to trace this source, I wrote to Bellamy seeking his help. He replied: "I fear Charles Newman got his index cards scrambled. I don't believe I ever said such a thing." In the absence of the original author, I've used Bellamy's name for convenience's sake in this discussion.
18. There are, of course, usages of *post-postmodern* that precede 1975. In 1974, for example, Campbell Tatham uses the term in a somewhat silly essay that also denies the existence of modernism and postmodernism, alongside post-postmodernism (79).
19. It should be noted that, for some critics, the mere existence of this resemblance is enough to discount the use of the term *post-postmodern*. In their introduction to *The Mourning After* (2007), for example, Josh Toth and Neil Brooks see post-postmodernism as a move toward "more grounded (or 'responsible') works of neo-realism" (5). Works that "seem to carry on a certain postmodern project while (all the while) critiquing elements of that project"—and Franzen and Wallace are the examples they offer—are classified as "renewalist writers" (7).
20. For more on *Infinite Jest's* intertextual dialogue with DeLillo, see my essay "The Machine-Language of the Muscles."
21. Powers echoes Pynchon elsewhere in his fiction, too. As Tom LeClair observes in his essay on "Prodigious Fiction" (36n1), a character in *Gold Bug* acknowledges that his "favorite living novelist notes, [that information has] replaced cigarettes as the universal medium of exchange" (468), an observation that also

comes from *Gravity's Rainbow* (158). In *The Time of Our Singing*, Powers diligently goes further back to identify his main modernist ancestor, too. "Have you ever read *Ulysses*, by James Joyce?" the novel's David Strom is asked by his father-in-law (230), and the reader is meant to recognize *The Time of Our Singing's* American variation on *Ulysses'* hybrid of Dubliner and Jew, a harmony that is quietly reinforced by the fact that the Strom's central son, Joey, is born on the anniversary of Bloomsday.

22 Critical readings of *Gold Bug* and *Infinite Jest* have begun to reveal just how carefully these novels are constructed. Jay Labinger, in particular, has offered an insightful account of *Gold Bug's* formal complexity in his essay "Encoding an Infinite Message" (1995).

23 Perhaps also linked to this aspect of post-postmodernism is the marked tendency of the younger writers to dilute their novelistic production by writing nonfiction that more obviously engages with wider social issues. With the 2005 release of *Consider the Lobster*, Wallace, for example, had written more books of nonfiction than he had novels. With *The Discomfort Zone*, Franzen boasts three novels to two collections of nonfiction.

24 Marshall Boswell usefully links "Octet" and "Westward" and suggests that the latter story's self-referential strategies are an attempt "to disclose the self-consciousness as manipulative and thereby enact an actual, two-way 'interrogation' with the reader" (187).

25 Indeed, Charles B. Harris has considered Powers's *Plowing the Dark* (2000) as an exemplary illustration of the way that Powers (despite his use of metafictional techniques) has allowed "realistic conventions" to become part of his "aesthetic repertoire," in his 2004 essay, "Technoromanticism and the Limits of Representation" (110).

26 It should be clear, both in this chapter and across the rest of this volume, that I agree substantially with McLaughlin's argument, but differ in my estimation of how Franzen's work relates to that argument.

27 This practice is more in line with DeLillo's *Underworld*, a fact that may explain why Franzen *initially* responded so positively to DeLillo's longest novel. He told Joanna Smith Rakoff, "I read [*Underworld*], loved it page by page, and concluded with this empty feeling of 'Wait a minute. That's not the book we need'" (32).

28 To be strictly correct, the years in Wallace's novel are partially obscured by the presence of what *Infinite Jest* calls "subsidized time," a parodic development in which years are named by corporate sponsors. Thus, 2010 becomes the "Year of Glad." I discuss this in more detail in my *Reader's Guide* to Wallace's novel.

29 Charles B. Harris offers a thorough and illuminating investigation into what he calls "neurological realism" in *The Echo Maker* in his essay "The Story of the Self." I discuss Wallace's consideration of theories of selfhood in "The Machine-Language of the Muscles."

Chapter 2

1 As I explain in Chapter 4, most of *Strong Motion*'s action takes place in 1990, but Renée compiles her list in 1989. A note about dates is also appropriate here:

while the temporal boundaries I outline above are accurate for books that Franzen *names* in this list, Renée also discards works by several authors without identifying a specific volume. Depending upon which works by these writers she discards, it would be feasible to argue for different dates. Since, however, there is obviously no way of establishing which exact unnamed works she discards, I am content to settle upon the dates of books that Franzen takes the trouble to name.

2. While Barth and Doctorow are frequently discussed in terms of metafiction and historiographic metafiction, respectively, Salinger may seem a surprising inclusion in this category, here, yet much of *Franny and Zooey* is given over to self-conscious discussion of writing.

3. England's geography has been distorted, here, for dramatic effect, since Newton is reputed to have made his famous discovery of gravity in Lincolnshire.

4. In "On Being Unable to Read," Cornell complains of her inability to read after a decade of arguing with Franzen about literature (409); Chetkovitch writes of her struggle to create in the face of Franzen's success that she has "met the circumstances that are larger than my capacity to be gracious" (87).

5. Franzen told me that they came up with "various silly title proposals ('Name Your Poison' etc.)" but never actually named this play.

6. In his first novel, Luisa Probst applies to Swarthmore (*TS* 57), while in *The Corrections* both Caroline and Denise go to school there (*C* 182, 300).

7. Knowles and Doctorow, of course, make Renée's list in *Strong Motion*. Walker's novel, *The Color Purple* (1982), is suggested by Chip's script, *The Academy Purple*, in *The Corrections* (*C* 27).

8. Franzen recalls Avery's influence in his essay on Gaddis (*A* 245), and at more length in his essay "The Foreign Language" in *The Discomfort Zone*.

9. Apart from the obvious "Joseph K." component of this name, the last name "Prager" is probably intended to suggest that the character is—like Kafka himself—from Prague (*Prag* in German).

10. All references to this interview with Eakin should be prefaced with the caveat that Franzen later described the profile as "painfully stupid" ("The Esquire Conversation").

11. Adam Haslett published a collection of stories, *You Are Not a Stranger Here* (2002); Max Watman, a reviewer for the *New Criterion*, offers a few reflections on his experience in Franzen's class in his review of *The Corrections*, "On the Hysterical Playground."

12. Because I offer a detailed account of the genesis of *The Corrections* in Chapter 5, I have omitted a lengthy discussion of the novel from this chapter.

13. In a perhaps intentional irony, Franzen's attempt to distinguish himself from his postmodern predecessors itself echoes Barth's attempt to distinguish postmodernism from modernism in "The Literature of Replenishment," where Barth describes himself as a writer "who cut his teeth on Eliot, Joyce, Kafka" (*Friday Book* 198).

14. *Strong Motion*'s epigraph is from Singer's 1972 novel, *Enemies* (96), while in *The Corrections*, Denise "steeped herself in I. B. Singer" (*C* 389), while Franzen also references Singer in his essays "Scavenging" (*A* 199) and "Two Ponies" (*DZ* 48).

15 In fact, Franzen himself seems to have doubted whether or not his other examples in this essay really expressed what he wanted them to. In the version of the essay that appeared in the *New Yorker*, for example, Franzen explained that: "With certain novels, of course, the distinction doesn't matter so much. *Pride and Prejudice, The House of Mirth*: you call them art, I call them entertainment" (100). But by the time the essay appeared in the paperback of *How to Be Alone*, Franzen had altered this to read: "With certain novels, of course, the distinction doesn't matter so much. *War and Peace, The House of Mirth*: you call them art, I call them entertainment" (*A* 240). The substitution of Tolstoy for Austen is mystifying, and—unless it serves simply to avoid the implication that this division is gendered—it's hard to see how the change helps clarify Franzen's terms.

16 Franzen made numerous changes to the essay between its first appearance in *Harper's* and its collection in *How to Be Alone*, but none of these revisions alters the fundamental issues I'm addressing here.

17 I'm aware that it may be misleading to cite Rebein's essay here, since his essay's stated conclusion—to demonstrate that "the generation of American writers that includes Franzen . . . promises to be the last to be directly influenced by the likes of a Pynchon or a Gaddis" (220) is less the result of a carefully explored critical investigation than an indication of his agenda against a kind of writing he clearly dislikes.

Chapter 3

1 I discuss the temporal arrangements of Franzen's next two novels in some detail in the subsequent chapters, but, in brief, the majority of the action of *Strong Motion* takes 4 months (April–July, 1990), while *The Corrections* principally covers 3 (October–December, c. 1999).

2 That the attempt to gain the "aerial view" is a crucial concept for Powers is reinforced by the fact that the phrase appears in each of his first seven novels. See *Three Farmers on Their Way to a Dance* (76), *Prisoner's Dilemma* (310), *Gold Bug* (313), *Operation Wandering Soul* (51), *Gain* (89), and *Plowing the Dark* (249).

3 The first epigraph from *Three Farmers on Their Way to a Dance* is taken from the end of vol. 5 of Proust's *In Search of Lost Time* (5: 754), though Powers relies upon the earlier unrevised translation, known as *Remembrance of Things Past*.

4 Donna Rifkind in the *Wall Street Journal*, Margo Jefferson in *Vogue*, and Michele Slung in the *Washington Post*, for example, all confidently placed the novel's action in 1984. Those reviewers and critics who dissent from this easy judgment make claims that are difficult to understand: David Keymer, who reviewed the book for the *Library Journal*, mysteriously chose to date the novel "in the late 1980s" (108), while, more recently, Daniel Grassian mistakenly insists in his study, *Hybrid Fictions* (2003), that the novel is one of several fictions that "envision a futuristic America" (143).

5 Franzen has clearly taken care over the accuracy of the novel's chronology, but he does make the odd error, such as when he dates the "morning of the day before

Halloween" as a Monday (*TS* 71). In fact, in 1984, Halloween occurred on a Wednesday.

6. It is worth noting that Franzen also alludes to Eliot's "The Hollow Men" (*TS* 67) and twice to the "objective correlative" that Eliot discusses in his 1919 essay on "*Hamlet*" (*TS* 392, 453).

7. In a further teasing reference, Franzen includes the name Shanti four times in the novel (*TS* 397 [twice], 398, 399), as if to imply that his book represents one step beyond Eliot's triple reference.

8. Laura Shapiro reports that Franzen told her that "he read Ved Mehta and V. S. Naipaul" for information about India (59).

9. Martin Probst probably owes his first name to Martin Beck, the detective-hero of a series of 10 novels by Maj Sjöwall and Per Wahlöö. Franzen describes these novels as particularly important to him because "things always go right, in the end, for Martin Beck" (qtd. in "Nourishing" 3). Of course, in the dark world of Franzen's novel, things have precisely stopped going right for Beck's modern counterpart.

10. Even Probst's illness seems to be couched in the syntax of *The Waste Land*. Just as Madame Sosostris "had a bad cold," so Franzen tells us that Probst "had a bad cold" (*TS* 209).

11. Spencer further notes that the theme of the first parade was the "Festival of Ceres," the Roman goddess of agriculture, while the Veiled Prophet ball served "as a courtship ritual for the daughters of St. Louis's wealthiest families" (3, 4).

12. The T. S. Eliot Society helped me to determine that a demolition permit was evidently issued to "wreck brick" at 2635 Locust Street in 1913. In 1917, a building permit records the construction of a "showroom" for Mary A. Bordeau. Southwestern Bell demolished this showroom in 1973. In February 2005, I wrote to Franzen and asked him about his knowledge of Eliot in St. Louis. Franzen responded somewhat coyly: "The Eliot references you've unearthed are so subtle and interesting that I'd be a fool to deny having placed all of them intentionally. Nor is it conceivable that an ambitious young writer from St. Louis could be unaware of sharing a hometown with both Eliot and Burroughs. But more than this I'd better not say." It should be noted that in recent years a plaque has been inserted into the sidewalk to mark the site of Eliot's birthplace (Cuoco and Gass 158).

13. Marshall Boswell has persuasively demonstrated that *The Broom of the System* is involved in an intertextual dialogue with John Updike's work, see, *Understanding David Foster Wallace*.

Chapter 4

1. I learnt of this essay from an article on Richard Powers's novel *Gain*, by Paul Maliszewski.

2. Aside from their obvious fascination with Boston, New England is contrasted with Basil Ransome's American south in James, and with Lauren Bowles's Texas in Franzen.

3. Debates around abortion also connect the two novels when, in the first book, Duane gives Luisa "the abortion quiz (it was going to turn out to be somehow hypocritical to be pro-choice)" (*TS* 437).
4. In the first novel in their series of 10 Beck stories, *Roseanna* (1965), the opening chapter details the discovery of a corpse, while the narrative lens in the second chapter pulls back to explain that "Motala is a medium-sized Swedish city in the province of Östergötland at the northern end of Lake Vättern. It has a population of 27,000" (4).
5. Because such patterns may seem speculative, I asked Franzen about the presence of anagrams and the repetition of letters in his characters. He confirmed that this was a deliberate strategy on his part, and that in terms of the play with Louis, Lauren, and Renée's names, "Rs and Ls had been in my mind during the writing of *Strong Motion*" (personal correspondence, 28 Nov. 2007).
6. Bressler's desire to purge his radio station of political content seems to parallel Franzen's critique of literature that takes no account of its social setting in *The Corrections*. See the discussion of Gunnar Myrdal in the next chapter.
7. Louis meets Renée on Sunday, April 15, 1990, and Lauren comes back into his life on Wednesday, June 6, 1990. To make it clear that Lauren and Renée represent different poles for Louis, Franzen has arranged his chronology as suggestively as possible, so that Louis meets Lauren almost exactly a year before he meets Renée, "during Easter Vacation" 1989 (*SM* 69).
8. In addition to quoting the Bible (as noted above), this section of the book also quotes "On Property," the fifth chapter of John Locke's 1690 work, *Second Treatise of Government* (*SM* 365).
9. It is worth noting that Powers's *The Gold Bug Variations* is similarly centered around a scientist who believes in order and isolation. For discussions of the scientific implications of order and isolation in Powers, see Scott Hermanson, "Chaos and Complexity," and Joseph Dewey, "Hooking the Nose of the Leviathan."
10. This praise of baseball represents a shift from Franzen's student journalism, where he describes "how dull the National Pastime really is" ("A Sunday" 6).
11. The length of this list gives some idea of how prevalent Franzen's tendency to describe humans in comparison to animals really is: 18, 33, 34, 36, 37, 43, 46, 71, 72, 78, 84, 121, 122, 123, 126, 128, 130, 162, 163, 164, 178, 187, 188, 234, 251, 292, 293, 331, 345, 386, 417, 456.

Chapter 5

1. See, DeLillo, "Silhouette City" (30).
2. In *Consider the Lobster*, he writes of Norman Mailer, Philip Roth, and John Updike: "it must seem to them no coincidence that the prospect of their own deaths appears backlit by the approaching millennium . . . When a solipsist dies, after all, everything goes with him" (51).
3. Powers told me that he had found in Cohn's book "a repeated source of narrative inspiration . . . especially the overwhelming account of the Siege of

Munster and the bizarre story of the pseudo-Baldwin" ("An Interview with Richard Powers" 169).

[4] Probably most significant, here, is Franzen's play with the idea of correction and intergenerational conflict, when he observes that "If his parents had survived to old age, had lived even just a year or two longer, there would surely have been a correction" (119). It is also worth noting, however, that Chip Lambert's faked experiment with Gibberellic acid (*C* 35) is assigned to the central character of this draft (116).

[5] As I note in Chapter 2, Franzen told Molly Mcquade in 1998 that *The Corrections* was narrated in the first person ("A Nonsmoker's Novel" 1865). In 2002 he told Kevin Canfield that he "wasted . . . more than a year" trying to get the first person voice to work out of "a sense of artistic duty having written two third person novels to show that I could do a voice novel."

[6] It's difficult to do anything more than speculate about the extent to which Swarthmore in the early 1990s provides a template for Franzen's presentation of D—College, yet while Franzen relates that Chip cannot be forgiven his sins by the faculty and students because he "was neither a lesbian nor a Filipina" (*C* 83), in 1994 the *Philadelphia Inquirer* suggested that Swarthmore may be a place where "political correctness [had] run amok" (McCullough 4).

[7] In actual fact, the evidence of Franzen's correspondence with DeLillo (held at the University of Texas at Austin) indicates that the changes Gessen identifies were actually suggested by one of Pynchon's "Progeny," DeLillo.

[8] For a valuable discussion of the way Franzen manipulates the idea of the prison in the novel, see T. M. McNally's essay in the *Yale Review*.

[9] Although critics such as Perry Meisel, Daniel Mark Fogel, and, of course, Sandra Gilbert and Susan Gubar have applied and adapted Bloom's theories to earlier literature, with the exception of Patricia Tobin's *John Barth and the Anxiety of Continuance* (1992), his work is rarely considered in relation to contemporary literature. In part this is probably because his approach seems so speculative, but (for the true believers) it is also presumably because the knowledge contemporary writers have of Bloom's notorious theories inevitably impacts upon the psychodynamics of the agonistic relationship. In my discussion above, however, I'd suggest that the very self-consciousness of the allusions by Wallace and Franzen to Bloom's theories is one way that these psychodynamics change.

[10] In his essay on *Infinite Jest*, Steven Moore notes that the quote is based on p. 122 of Bloom's book.

[11] When Chip writes in the margin of a student paper that "*Cressida's character may inform Toyota's choice of product name; that Toyota's Cressida informs the Shakespearean text requires more argument than you present here*" (*C* 48), he outlines the kind of Borgesian reversal of priority that characterizes Bloom's *apophrades*.

[12] Compare the list at the beginning of this chapter with Babette's belief that "a person can change a harmful condition by . . . mak[ing] lists" (*White Noise* 191).

[13] Brian Passafaro's product "Eigenmelody" (*C* 345) seems to be a nod towards *JR*'s Thomas Eigen, who "wrote an important novel once" but whose creativity has since been increasingly consumed by working (like Chip) for big corporations (279).

14 Franzen writes about *Desperate Characters* in "Why Bother?" and "No End to It: Rereading *Desperate Characters*," an introduction to the 1999 reprint of Fox's novel.

15 In the context of the previous discussion of literary paternity, it seems worth noting that since Otto was probably born in 1928, he is likely to be only six years younger than Chip's father, Alfred.

16 While the action of *The Corrections* clearly takes place in the 1990s, it is, in the first instance, impossible to locate the exact year when the major action takes place. The novel opens, for example, on Thursday, September 30, which suggests that the novel must be set in either 1993 or 1999, the latter of which would reinforce the novel's millennial atmosphere. But the Christmas day that provides the novel's climax is also a Thursday, while in 1993 and 1999, December 25 fell on a Saturday. Franzen explains the reason for this inconsistency: "The chronologies aren't designed to bear up under close scrutiny. I try to make the day-to-day and month-to-month progressions fairly plausible, but with the larger chronologies (year of the present action; birth dates of the main characters), I am often stretching Twister-like to reconcile the fixed coordinates of my back story with the hideously rapid progress of contemporaneity. This is one reason I try to keep the particular year of the present action unidentifiable or at least blurry: I need wiggle room" (personal correspondence, 30 July 2006).

17 Pages 171–8 recall Jonah and Gary's trip to St. Jude in March, and pages 196–8 shift back from Monday, October 4, to Friday, October 1.

18 DeLillo works variations on this refrain on three other occasions in the novel (289, 408, 465) and critics normally trace the phrase's lineage (as Franzen's fascination with connection might also be traced) back to Pynchon's *Gravity's Rainbow*, where a drug-induced paranoia sparks "the discovery that *everything is connected*" (703).

19 In their inability to identify Myrdal, there is a link back to *Strong Motion* where an incredulous Louis Holland says to his sister "You're asking me if I remember the name of last year's Nobel Prize winner in economics?" (*SM* 201).

20 Barth also draws on quantum physics in his massive novel, *LETTERS* (1979), where he paraphrases physics' recognition of the reciprocal relationship between observer and observed in terms of metafiction, by reflecting "thus has chronicling transformed the chronicler" (80).

21 There are similar passages in *Once Upon a Time*, *On With the Story*, and *The Book of Ten Nights and a Night* (2004).

22 See, "Once Upon a Time: Storytelling Explained" (*Further Fridays* 183–96).

23 Outside the narrow group of writers I consider here, Lynne Tillman also seems to adopt Dennett's model in *American Genius* (2006), a novel that is fascinated by the "neural routes of the brain," and which describes characters who "narrate the events of [their] beleaguered life" (132, 49).

24 The scene in Gary's room takes place when Enid is pregnant with Denise and, since Gary is eleven years older than Denise, it seems reasonable to assume that he is eleven years old at this point.

25 In *Late Postmodernism*, Green offers such a binary opposition when he argues that the novel is divided between "two divergent models of the subject . . .

a therapeutic conception of the self, wherein misery simply suggests a neurochemical imbalance" and Alfred's conception of identity in terms of privacy and self-control (112). It should be clear from my account that while I appreciate many aspects of his study, I have substantive differences with Green on this score.

26. Franzen made this point in an interview with Birkerts. When Birkerts asked him about his supposed revival of character in *The Corrections*, Franzen responded: "the question is: what exactly do we mean by a renewed focus on character?" ("The Esquire Conversation").

27. There's a parallel, here, to Powers's later neurologist, Gerald Weber, in *The Echo Maker* who descends from the cortex to the lower structures of his brain, slipping "down into limbic back alleys, corners that survived when the massive neocortex came through like a superhighway" (428).

28. In "What the Dickens," Wood argues that *The Corrections* can be understood as basically a DeLillo novel with the addition of "human beings" at its center.

29. I am grateful to Jason Shrontz for pointing this reversal out to me, along with the near anagram of *Frolic* in *Orfic*.

30. Franzen has twice begun reading *In Search of Lost Time*.

31. Although Franzen worked out many of the aesthetic problems he was wrestling with in the 1990s in conversation with, and writing to, David Foster Wallace, I do not include Wallace in the following discussion because—unlike Powers—Wallace ends each of his first three books in a different manner. An argument could be made to connect certainly the end of *The Broom of the System* and possibly the end of *Girl with Curious Hair* to the end of Powers's novels, but to introduce Wallace into the equation would require entangling this argument in the thorny complications of Wallace's development as a writer.

Bibliography of Works by Franzen

I: Books

The Twenty-Seventh City. 1988. New York: Noonday-Farrar, 1997.
Strong Motion. New York: Picador-Farrar, 1992.
The Corrections. 2001. New York: Picador-Farrar, 2002.
How to Be Alone. Rev. ed. New York: Farrar, 2003.
The Discomfort Zone. 2006. New York: Picador-Farrar, 2007.

II: Juvenilia

With Kathy Siebert. *The Fig Connection.* Woodstock, IL: Dramatic, 1977.
"An African Correspondence on the World as Serengeti." *Nulset Review* 2.1 (1977): 7.
"Firemen Fight Fires for Free." *Phoenix* 21 Sept. 1977: 4.
"Dick Falls, Kathy Triumphs." *Phoenix* 28 Sept. 1977: 4.
"Tint and Reflection." *Phoenix* 12 Oct. 1977: 3.
"What's in Vogue this Fall for Stylish Students." *Phoenix* 19 Oct. 1977: 3.
With Tom Hjelm. "Union Maids in College's Future?" *Phoenix* 26 Oct. 1977: 1+.
With Nick Burbank. "SAGA Slaughter Protested." Letter to the Editor. *Phoenix* 16 Nov. 1977: 2.
"Pol. Sci. Leads Sex Imbalance in Honors." *Phoenix* 7 Dec. 1977: 5.
"Board of Managers Displays Diversity." *Phoenix* 25 Jan. 1978: 3.
"South African Investments Questioned." *Phoenix* 1 Feb. 1978: 1+.
"Sproul Justifies Its Fame." *Phoenix* 22 Mar. 1978: 1+.
Untitled Poem. *Nulset Review* 2.2 (1978): 5.
"Rainy Season." *Nulset Review* 2.2 (1978): 10.
"Italian Market Abounds with Scents of Food." *Phoenix* 5 Apr. 1978: 4.
"Marriages Made in Swats." *Phoenix* 5 Apr. 1978: 5.
"Fleisher and Heubert: A Bridge Two Far." *Phoenix* 26 Apr. 1978: 3.
"Fashion: Tips and Comment." *Phoenix* 26 Apr. 1978: 5.
With Nick Burbank. "Attention Staffers: The Phoenix Style." *Phoenix* 26 Apr. 1978: 6.
With Tom Hjelm. "A Sunday at the Vet: Circus 10, Baseball 0." *Phoenix* 29 Sept. 1978: 6.
"Oktoberfest Hin und Her." *Phoenix* 27 Oct. 1978: 5.
With Gwen Aldridge. "Campus in Style." *Phoenix* 3 Nov. 1978: 4.

With Tom Hjelm. "Jan. '69: Swarthmore's Time of Crisis." *Phoenix* 26 Jan. 1979: 1+.
With Ann Cudd. "Inflation (of Grades) Passes by Swarthmore." *Phoenix* 26 Jan. 1979: 4.
With Tom Hjelm. "The SASS Crisis: 1969 and Beyond." *Phoenix* 9 Feb. 1979: 1+.
"Adventures in the Pizza Trade." *Phoenix* 23 Feb. 1979: 5.
"CEP Considering Core Curriculum." *Phoenix* 6 Apr. 1979: 3.
"Core is Fashionable, But is it Necessary." *Phoenix* 20 Apr. 1979: 2+.
"This is Not a Play." *Sparrowfart* 1979: 27–31.
"Mixed Review." *Small Craft Warnings* 1.1 (1980): n. pag.
Untitled Photograph. *Small Craft Warnings* 1.1 (1980): n. pag.
"Crime at a Glance." *Small Craft Warnings* 1.1 (1980): n. pag.
"Issues and Issues: Cheap, Sudden Death." *Phoenix* 19 Sept. 1980: 6.
"Issues and Issues: Vice in the Rat Race." *Phoenix* 26 Sept. 1980: 9.
"Issues and Issues: Fire and Forget." *Phoenix* 10 Oct. 1980: 8.
"From 1810 to 1980, Oktoberfest Offers Oompah Bands and Beer." *Phoenix* 17 Oct. 1980: 5.
"Issues and Issues: Fresh Frozen." *Phoenix* 12 Dec. 1980: B5.
"Issues and Issues: Let's All Work a Little Harder." *Phoenix* 23 Jan. 1981: 2.
"Issues and Issues: A New Vietnam." *Phoenix* 6 Feb. 1981: 5.
"Issues and Issues: The Man Everyone Dreams About." *Phoenix* 27 Feb. 1981: 4.
"Issues and Issues: Dateline: International." *Phoenix* 27 Mar. 1981: 4.
"Issues and Issues: What's Growing." *Phoenix* 16 Apr. 1981: 3.
Untitled Photograph. *Small Craft Warnings* 1.2 (1981): n. pag.
"Facts." *Fiction International* 17.1 (1986): 144–51.

III: Coauthored scientific articles

With A. M. Dziewonski, and J. H. Woodhouse. "Centroid-Moment Tensor Solutions for April–June, 1983." *Physics of the Earth and Planetary Interiors* 33.4 (1983): 243–49.
With A. M. Dziewonski, and J. H. Woodhouse. "Centroid-Moment Tensor Solutions for July–September, 1983." *Physics of the Earth and Planetary Interiors* 34.1-2 (1984): 1–8.
With A. M. Dziewonski, and J. H. Woodhouse. "Centroid-Moment Tensor Solutions for October–December, 1983." *Physics of the Earth and Planetary Interiors* 34.3 (1984): 129–36.
With A. M. Dziewonski, and J. H. Woodhouse. "Centroid-Moment Tensor Solutions for January–March, 1984." *Physics of the Earth and Planetary Interiors* 34.4 (1984): 209–19.
With A. M. Dziewonski, and J. H. Woodhouse. "Centroid-Moment Tensor Solutions for April–June, 1984." *Physics of the Earth and Planetary Interiors* 37.2-3 (1985): 87–96.

With A. M. Dziewonski, and J. H. Woodhouse. "Centroid-Moment Tensor Solutions for July–September, 1984." *Physics of the Earth and Planetary Interiors* 38.4 (1985): 203–13.

With A. M. Dziewonski, and J. H. Woodhouse. "Centroid-Moment Tensor Solutions for October–December, 1984." *Physics of the Earth and Planetary Interiors* 39.3 (1985): 147–56.

With A. M. Dziewonski, and J. H. Woodhouse. "Centroid-Moment Tensor Solutions for January–March, 1985." *Physics of the Earth and Planetary Interiors* 40.4 (1985): 249–58.

With A. M. Dziewonski, and J. H. Woodhouse. "Centroid-Moment Tensor Solutions for April–June, 1985." *Physics of the Earth and Planetary Interiors* 41.4 (1986): 215–24.

With A. M. Dziewonski, and J. H. Woodhouse. "Centroid-Moment Tensor Solutions for July–September, 1985." *Physics of the Earth and Planetary Interiors* 42.4 (1986): 205–14.

With A. M. Dziewonski, and J. H. Woodhouse. "Centroid-Moment Tensor Solutions for October–December, 1985." *Physics of the Earth and Planetary Interiors* 43.3 (1986): 185–95.

With A. M. Dziewonski, G. Ekstrom, and J. H. Woodhouse. "Centroid-Moment Tensor Solutions for January–March, 1986." *Physics of the Earth and Planetary Interiors* 45.1 (1987): 1–10.

With A. M. Dziewonski, G. Ekstrom, and J. H. Woodhouse. "Global Seismicity of 1977: Centroid-Moment Tensor Solutions for 471 Earthquakes." *Physics of the Earth and Planetary Interiors* 45.1 (1987): 11–36.

With A. M. Dziewonski, G. Ekstrom, and J. H. Woodhouse. "Centroid-Moment Tensor Solutions for April–June, 1986." *Physics of the Earth and Planetary Interiors* 45.3 (1987): 229–39.

With A. M. Dziewonski, G. Ekstrom, and J. H. Woodhouse. "Centroid-Moment Tensor Solutions for July–September, 1986." *Physics of the Earth and Planetary Interiors* 46.4 (1987): 305–15.

With A. M. Dziewonski, G. Ekstrom, and J. H. Woodhouse. "Global Seismicity of 1978: Centroid-Moment Tensor Solutions for 512 Earthquakes." *Physics of the Earth and Planetary Interiors* 46.4 (1987): 316–42.

With A. M. Dziewonski, G. Ekstrom, and J. H. Woodhouse. "Global Seismicity of 1979: Centroid-Moment Tensor Solutions for 524 Earthquakes." *Physics of the Earth and Planetary Interiors* 48.1–2 (1987): 18–46.

With A. M. Dziewonski, G. Ekstrom, and J. H. Woodhouse. "Global Seismicity of 1980: Centroid-Moment Tensor Solutions for 515 Earthquakes." *Physics of the Earth and Planetary Interiors* 50.2 (1988): 127–54.

With A. M. Dziewonski, G. Ekstrom, and J. H. Woodhouse. "Global Seismicity of 1981: Centroid-Moment Tensor Solutions for 542 Earthquakes." *Physics of the Earth and Planetary Interiors* 50.2 (1988): 155–82.

With A. M. Dziewonski, G. Ekstrom, and J. H. Woodhouse. "Global Seismicity of 1982 and 1983: Additional Centroid-Moment Tensor Solutions for 533 Earthquakes." *Physics of the Earth and Planetary Interiors* 53.1–2 (1988): 17–45.

IV: Uncollected writing

"The Richest Man in Spain." Rev. of *The City of Marvels* by Eduardo Mendoza. *Los Angeles Times Book Review* 8 Jan. 1989: 2+.

"I, Spy." Rev. of *Harlot's Ghost*, by Norman Mailer. *Los Angeles Times Book Review* 29 Sept. 1991: 1+.

"Skeleton Key to the Phelans." Rev. of *Very Old Bones*, by William Kennedy. *Los Angeles Times Book Review* 26 Apr. 1992: 2+.

"Anger is My Business." Rev. of *The Night Manager*, by John Le Carré. *Los Angeles Times Book Review* 27 June 1993: 1+.

"Where Our Troubles Began." Rev. of *The Waterworks*, by E. L. Doctorow. *Los Angeles Times Book Review* 19 June 1994: 1+.

"Hitting the Road." Rev. of *Rule of the Bone*, by Russell Banks. *New York Times Book Review* 7 May 1995: 13.

"The Fifth Column: A Novel." *Village Voice* 14 Nov. 1995: 8, 10. Rpt. as Jonathan Franzen et al. "The Fifth Column: A Novel." *Village Voice* 26 Mar. 1996: 33–38.

"Somewhere North of Wilmington." *Blind Spot* 8 (1996): n. pag.

"FC2." *New Yorker* 18 Mar. 1996: 116.

"I'll Be Doing More of Same." *Review of Contemporary Fiction* 16.1 (1996): 34–38.

"How He Came to Be Nowhere." *Granta* 54 (1996): 111–23.

"At the Part for the Artist with No Last Name." *Blind Spot* 14 (1999): n. pag.

"No End to It: Rereading *Desperate Characters*." Introduction. *Desperate Characters*. By Paula Fox. New York: Norton, 1999. vii–xiv.

"Freeloading Man." Rev. of *John Henry Days*, by Colson Whitehead. *New York Times Book Review* 13 May 2001: 8–9.

Franzen responds to the attack on the World Trade Center. *New Yorker* 24 Sept. 2001: 29.

National Book Award Acceptance Speech. 14 Nov. 2001. 8 Nov. 2003 http://www.nationalbook.org/nbaacceptspeech_jfranzen.html.

Introduction. *The Man in the Gray Flannel Suit*. By Sloan Wilson. New York: Four Walls, 2002. n. pag.

With Michael Cunningham et al. "Murder at the Beau Rivage." *Paris Review* 164 (2002–3): 217–36.

"The Quitter's Lament." *Across the Board* Jan.–Feb. 2003: 9.

"From *The Corrections*." *Paris Review* 167 (2003): 246–48.

"The Listener." *New Yorker* 6 Oct. 2003: 85–99.

"Hush Club," "Misteak," and "Silence Parlor." *The Future Dictionary of America*. Ed. Jonathan Safran Foer, et al. Wisconsin: McSweeney's, 2004. 67, 87, 125.

"Breakup Stories." *New Yorker* 8 Nov. 2004: 104–8.

"Alice's Wonderland." Rev. of *Runaway*, by Alice Munro. *New York Times Book Review* 14 Nov. 2004: 1+.

"Countdown." *New Yorker* 18 Apr. 2005: 155.

Swarthmore Commencement Address. 29 May 2005. 3 Mar. 2006 http://www.swarthmore.edu/news/commencement/2005/franzen.html

"Two's Company." *New Yorker* 23 May 2005: 78–81.

"Tomes That Can Trigger a Writer's Wanderlust." *New York Times* 14 May 2006, Travel sec.: 9+.

"Ambition." *Guardian* 15 July 2006, Weekend sec.: 17–21.

List of Top Ten Books. *The Top Ten: Writers Pick Their Favorite Books.* Ed. J. Peder Zane. New York: Norton, 2007. 65.

"Authentic but Horrible: An Introduction to *Spring Awakening*." Introduction. *Spring Awakening: A Children's Tragedy.* By Frank Wedekind. Trans. Franzen. New York: Faber-Farrar, 2007. vii–xvii.

Works Cited

Adams, Robert Martin. "What Was Modernism?" *Hudson Review* 31 (1978): 19–33.
Altieri, Charles. "From Experience to Discourse: American Poetry and Poetics in the Seventies." *Contemporary Literature* 21 (1980): 191–224.
Amsden, David. "The Write Start." *New York Metro.com.* 21 July 2003. 13 Oct. 2004 http://www.newyorkmetro.com/nymetro/news/media/features/n_8974/
Anderson, Perry. *The Origins of Postmodernity.* London: Verso, 1998.
Andrews, Peter. "Jammu Has Plans for St. Louis." Rev. of *The Twenty-Seventh City*, by Jonathan Franzen. *New York Times Book Review* 9 Oct. 1988: 22.
Annesley, James. "Market Corrections: Jonathan Franzen and the 'Novel of Globalization.'" *Journal of Modern Literature* 29.2 (2006): 111–28.
Baraka, Amiri. "Amiri Baraka: An Interview." With Kimberly W. Benston. *Boundary 2* 6 (1978): 303–18.
Barth, John. *The Sot-Weed Factor.* 1960. London: Secker, 1961.
———. *Giles Goat-Boy or, the Revised New Syllabus.* New York: Doubleday, 1966.
———. *LETTERS.* 1979. London: Secker, 1980.
———. *The Friday Book: Essays and Other Nonfiction.* 1984. Baltimore: Johns Hopkins University Press, 1997. 64–76.
———. *Once Upon a Time: A Floating Opera.* Boston: Little, 1994.
———. *Further Fridays: Essays, Lectures, and Other Nonfiction: 1984–94.* Boston: Little, 1995.
———. *On with the Story.* Boston: Little, 1996.
———. *Coming Soon!!!* Boston: Houghton, 2001.
Barthes, Roland. "The Death of the Author." *Image-Music-Text.* Trans. and ed. Stephen Heath. London: Fontana, 1977. 142–48.
Bateson, Gregory. *Steps to an Ecology of Mind: Collected Essays in Anthropology, Psychiatry, Evolution, and Epistemology.* San Francisco: Chandler, 1972.
Begley, Adam. "'But Dad!' The Joys of Family, Up Close and Scarily Lifelike." Rev. of *The Corrections*, by Jonathan Franzen. *New York Observer* 27 Aug. 2001: 10.
Bradbury, Malcolm. "Saul Bellow's Intellectual Heroes." *Saul Bellow at Seventy-Five: A Collection of Critical Essays.* Ed. Gerhard Bach. Tubingen: Verlag, 1991. 33–39.
Bell, Bernard Iddings. *Postmodernism and Other Essays.* Milwaukee: Morehouse, 1926.
Bernstein, Michael André. "Making Modernist Masterpieces." *Modernism/Modernity* 5.3 (1998): 1–17.
Birkerts, Sven. "The Novel We've Been Waiting For." Rev. of *The Corrections*, by Jonathan Franzen. *Esquire* Sept. 2001: 71.
Blades, John. "Wild Urban Flight of Fancy." Rev. of *The Twenty-Seventh City*, by Jonathan Franzen. *Chicago Tribune* 21 Aug. 1988, sec. 14: 1+.

Bloom, Harold. *The Anxiety of Influence: A Theory of Poetry*. 1973. London: Oxford University Press, 1975.

Borges, Jorge Luis. "On Exactitude in Science." *Collected Fictions*. Trans. Andrew Hurley. New York: Penguin, 1998. 325.

Boswell, Marshall. *Understanding David Foster Wallace*. Understanding Contemporary American Literature. Columbia, SC: University of South Carolina Press, 2003.

Buell, Lawrence. *Writing for an Endangered World: Literature, Culture, and Environment in the U.S. and Beyond*. Cambridge, MA: Belknap-Harvard, 2001.

Bukiet, Melvin Jules. "Crackpot Realism: Fiction for the Forthcoming Millennium." *Review of Contemporary Fiction* 16.1 (1996): 13–22.

Burn, Stephen. *David Foster Wallace's Infinite Jest: A Reader's Guide*. Continuum Contemporaries. New York: Continuum, 2003.

———. "'The Machine-Language of the Muscles': Reading, Sport, and the Self in *Infinite Jest*." *Upon Further Review: Essays on American Sports Literature*. Ed. Michael Cocchiarale and Scott D. Emmert. Westport, CO: Praeger-Greenwood, 2004. 41–50.

———. "The Collapse of Everything: William Gaddis and the Encyclopedic Novel." *Paper Empire: William Gaddis and the World System*. Ed. Joseph Tabbi and Rone Shavers. Tuscaloosa: University of Alabama University, 2007. 46–62.

Butler, Christopher. *After the Wake: An Essay on the Contemporary Avant-Garde*. Oxford: Clarendon, 1980.

Calvino, Italo. *Six Memos for the Next Millennium*. 1988. Trans. Patrick Creagh. London: Vintage-Random, 1996.

Carlyle, Thomas. Preface. *Essays*. By Ralph Waldo Emerson. London: Fraser, 1841. v–xiii.

Chetkovitch, Kathy. "Envy." *Granta* 82 (2003): 67–87.

Clayton, Jay. *The Pleasures of Babel: Contemporary American Literature and Theory*. New York: Oxford University Press, 1993.

Conte, Joseph M. *Design and Debris: A Chaotics of Postmodern American Fiction*. Tuscaloosa: University of Alabama Press, 2002.

Cooper, James Fenimore. *The Pathfinder, or The Inland Sea*. 1840. Introd. Kay Seymour House. New York: Penguin, 1989.

———. *The American Democrat and Other Political Writings*. Ed. Bradley J. Birzer and John Wilson. Washington, DC: Regnery, 2000.

Coover, Robert. *Pricksongs and Descants*. New York: Dutton, 1969.

———. *The Public Burning*. New York: Viking, 1977.

———. "An Interview with Robert Coover." With Larry McCaffery. *Anything Can Happen: Interviews with Contemporary American Novelists*. Ed. Tom LeClair and Larry McCaffery. Urbana: University of Illinois Press, 1983. 63–78.

———. "The End of Books." *New York Times Book Review* 21 June 1992: 1+.

———. "I am an Intransigent Realist." Interview with Susana Pajares Tosca. *Espéculo*. Oct. 1999. 6 Jan. 2005 http://www.ucm.es/info/especulo/numero12/cooverin.html

———. "The Public Burning Log 1966–77." *Critique* 42.1 (2000): 84–114.

———. *The Adventures of Lucky Pierre: Directors' Cut*. New York: Grove, 2002.

Cornell, Valerie. "On Being Unable to Read." *By Herself: Women Reclaim Poetry*. Ed. Molly McQuade. Saint Paul, MN: Graywolf, 2000. 403–20.

Cowart, David. *Don DeLillo: The Physics of Language*. Athens, GA: University of Georgia Press, 2002.

Cuoco, Lorin and William H. Gass, eds. *Literary St. Louis: A Guide*. St. Louis: Missouri Historical Society, 2000.

Darwin, Charles. *The Origin of Species*. 1859. Ed. and Introd. J. W. Burrow. Harmondsworth: Penguin, 1968.

Davion, Victoria. "Is Ecofeminism Feminist?" *Ecological Feminism*. Ed. Karen Warren. Environmental Philosophies. London: Routledge, 1994. 8–28.

Davis, Scott D. and Cliff Frolhlich. "Did (or Will) Fluid Injection Cause Earthquakes? Criteria for a Rational Assessment." *Seismological Research Letters* 64.3–4 (1993): 207–24.

DeLillo, Don. *Great Jones Street*. Boston: Houghton, 1973.

———. *Ratner's Star*. New York: Knopf, 1976.

———. *The Names*. New York: Knopf, 1982.

———. *White Noise*. New York: Viking-Penguin, 1985.

———. *Libra*. New York: Viking-Penguin, 1988.

———. "Silhouette City: Hitler, Manson and the Millennium." *Dimensions: A Journal of Holocaust Studies* 4.3 (1988): 29–34.

———. *Mao II*. New York: Viking-Penguin, 1991.

———. *Underworld*. New York: Scribner-Simon, 1997.

Dennett, Daniel C. *Consciousness Explained*. Boston: Little, 1991.

Derrida, Jacques. *Of Grammatology*. Trans. Gayatri Chakravorty Spivak. Baltimore: Johns Hopkins University Press, 1976.

Dewey, Joseph. "Hooking the Nose of the Leviathan: Information, Knowledge, and the Mysteries of Bonding in *The Gold Bug Variations*." *Review of Contemporary Fiction* 18.3 (1998): 51–66.

———. *Understanding Richard Powers*. Understanding Contemporary American Literature. Columbia, SC: University of South Carolina Press, 2002.

Eagleton, Terry. *The Illusions of Postmodernism*. Malden, MA: Blackwell, 1996.

Eliot, George. *The George Eliot Letters*. Ed. Gordon S. Haight. Vol. 2. New Haven: Yale University Press, 1954.

Eliot, T. S. *The Complete Poems and Plays*. London: Faber, 1969.

———. "Letter to Edna McCourt." Sandweiss 554.

Emerson, Ralph Waldo. "The American Scholar." *Selected Essays*. Ed. and Introd. Larzer Ziff. New York: Penguin, 1982. 83–105.

Evans, David M. "Man-Made Earthquakes in Denver." *Geotimes* May–June 1966: 11–18.

Evenson, Brian. *Understanding Robert Coover*. Understanding Contemporary American Literature. Columbia, SC: University of South Carolina Press, 2003.

Federman, Raymond. "Surfiction—Four Propositions in Form of an Introduction." *Surfiction: Fiction Now . . . and Tomorrow*. 2nd ed. Ed. Federman. Chicago: Swallow, 1981. 5–15.

Fiedler, Leslie A. "Cross the Border—Close that Gap: Post-Modernism." *American Literature since 1900*. Ed. Marcus Cunliffe. 1975. Harmondsworth: Penguin, 1987. 329–51.

Fitzpatrick, Kathleen. *The Anxiety of Obsolescence: The American Novel in the Age of Television*. Nashville: Vanderbilt University Press, 2006.

Ford, Richard. *A Multitude of Sins.* 2001. New York: Vintage-Random, 2002.
Forrest, David V. and Lucien J. Côté. "The Mortal Stage of Late Life." *Journal of the American Academy of Psychoanalysis and Dynamic Psychiatry* 30 (2002): 329–40.
Foster, Hal. *The Return of the Real: The Avant-Garde at the End of the Century.* October Book. Cambridge, MA: MIT, 1996.
Fox, Paula. *Desperate Characters.* 1970. Introd. Jonathan Franzen. New York: Norton, 1999.
———. *Western Wind.* New York: Orchard, 1993.
Frank, Joseph. "Spatial Form in Modern Literature." *The Widening Gyre: Crisis and Mastery in Modern Literature.* Fwd. Allen Tate. New Brunswick, NJ: Rutgers University Press, 1963. 3–62.
Franzen, Jonathan. "Don't Judge by Cover: Author Likes Hometown." Interview with Clarence E. Olson. *St. Louis Post-Dispatch* 28 Aug. 1988: 3+.
———."PW Interviews: Jonathan Franzen." With Michael Coffey. *Publishers Weekly* 6 Dec. 1991: 53–54.
———. "A Writer Basking in the Raves." Interview with Carlin Romano. *Philadelphia Inquirer* 25 Jan. 1992: D1+.
———. "Chez Lambert." *Paris Review* 139 (1996): 29–41.
———. "A Nonsmoker's Novel by Jonathan Franzen." Interview with Molly McQuade. *Booklist* July 1998: 1865.
———. "Jonathan Franzen." Interview with Donald Antrim. *Bomb* 77 (2001): 72–78.
———. "Making *The Corrections*: An Interview with Jonathan Franzen." With Joanna Smith Rakoff. *Poets and Writers* 29.5 (2001): 27–33.
———. "Jonathan Franzen's Big Book." Interview with Emily Eakin. *New York Times Magazine* 2 Sept. 2001: 18–21.
———. "Only Correct." Interview with Laura Miller. *Salon* 7 Sept. 2001. 16 Nov. 2007 http://archive.salon.com/books/int/2001/09/07/franzen/index.html
———. "In the Mind's Eye of Jonathan Franzen." Interview with Jane Henderson. *St. Louis Post-Dispatch* 23 Sept. 2001: G1+.
———. "Mainstream and Meaningful." Interview with Jessica Murphy. *Atlantic Unbound* 3 Oct. 2001. 16 June 2004 www.theatlantic.com/unbound/interviews/int2001-10–03.htm
———. "This Year's Great American Novel." Interview. *New Yorker Online Only* 17 Dec. 2001. 14 Dec. 2004 http://www.newyorker.com/online/content/articles/011224on_onlineonly01
———. "Having Difficulty with Difficulty." Interview with Ben Greenman. *New Yorker Online Only* 23 Sept. 2002. 24 Sept. 2002 www.newyorker.com
———. "Jonathan Franzen on *How to Be Alone* (and Less Angry)." Interview with Kevin Canfield. *Poets and Writers Online Only* 11 Oct. 2002. 13 Oct. 2004 http://www.pw.org/mag/dq_franzen.htm
———. "A Difficult Haven: An Interview with Jonathan Franzen." With Trey Strecker. *Raintaxi* 8.3 (2003): 12–13.
———. "Intimately Connected to the Zeitgeist." Interview with Bernadette Conrad. *Sign and Sight* 24 Aug. 2005. 4 Aug. 2006 http://www.signandsight.com/features/321.html
———. "The Esquire Conversation: Jonathan Franzen." With Sven Birkerts. *Esquire* 10 Aug. 2006 www.esquire.com

Frow, John. *Time and Commodity Culture: Essays in Cultural Theory and Postmodernity.* Oxford: Clarendon, 1997.
Frye, Northrop. *Anatomy of Criticism: Four Essays.* 1957. Fwd. Harold Bloom. Princeton, NJ: Princeton University Press, 2000.
Gaddis, William. *The Recognitions.* 1955. Introd. William H. Gass. Harmondsworth: Penguin, 1993.
——. *JR.* 1975. Introd. Frederick R. Karl. Harmondsworth: Penguin, 1993.
——. *A Frolic of His Own.* New York: Poseidon-Simon, 1994.
Gass, William H. *Fiction and the Figures of Life.* New York: Knopf, 1970.
——. "William H. Gass." Interview with Carole Spearin McCauley. *The New Fiction: Interviews with Innovative American Writers.* Ed. Joe David Bellamy. Urbana: University of Illinois Press, 1974. 32–44.
——. *The Tunnel.* New York: Knopf, 1995.
——. *Tests of Time.* Chicago: University of Chicago Press, 2002.
Gessen, Keith. "A Literary Correction." Rev. of *The Corrections,* by Jonathan Franzen. *American Prospect* 5 Nov. 2001: 33–35.
Goeglein, Timothy. "Poetic Injustice." *National Review* 29 May 1995: 64–5.
Grassian, Daniel. *Hybrid Fictions: American Literature and Generation X.* Jefferson, NC: McFarland, 2003.
Green, Jeremy. *Late Postmodernism: American Fiction at the Millennium.* New York: Palgrave, 2005.
Harrington, Anne. "Beyond Phrenology: Localization Theory in the Modern Era." *The Enchanted Loom: Chapters in the History of Neuroscience.* Ed. Pietro Corsi. History of Neuroscience no. 4. New York: Oxford University Press, 1991. 207–39.
Harris, Charles B. "PoMo's Wake, I." *American Book Review* 23.2 (2002): 1+.
——. "Technoromanticism and the Limits of Representation: Richard Powers's *Plowing the Dark.*" *The Holodeck in the Garden: Science and Technology in Contemporary American Fiction.* Ed. Peter Freese and Harris. Normal, IL: Dalkey, 2004. 110–29.
——. "The Story of the Self: *The Echo Maker* and Neurological Realism." *Intersections: Essays on Richard Powers.* Ed. Stephen J. Burn and Peter Dempsey. Champaign, IL: Dalkey, 2008. 230–59.
Hawthorne, Nathaniel. *The House of the Seven Gables.* 1851. Ed. and Introd. Milton R. Stern. New York: Penguin, 1981.
——. *The Blithedale Romance.* 1852. Introd. Annette Kolodny. New York: Penguin, 1983.
Hayles, N. Katherine. *The Cosmic Web: Scientific Field Models and Literary Strategies in the Twentieth Century.* Ithaca: Cornell University Press, 1984.
——. *Chaos Bound: Orderly Disorder in Contemporary Literature and Science.* Ithaca: Cornell University Press, 1990.
——. "Introduction: Complex Dynamics in Literature and Science." *Chaos and Order: Complex Dynamics in Literature and Science.* Ed. Hayles. Chicago: University of Chicago Press, 1991. 1–33.
Heise, Ursula K. *Chronoschisms: Time, Narrative, and Postmodernism.* Cambridge: Cambridge University Press, 1997.

Hermanson, Scott. "Chaos and Complexity in Richard Powers's *The Gold Bug Variations.*" *Critique* 38 (1996): 38–51.

———. "Just Behind the Billboard: The Instability of *Prisoner's Dilemma.*" *Intersections: Essays on Richard Powers.* Ed. Stephen J. Burn and Peter Dempsey. Champaign, IL: Dalkey, 2008. 60–74.

Horgan, John. *The Undiscovered Mind: How the Brain Defies Explanation.* London: Weidenfeld, 1999.

Hunt, Anne Lucas. "Early Recollections." Sandweiss. 269–75.

James, Henry. *The Bostonians.* 1886. Ed. and Introd. Charles R. Anderson. Harmondsworth: Penguin, 1986.

———. *The Notebooks of Henry James.* 1947. Ed. F. O. Matthiessen and Kenneth B. Murdock. Chicago: University of Chicago Press, 1974.

———. "The Question of the Opportunities." *The American Essays.* Ed. and Introd. Leon Edel. New York: Vintage, 1956. 197–204.

———. "The Art of Fiction." *The Critical Muse: Selected Literary Criticism.* Ed. and Introd. Roger Gard. Harmondsworth: Penguin, 1987. 186–206.

Jameson, Fredric. *Postmodernism, or, the Cultural Logic of Late Capitalism.* London: Verso, 1991.

Jefferson, Margo. "A Go-For-Broke First Novel." Rev. of *The Twenty-Seventh City*, by Jonathan Franzen. *Vogue* Sept. 1988: 454.

Joyce, James. *Finnegans Wake.* 1939. 3rd ed. London: Faber, 1964.

Kenner, Hugh. *A Homemade World: The American Modernist Writers.* New York: Morrow, 1975.

Keymer, David. Rev. of *The Twenty-Seventh City*, by Jonathan Franzen. *Library Journal* 1 Nov. 1988: 108.

Knowles, John. *A Separate Peace.* 1959. New York: Scribner-Simon, 2003.

Kostelanetz, Richard. *An ABC of Contemporary Reading.* San Diego: San Diego University Press, 1995.

Kraus, Karl. *Dicta and Contradicta.* Trans. Jonathan McVity. Urbana: University of Illinois Press, 2001.

Labinger, Jay A. "Encoding an Infinite Message: Richard Powers's *Gold Bug Variations.*" *Configurations* 3 (1995): 79–93.

LeClair, Tom. "The Systems Novel." Rev. of *Prisoner's Dilemma*, by Richard Powers. *New Republic* 25 Apr. 1988: 40–42.

———. *The Art of Excess: Mastery in Contemporary American Fiction.* Urbana: University of Illinois Press, 1989.

———. "The Prodigious Fiction of Richard Powers, William Vollmann, and David Foster Wallace." *Critique* 38 (1996): 12–37.

———. "Shortfall." Rev. of *The Corrections*, by Jonathan Franzen. *American Book Review* 23.2 (2002): 1+.

Levin, Harry. "What Was Modernism?" *Refractions: Essays in Comparative Literature.* New York: Oxford University Press, 1966. 271–95.

Leyner, Mark. "Geraldo, Eat Your Avant-Pop Heart Out." *New York Times* 21 Dec. 1997, sec. 4: 11.

Luhmann, Niklas. *Art as a Social System.* Trans. Eva M. Knodt. Stanford, CA: Stanford University Press, 2000.

MacLean, Paul D. *A Triune Concept of the Brain and Behaviour*. Ed. T. J. Boag and D. Campbell. The Clarence M. Hincks Memorial Lectures, 1969. Toronto: University of Toronto Press, 1973.

Maliszewski, Paul. "The Business of *Gain*." *Intersections: Essays on Richard Powers*. Ed. Stephen J. Burn and Peter Dempsey. Champaign, IL: Dalkey, 2008. 162–86.

McCaffery, Larry. "Introduction." *Postmodernism: A Bio-bibliographical Guide*. Ed. Larry McCaffery. Movements in the Arts 2. New York: Greenwood, 1986. xi–xxviii.

———. *Avant-Pop: Fiction for a Daydream Nation*. Normal, IL: Black Ice, 1993.

———. "Avant-Pop: Still Life After Yesterday's Crash." *After Yesterday's Crash: The Avant-Pop Anthology*. Ed. Larry McCaffery. Harmondsworth: Penguin, 1995. xi–xxix.

McCullough, Marie. "Swarthmore in '94?" *Philadelphia Inquirer* 22 June 1994, sec. B: 4.

McElroy, Joseph. *Lookout Cartridge*. New York: Knopf, 1974.

McHale, Brian. *Constructing Postmodernism*. London: Routledge, 1992.

———. "What Was Postmodernism?" *electronic book review* 20 Dec. 2007. 20 Dec. 2007 www.electronicbookreview.com/thread/fictionspresent/tense

McLaughlin, Robert L. "Post-Postmodern Discontent: Contemporary Fiction and the Social World." *Symplokē* 12.1–2 (2004): 53–68.

McNally, T. M. Rev. of *The Corrections*, by Jonathan Franzen. *Yale Review* 90.2 (2002): 161–69.

Maltby, Paul. Rev. of *Memorius Discourse*, by Christian Moraru. *Ariel* 37 (2006): 99–102.

Meeker, Joseph W. *The Comedy of Survival: Literary Ecology and a Play Ethic*. 3rd ed. Tucson: University of Arizona Press, 1997.

Mehta, Ved. *Portrait of India*. New York: Farrar, 1970.

Melville, Herman. *White-Jacket or, the World in a Man-of-War*. 1850. Ed. Harrison Hayford, Hershel Parker, and G. Thomas Tanselle. Evanston: Northwestern University Press, 1970.

Meyer, Leonard B. "The End of the Renaissance? Notes on the Radical Empiricism of the Avant-Garde." *Hudson Review* 16 (1963): 169–86.

Mills, Megan. "Jonathan Franzen Returns to Swat; Dedicates Reading to Late George Avery." *Daily Gazette* 2 Apr. 2004. 2 Aug. 2006 http://www.sccs.swarthmore.edu/org/daily/archive/spring_2004/20040402.html

Moore, Steven. "The First Draft Version of *Infinite Jest*." *The Howling Fantods* 11 May 2003. 11 Aug. 2004 www.thehowlingfantods.com/ij_first.htm

Myrdal, Gunnar. *An American Dilemma: The Negro Problem and Modern Democracy*. 1944. New York: Harper, 1962.

Newman, Charles. *The Post-Modern Aura: The Act of Fiction in an Age of Inflation*. 1984. Evanston: Northwestern University Press, 1985.

Norfolk, Lawrence. "Closing Time in the Fun-House." Rev. of *Brief Interviews with Hideous Men*, by David Foster Wallace. *Times Literary Supplement* 14 Jan. 2000: 25–26.

"Nourishing the Spirit." *Washington Post* 2 Dec. 2001, Book World sec.: 3–4.

Osborne, David. "The Origin of Petroleum." *Atlantic Monthly* Feb. 1986: 39–54.

Osteen, Mark. *American Magic and Dread: Don DeLillo's Dialogue with Culture*. Penn Studies in Contemporary American Fiction. Philadelphia: University of Pennsylvania Press, 2000.

Ovid. *Metamorphoses.* Trans. Charles Martin. Introd. Bernard Knox. New York: Norton, 2004.

Ozick, Cynthia. *The Din in the Head.* Boston: Houghton, 2006.

Pessl, Marisha. *Special Topics in Calamity Physics.* New York: Viking-Penguin, 2006.

Pinker, Steven. *How the Mind Works.* 1997. Harmondsworth: Lane-Penguin, 1998.

Poe, Edgar Allan. *Essays and Reviews.* Ed. G. R. Thompson. New York: Library of America, 1984.

——. "The Fall of the House of Usher." *The Fall of the House of Usher and Other Writings.* Ed. and Introd. David Galloway. New York: Penguin, 1986. 138–57.

Porush, David. "Eudoxical Discourse: A Post-Postmodern Model for the Relations Between Science and Literature." *Modern Language Studies* 20.4 (1990): 40–64.

Pound, Ezra. *The Cantos.* 4th ed. London: Faber, 1987.

Powers, Richard. *Three Farmers on Their Way to a Dance.* New York: Beech Tree-Morrow, 1985.

——. *Prisoner's Dilemma.* New York: Beech Tree-Morrow, 1988.

——. *The Gold Bug Variations.* New York: Morrow, 1991.

——. *Operation Wandering Soul.* New York: Morrow, 1993.

——. *Galatea 2.2.* New York: Farrar, 1995.

——. *Gain.* New York: Farrar, 1998.

——. "An Interview with Richard Powers." With Jim Neilson. *Review of Contemporary Fiction* 18.3 (1998): 13–23.

——. "The Salon Interview: Richard Powers." With Laura Miller. *Salon* 23 July 1998. 1 Feb. 2006 http://dir.salon.com/books/int/1998/07/cov_si_23inta.html

——. "Being and Seeming: The Technology of Representation." *Context* 3 (2000): 15–17.

——. "A Dialogue." With Bradford Morrow. *Conjunctions* 34 (2000): 171–88.

——. *Plowing the Dark.* New York: Farrar, 2000.

——. "A Conversation with Richard Powers." With Harvey Blume. *Atlantic Unbound* 28 Jun. 2000. 13 Aug. 2000 www.theatlantic.com/unbound/interviews/ba2000-06-28.htm

——. "Literary Devices." *Zoetrope: All-Story* 6.4 (2002): 8–15.

——. *The Time of Our Singing.* New York: Farrar, 2003.

——. "Pynchon Appreciation." *Bookforum* (Summer 2005): 40.

——. *The Echo Maker.* New York: Farrar, 2006.

——. "An Interview with Richard Powers." With Stephen J. Burn. *Contemporary Literature* 49 (2008): 162–78.

Prigogine, Ilya. *The End of Certainty: Time, Chaos, and the New Laws of Nature.* New York: Free-Simon, 1996.

Proust, Marcel. *In Search of Lost Time.* Vol. 2. Trans. C. K. Scott Moncrieff, Terence Kilmartin, and D. J. Enright. London: Vintage-Random, 1992.

——. *In Search of Lost Time.* Vol. 5. Trans. C. K. Scott Moncrieff, Terence Kilmartin, and D. J. Enright, London: Vintage-Random, 1992.

Pynchon, Thomas. *V..* Philadelphia: Lippincott, 1963.

——. *Slow Learner: Early Stories.* Boston: Little, 1984.

——. "Is it O.K. to Be a Luddite?" *New York Times Book Review* 28 Oct. 1984: 1+.

——. *Gravity's Rainbow.* 1973. New York: Penguin, 1995.

——. *Mason & Dixon.* New York: Holt, 1997.

Rebein, Robert. "Turncoat: Why Jonathan Franzen Finally Said 'No' to Po-Mo." *The Mourning After: Attending the Wake of Postmodernism*. Ed. Neil Brooks and Josh Toth. Postmodern Studies. 40. Amsterdam: Rodopi, 2007. 201–21.

Restak, Richard M. *The Brain*. Toronto: Bantam, 1984.

Ribbat, Christopher. "Handling the Media, Surviving *The Corrections*." *Amerikastudien/American Studies* 47.4 (2002): 555–66.

Riding, Laura and Robert Graves. *A Survey of Modernist Poetry*. London: Heinemann, 1927.

Rifkind, Donna. "Something's Up in St. Louis." Rev. of *The Twenty-Seventh City*, by Jonathan Franzen. *Wall Street Journal* 13 Sept. 1988: 34.

Robbins, Tom. *Even Cowgirls Get the Blues*. 1976. Toronto: Bantam, 1991.

Robinson, Douglas. *American Apocalypses: The Image of the End of the World in American Literature*. Baltimore: Johns Hopkins University Press, 1985.

Rooney, Kathleen. *Reading with Oprah: The Book Club that Changed America*. Fayetteville: University of Arkansas Press, 2005.

Rorty, Richard et al. "Lofty Ideas that May Be Losing Altitude." *New York Times* 1 Nov. 1997, sec. B: 13.

Rusk, William S. "Education Through the Fine Arts." *Journal of Higher Education* 7 (1936): 377–82.

Sagan, Carl. *The Dragons of Eden: Speculations on the Evolution of Human Intelligence*. New York: Random, 1977.

Sandweiss, Eric, "Introduction." *Seeking St. Louis: Voices from a River City, 1670–2000*. Ed. Lee Ann Sandweiss. St. Louis: Missouri Historical Society, 2000. xvii–xxxiii.

Schindehette, Susan. "Novel Approach: Author Jonathan Franzen Insults Oprah—and Gets Dumped from Her Show." *People* 12 Nov. 2001: 83–84.

Schneck, Peter. "Pop Goes the Novel: Avant-Pop Literature and the Tradition of the New." *Simulacrum America: The USA and the Popular Media*. Ed. Elisabeth Kraus and Carolin Auer. European Studies in American Literature and Culture. New York: Camden-Boydell, 2000. 64–74.

Shapiro, Fred R. "Prehistory of *Postmodern* and Related Terms: Evidence from the JSTOR Electronic Journal Archive and Other Sources." *American Speech* 76 (2001): 331–34.

Shapiro, Laura. "A Lavish Novel by a Newcomer." Rev. of *The Twenty-Seventh City*, by Jonathan Franzen. *Newsweek* 29 Aug. 1988: 59.

Shinkle, Jim. Letter. *Phoenix* 14 Dec. 1977: 2.

Siegel, Lee. *Love and Other Games of Chance: A Novelty*. New York: Penguin, 2003.

Singer, Isaac Bashevis. *Enemies: A Love Story*. 1972. Harmondsworth: Penguin, 1977.

——. "I.B. Singer, Storyteller." Interview with Herbert R. Lottman. *Isaac Bashevis Singer: Conversations*. Ed. Grace Farrell. Jackson: University Press of Mississippi, 1992. 116–23.

——. "Nobel Lecture." *Nobel Lectures: Literature, 1968–1980*. Ed. Tore Frangsmyr and Sture Allen. Singapore: World Scientific, 1993. 163–65.

Sjöwall, Maj and Per Wahlöö. *Roseanna*. Trans. Lois Roth. New York: Vintage-Random, 1967.

Sloan, De Villo. "The Decline of American Postmodernism." *SubStance* 16.3 (1987): 29–43.

Slung, Michelle. "Meet Them in St. Louis." Rev. of *The Twenty-Seventh City*, by Jonathan Franzen. *Washington Post* 4 Sept. 1988: 1+.

Smith, Richard. "Spend (Slightly) Less on Health and More on the Arts." *British Medical Journal* 325 (2002): 1432–33.

Spanos, William V. "The Detective and the Boundary: Some Notes on the Postmodern Literary Imagination." *Early Postmodernism: Foundational Essays*. Ed. Paul A. Bové. Durham, NC: Duke University Press, 1995. 17–39.

Spencer, Thomas M. *The St. Louis Veiled Prophet Celebration: Power on Parade, 1877–1995*. Columbia, MO: University of Missouri Press, 2000.

Spoto, Daniel. *The Kindness of Strangers: The Life of Tennessee Williams*. Boston: Little, 1985.

Steiner, Wendy. "Postmodern Fictions, 1970–1990." *The Cambridge History of American Literature*. Vol. 7. Ed. Sacvan Bercovitch. Cambridge: Cambridge University Press, 1999. 425–538.

Stevens, Wallace. *The Collected Poems of Wallace Stevens*. New York: Knopf, 1967.

Tabbi, Joseph. *Cognitive Fictions*. Electronic Meditations 8. Minneapolis: University of Minnesota Press, 2002.

"Talk of the Town." *New Yorker* 11 Aug. 1975: 19.

Tatham, Campbell. "Language Games: (Post)Modern(Isms)." *SubStance* 4.10 (1974): 67–80.

Thiher, Allen. "Postmodernism's Evolution as Seen by Ihab Hassan." Rev. of *The Postmodern Turn*, by Ihab Hassan. *Contemporary Literature* 31 (1990): 236–39.

Tillman, Lynne. *American Genius, a Comedy*. Brooklyn: Soft Skull, 2006.

Toal, Catherine. "Corrections: Contemporary American Melancholy." *Journal of European Studies* 33 (2003): 305–22.

Toth, Josh and Neil Brooks. "Introduction: A Wake and Renewed?" *The Mourning After: Attending the Wake of Postmodernism*. Ed. Brooks and Toth. Postmodern Studies 40. Amsterdam: Rodopi, 2007. 1–13.

Turner, Tom. *City as Landscape: A Post-Postmodern View of Design and Planning*. London: Spon-Chapman, 1996.

The Twenty-Seventh City. Advertisement. *New York Times Book Review* 25 Sept. 1988: 28–9.

Verhoeven, W. M. "What We Talk About When We Talk About Raymond Carver: Or, Much Ado About Minimalism." *Narrative Turns and Minor Genres in Postmodernism*. Ed. Theo D'haen and Hans Bertens. Postmodern Studies 11. Amsterdam: Rodopi, 1995. 41–58.

Vidal, Gore. "American Plastic: The Matter of Fiction." *New York Review of Books* 15 July 1976: 31–39.

Virgil. *The Aeneid*. Trans. and Introd. David West. Harmondsworth: Penguin, 1990.

Vollmann, William T. *You Bright and Risen Angels: A Cartoon*. 1987. New York: Penguin, 1988.

———. "American Writing Today: Diagnosis of the Disease." *Conjunctions* 15 (1990): 355–58.

———. "An Interview with William T. Vollmann." With Larry McCaffery. *Review of Contemporary Fiction* 13.2 (1993): 9–24.

Wallace, David Foster. *The Broom of the System*. 1987. New York: Penguin, 2004.

———. *Girl with Curious Hair*. New York: Norton, 1989.

———. "Order and Flux in Northampton." *Conjunctions* 17 (1991): 91–118.

———. "An Interview with David Foster Wallace." With Larry McCaffery. *Review of Contemporary Fiction* 13.2 (1993): 127–50.

———. "E Unibus Pluram: Television and U.S. Fiction." *Review of Contemporary Fiction* 13.2 (1993): 151–94.

———. "Quo Vadis—Introduction." *Review of Contemporary Fiction.* 16.1 (1996): 7–8.

———. *Infinite Jest.* 1996. Fwd. Dave Eggers. New York: Back-Little, 2006.

———."The Salon Interview: David Foster Wallace." With Laura Miller. *Salon* 1996. 16 Dec.1997, www.salon.com/09/features/wallace2.html

———. Interview with David Wiley. *Minnesota Daily* 27 Feb. 1997. 5 Jan. 2006 http://www.ptwi.com/~bobkat/jestwiley2.html

———. *Oblivion.* Boston: Little, 2004.

———. *Consider the Lobster and Other Essays.* Boston: Little, 2005.

Warren, Karen J. "The Power and the Promise of Ecological Feminism." *Environmental Ethics* 12 (1990): 125–46.

Watman, Max. "On the Hysterical Playground." Rev. of *The Corrections*, by Jonathan Franzen, *After the Plague*, by T. C. Boyle, *Up in the Air*, by Walter Kirn, *John Henry Days*, by Colson Whitehead, *The Amazing Adventures of Kavalier and Clay*, by Michael Chabon, and *Pafko at the Wall*, by Don DeLillo. *New Criterion* Nov. 2001: 67–72.

Waugh, Patricia. "Introduction." *Postmodernism: A Reader.* Ed. Waugh. London: Arnold-Hodder, 1992. 1–10.

Weston, Jessie L. *From Ritual to Romance.* 1920. Fwd. Robert A. Segal. Princeton, NJ: Princeton University Press, 1993.

Wilde, Alan. "Barthelme Unfair *to* Kierkegaard: Some Thoughts on Modern and Postmodern Irony." *Boundary* 25 (1976): 45–70.

Wilden, Anthony. *System and Structure: Essays in Communication and Exchange.* London: Tavistock, 1972.

Williams, Tennessee. *Memoirs.* New York: Doubleday, 1975.

Wood, James. "What the Dickens." Rev. of *The Corrections*, by Jonathan Franzen. *Guardian* 9 Nov. 2001. 10 Nov. 2001 http://books.guardian.co.uk

Woolf, Virginia. *The Waves.* 1931. Ed. and Introd. Kate Flint. Harmondsworth: Penguin, 1992.

———. "Mr Bennett and Mrs Brown." *A Woman's Essays.* Selected Essays Vol. 1. Ed. and Introd. Rachel Bowlby. Harmondsworth: Penguin, 1992. 69–87.

Worster, Donald. *Nature's Economy: A History of Ecological Ideas.* 2nd ed. Studies in Environment and History. Cambridge: Cambridge University Press, 1994.

Ziegler, Heide. "The End of Postmodernism: New Directions." *The End of Postmodernism: New Directions.* Proceedings of the First Stuttgart Seminar in Cultural Studies, Aug. 1991. Stuttgart: Verlag, 1993. 5–10.

Index

Adams, Robert Martin 130n3
Altieri, Charles 18
Amelio, Gianni 31
Amerika, Mark 11
Anderson, Perry 130n1
Antrim, Donald 2, 45, 50, 60, 92, 124

Barth, John 2, 11–14, 19, 23, 47–48,
    88–89, 113–14, 132n11, 132n13,
    134n13, 139n20–22
Barthelme, Donald 16
Bateson, Gregory 15
Beckett, Samuel 34, 35, 40
Begley, Adam 108
Bell, Bernard Iddings 3
Bellamy, Joe David 17–18, 132n17
Bernstein, Michael André 131n6
Birkerts, Sven 129n2, 140n26
Bloom, Harold 97–100, 138n9–11
Borges, Jorge Luis 16
Boswell, Marshall 129n3, 133n24,
    136n13
Brooks, Neil 132n19
Buell, Lawrence 22
Bukiet, Melvin Jules x–xi
Butler, Christopher 5

Calvino, Italo 88–90
Carlyle, Thomas 1
chaos theory 71, 81–84, 94
Chetkovitch, Kathy 34, 134n4
Clayton, Jay 9
Cohn, Norman 89, 137–38n3
Cooper, James Fenimore 72
Coover, Robert 2, 6–9, 13–14, 24,
    29–30, 126, 131n5

Cornell, Valerie 31–32, 34, 134n4
Cowart, David 108–9

Darwin, Charles 87, 119–20
DeLillo, Don 1, 17, 19, 24, 25–26, 32,
    45, 55, 68, 79, 89, 97–98, 108–9,
    110, 119, 123, 133n27, 137n1,
    138n7, 138n12, 139n18, 140n28
Dennett, Daniel 114–18, 139n23
Derrida, Jacques 20
Doctorow, E.L. 35, 134n7

Eagleton, Terry 4
ecofeminism 73–74, 82
Eliot, George 125
Eliot, T. S. 62–66, 68–69, 136n6–7,
    136n10, 136n12
Emerson, Ralph Waldo 1
encyclopedic novel 5–9, 20, 94–96, 115
Evenson, Brian 7

Federman, Raymond 5
Fiedler, Leslie 130n2
Ford, Richard 52
Foster, Hal 11
Fox, Paula 44, 88, 100, 139n14–15
Frank, Joseph 78, 104
Franzen, Jonathan:
    The Corrections 19, 21–22, 24, 26, 27,
        29, 31, 32, 36, 45–46, 50–51, 76,
        88–128, 129n2, 134n6, 135n1,
        137n6
    The Discomfort Zone 33, 34, 39, 46,
        133n23, 134n8
    How to Be Alone 45, 47–49, 98–99,
        122, 135n15

"Perchance to Dream" / "Why
  Bother?" 11, 45, 50–51, 61,
  112–13, 135n16
Strong Motion 19, 22, 27, 28–32,
  42, 44, 46–48, 55, 68–87, 88,
  91–92, 93, 118, 126–27, 128,
  133–34n1, 134n14, 135n1,
  139n19
The Twenty-Seventh City 16, 19, 27, 32,
  33, 34, 41, 43, 46, 52–67, 68–72,
  76, 93, 115, 118, 126, 129n2,
  134n6, 137n3
Frazer, Sir James 4, 64
Frow, John 28
Frye, Northrop 5, 31

Gaddis, William 5, 6, 17, 19, 24, 48, 66,
  98–100, 122, 126, 138n13
Gardner, Howard 25
Gass, William H. 6, 28, 122–23
Geertz, Clifford 25
Grassian, Daniel 135n4
Graves, Robert 3
Green, Jeremy 50, 92, 100, 104, 113,
  139–40n25

Harrington, Anne 119
Harris, Charles B. ix, 11, 19, 129n1,
  133n25, 133n29
Hassan, Ihab 130n2
Hawthorne, Nathaniel 89, 118
Hayles, N. Katherine 81
Heise, Ursula 24
Hermanson, Scott 22, 137n9

James, Henry 68–69, 73, 125, 136n2
Jameson, Fredric 14, 132n13
Joyce, James 4, 61, 78, 97, 132–33n21

Kafka, Franz 41, 134n9
Kennedy, William 60
Kenner, Hugh 9, 130n6

Knowles, John 31, 134n7
Kostelanetz, Richard 5
Kraus, Karl 41–42, 43, 72–73

Labinger, Jay 133n22
Lahiri, Jhumpa 15
LeClair, Tom xi, 75, 92, 131n6, 132n21
Levin, Harry 9, 130n3
Lewin, Roger 84
Leyner, Mark 14–15
Locke, John 137n8

MacLean, Paul D. 118–22
McCaffery, Larry 10, 11, 18, 131n9
McElroy, Joseph 25, 58
McHale, Brian 2, 4
McLaughlin, Robert L. ix, 22, 49–50,
  129n1, 133n26
Maltby, Paul 9
Meeker, Joseph W. 22
Mehta, Ved 63, 136n8
Melville, Herman 89
metafiction 10–16, 20–22, 60, 113–15,
  127–28
Meyer, Leonard B. 5
modernism 3–5, 23, 78–79
Moore, Steven 19, 138n10
Myrdal, Gunnar 111–12

neuroscience 25–26, 91, 114–22
Newman, Charles 132n17

Olsen, Lance 11
Orwell, George 46
Osteen, Mark 108
Ovid 39

Passer, Ivan 31
Pessl, Marisha 15–16
Pinker, Steven 115, 117, 119
Poe, Edgar Allan 89, 96, 118
Porush, David 18

postmodernism 1–27, 46–51, 58, 60–61, 66, 75–76, 79, 88–89, 92–93, 97–100, 122–23, 125–26
post-postmodernism 10–27, 54–55, 56–58, 66–67, 71–72, 79, 89–90, 93, 94–100, 126–28, 132n11, 132n19
Pound, Ezra 4, 52
Powers, Richard ix, x, 16–17, 19–27, 52, 54, 55, 56–58, 60, 67, 71, 87, 89–90, 94–96, 114–15, 119, 127–28, 132–33n21–22, 135n2, 137n9, 137–38n3, 140n27
Prigogine, Ilya 82
Proust, Marcel 32, 57, 86, 125, 135n3, 140n30
Pynchon, Thomas x, 1, 6, 7, 17, 19, 23–24, 58, 61, 66, 94, 96, 126, 132–33n21, 138n7, 139n18

Rebein, Robert 50, 59, 130n7, 135n17
Riding, Laura 3
Robbins, Tom 25
Robinson, Douglas 88–89
Rorty, Richard 11, 14

Sandweiss, Eric 59, 61
Schneck, Peter 131n9
Schopenhauer, Arthur 117
Siegel, Lee 5
Singer, Isaac Bashevis ix, 48–49, 134n14
Sjöwall, Maj 70, 136n9, 137n4
Sloan, De Villo 5
Spanos, William V. 130n2
Spencer, Thomas M. 63, 136n11

Steiner, Wendy 9, 131n7
Stendhal 107, 114
Stevens, Wallace 1
systems novel 75–78

temporal form 20, 78–81, 101–8
Tillman, Lynne 139n23
Toal, Catherine 50
Toth, Josh 132n19
Turner, Tom 11

Vidal, Gore x
Virgil 39
Vollmann, William T. 10, 22, 56–58, 67, 132n16
Vonnegut, Kurt 39, 47

Wahlöö, Per 70, 136n9, 137n4
Walker, Alice 35, 134n7
Wallace, David Foster ix, 11, 12–15, 16–17, 19–27, 43, 44, 52, 56–58, 60, 66, 71–72, 79, 89–90, 94–97, 119, 124–25, 132n12, 132n14, 132n20, 133n22–24, 133n28, 137n2, 140n31
Warren, Karen 73–74
Waugh, Patricia 26–27
Wenders, Wim 31
Weston, Jessie 63–64
Wilden, Anthony 82
Williams, Tennessee 39, 93
Winfrey, Oprah x, 45–46, 130n6
Wood, James 108, 123, 140n28
Woolf, Virginia 23, 85
Worster, Donald 87

Ziegler, Heide 10

Printed in Great Britain
by Amazon.co.uk, Ltd.,
Marston Gate.